OECD Economic Surveys:
Indonesia
2018

This document, as well as any data and any map included herein, are without prejudice to the status of or sovereignty over any territory, to the delimitation of international frontiers and boundaries and to the name of any territory, city or area.

Please cite this publication as:

OECD (2018), *OECD Economic Surveys: Indonesia 2018*, OECD Publishing, Paris.
https://doi.org/10.1787/eco_surveys-idn-2018-en

ISBN 978-92-64-30492-5 (print)
ISBN 978-92-64-30493-2 (pdf)

Series: OECD Economic Surveys
ISSN 0376-6438 (print)
ISSN 1609-7513 (online)

OECD Economic Surveys: Indonesia
ISSN 2072-5116 (print)
ISSN 2072-5108 (online)

The statistical data for Israel are supplied by and under the responsibility of the relevant Israeli authorities. The use of such data by the OECD is without prejudice to the status of the Golan Heights, East Jerusalem and Israeli settlements in the West Bank under the terms of international law.

Photo credits: Cover © Teguh Hardi Sujono/Dreamstime.com.

Corrigenda to OECD publications may be found on line at: *www.oecd.org/publishing/corrigenda*.

Table of contents

Chapter 2. Making the most of tourism to promote sustainable regional development **113**

Tables

Figures

Boxes

This Survey was prepared in the Economics Department by Christine Lewis and Patrice Ollivaud under the supervision of Peter Jarrett and Vincent Koen. It has benefited from valuable background research by Rita Helbra Tenrini, seconded from the Indonesian Ministry of Finance. Peter Haxton and Jarmila Botev also contributed to the Survey. *Statistical research assistance was provided by Klaus Pedersen and editorial assistance was provided by Elisabetta Pilati. The previous* Survey *of Indonesia was issued in October 2016.*

The Survey *was discussed at a meeting of the Economic and Development Review Committee on 10 September 2018 with participation of representatives of the Indonesian government and representatives of France and Hungary as lead speakers.*

The Survey *is published under the responsibility of the Secretary-General of the OECD.*

Information about the latest as well as previous Surveys *and more information about how* Surveys *are prepared is available at* www.oecd.org/eco/surveys.

Follow OECD Publications on:

> *http://twitter.com/OECD_Pubs*

> *http://www.facebook.com/OECDPublications*

> *http://www.linkedin.com/groups/OECD-Publications-4645871*

> *http://www.youtube.com/oecdilibrary*

> *http://www.oecd.org/oecddirect/*

This book has...   StatLinks

A service that delivers Excel® files from the printed page!

Look for the *StatLinks* ▄ﻼ﹖ at the bottom of the tables or graphs in this book. To download the matching Excel® spreadsheet, just type the link into your Internet browser, starting with the *http://dx.doi.org* prefix, or click on the link from the e-book edition.

Basic Statistics of Indonesia, 2017

(Numbers in parenthesis refer to the OECD average)[a]

LAND, PEOPLE AND ELECTORAL CYCLE

Population (million)	261.9		Population density per km²	137.5	(35.6)
Under 15 (%)	27.2	(17.9)	Life expectancy (years, 2016)	69.1	(80.6)
Over 65 (%)	5.4	(16.9)	Men	67.0	(77.8)
			Women	71.2	(83.2)
Latest 5-year average growth (%)	1.3	(0.6)	Latest general election	July	2014

ECONOMY

Gross domestic product (GDP)			Value added shares (%)		
In current prices (billion USD)	1,016		Primary sector	21.5	(2.5)
In current prices (billion IDR)	13589		Industry including construction	33.1	(26.8)
Latest 5-year average real growth (%)	5.1	(2.1)	Services	45.4	(70.7)
Per capita (000 USD PPP)	12.4	(43.7)			

GENERAL GOVERNMENT
Per cent of GDP

Expenditure	16.5	(41.3)	Gross financial debt	28.9	(109.9)
Revenue	14.0	(39.1)			

EXTERNAL ACCOUNTS

Exchange rate (IDR per USD)	13381		Main exports (% of total merchandise exports)		
PPP exchange rate (USA = 1)	4190		Mineral fuels, lubricants and related materials	21.8	
In per cent of GDP			Manufactured goods classified chiefly by material	13.3	
Exports of goods and services	20.4	(55.7)	Animal and vegetable oils, fats and waxes	13.0	
Imports of goods and services	19.2	(51.3)	Main imports (% of total merchandise imports)		
Current account balance	-1.7	(0.4)	Machinery and transport equipment	28.5	
Net international investment position	-33.5		Mineral fuels, lubricants and related materials	17.8	
			Manufactured goods classified chiefly by material	16.0	

LABOUR MARKET, SKILLS AND INNOVATION

Employment rate for 15-64 year-olds (%)	66.1	(67.7)	Unemployment rate, Labour Force Survey (age 15 and over) (%)	5.6	(5.8)
Men	80.0	(75.4)	Youth (age 15-24, %)	17.8	(11.9)
Women	52.1	(60.1)			
Participation rate for 15-64 year-olds (%)	70.0	(72.0)	Tertiary educational attainment 25-64 year-olds (%, 2016)	9.8	(35.7)

ENVIRONMENT

Total primary energy supply per capita (toe, 2015)	0.9	(4.1)	CO_2 emissions from fuel combustion per capita (tonnes, 2015)	1.7	(9.2)
Renewables (%, 2015)	33.4	(9.6)	Energy intensity (toe per thousand 2010 USD PPP, 2015)	0.1	(0.1)
Fine particulate matter concentration (PM2.5, µg/m3, 2015)	17.9	(14.5)	Self suffiency (%, 2015)	189	(79)

SOCIETY

Income inequality (Gini coefficient, 2015)	0.391	(0.314)	Education outcomes (PISA score, 2015)		
Relative poverty rate (%, 2015)	36.4	(11.8)	Reading	397	(493)
			Mathematics	386	(490)
Public and private spending (% of GDP)			Science	403	(493)
Health care (2015)	3.4	(8.8)	Share of women in parliament (%)	19.8	(28.8)
Education (2014)	2.7	(3.6)			

Better life index: www.oecdbetterlifeindex.org

a. where the OECD aggregate is not provided in the source database, a simple OECD average of latest available data is calculated where data exists for at least 29 member countries.

Source: Calculations based on data extracted from the databases of the following organisations: OECD, International Energy Agency, Eurostat, World Bank, International Monetary Fund, Eurostat and Inter-Parliamentary Union.

Executive summary

Living standards are rising steadily

Thanks to a steady economic expansion and helpful government policies, poverty rates and inequality are falling, and access to public services is broadening. Income per capita growth is strong. Yet, the infrastructure gap remains large, and more spending on health and social assistance is needed to enhance inclusiveness. Well-being would also benefit from greater attention to environmental outcomes.

Economic growth has been solid at around 5% per year since 2013, driven by consumption but also, more recently, by much-needed infrastructure investment (Figure A). The recovery in global trade has boosted exports. The import bill has also risen due to higher oil prices and capital goods purchases, contributing to the current account deficit. Annual inflation is well within the target band of 3.5% +/-1%.

Figure A. Economic growth is solid

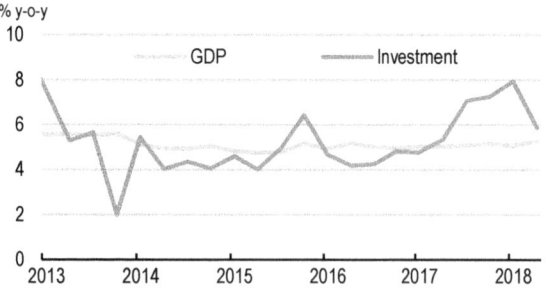

Source: CEIC.

StatLink https://doi.org/10.1787/888933832685

Macroeconomic policies are finely balancing growth and stability. After lowering policy interest rates during 2016-17 to support economic growth, Bank Indonesia has started to raise them to temper capital outflows. The budget deficit is expected to narrow in 2018 and 2019, expanding the buffer *vis-à-vis* the legislated cap of 3% of GDP.

GDP growth is projected to remain healthy (Table A). Rising incomes and consumer confidence will support a pick-up in private consumption. Investment is projected to remain robust. Improvements in logistics and price competitiveness will support export growth even as trading partner growth slows.

Table A. Growth is projected to remain healthy

Percentage change unless indicated

	2017	2018	2019
Gross domestic product	5.1	5.2	5.3
Private consumption	5.0	5.2	5.4
Government consumption	2.1	4.7	3.6
Gross fixed capital formation	6.2	6.5	5.9
Exports	9.1	5.5	5.6
Imports	8.1	10.3	5.7
Consumer price index	3.8	3.5	3.9
Fiscal balance (% of GDP)	-2.5	-2.2	-2.0
Current account balance (% of GDP)	-1.7	-2.5	-2.5

Source: *OECD Interim Economic Outlook*, September 2018.

A key downside risk to the outlook stems from capital outflows related to US monetary tightening. Large outflows would require a steeper path for interest rates, slowing growth. On the upside, past regulatory reforms and the expansion of infrastructure could boost investment and exports faster than expected.

Government debt is low and sustainable

The deficit rule is containing the growth of debt. But additional spending on infrastructure, health and social assistance is limited by low revenues. Accordingly, resources must be found through greater efficiency and higher revenues. Growth in the public wage bill was curbed in 2017, and targeting of sub-national transfers is improving. However, spending on energy subsidies has risen anew after falling over 2014-17. Shifting social assistance more towards conditional cash and non-cash transfers would improve targeting.

State-owned enterprises are contributing to the development agenda through infrastructure investment, loans to small businesses and price restraint. Yet, growing financial vulnerabilities might in time require public capital injections. SOEs' dominance in some sectors crowds out private capital. Governance would benefit from increased disclosure, strengthened procedures for board appointments and more explicit mandates with adequate independence to pursue them. Implicit fiscal risks from SOE losses and rising debt at some require more attention.

Raising revenues is the key fiscal challenge

Tax revenues are low relative to other emerging economies (Figure B). Registration has expanded but compliance remains a major challenge.

Figure B. Tax revenues are low

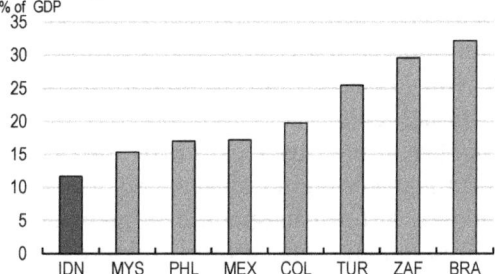

Source: OECD, *Revenue Statistics Database.*

StatLink ᠁ https://doi.org/10.1787/888933832704

Strengthening the tax administration is a government priority and is crucial for improving compliance. Modernising IT systems and processes can promote compliance and improve enforcement. But it will increase demands for highly skilled staff who are in short supply. Effectively using the swathes of new data is crucial to deter future evasion and could help boost revenues. Complexity and frequent policy changes make compliance more difficult. Wider public consultation ahead of proposed changes to tax legislation would enhance the quality of legislation over time.

Low incomes and widespread informality imply that the personal income tax net currently includes few individuals and raises scant revenue. The initial income threshold for paying income tax is relatively high. At medium-to-high incomes, marginal tax rates are well below those in other emerging economies. Gradually lowering the top income tax thresholds would make the system more progressive and raise additional revenue. High-income earners disproportionately benefit from the tax-free treatment of fringe benefits within personal income tax.

The corporate income tax base is also reduced by informality and the prevalence of small firms. Tax holidays and other incentives target specific sectors and locations and have been expanded recently to attract new investment. However, these risk eroding the tax base, creating distortions and spurring further regional tax competition. The recent publication of revenue forgone due to tax incentives improves transparency. These estimates should be published annually, as planned. Shifting to cost-based tax incentives would sharpen investment incentives. Competitiveness concerns could be addressed through greater regional co-operation.

Value-added tax generates sizeable revenue but its revenue-raising potential is undermined by exemptions, including for hotels and restaurants, which are subject to local sales tax, and some intermediate inputs. A high threshold for compulsory registration for firms weakens the self-enforcement mechanism embodied in the tax. A reform package removing most exemptions, replacing local sales tax by VAT, compensating local governments for lost sales tax revenue, and lowering the registration threshold would raise compliance. An accommodation tax for local governments would incentivise them to develop tourism.

There is scope to better use taxes for health and environmental aims. Smoking rates are high and tobacco taxes are lower than elsewhere. Motor vehicle taxes can be better linked to environmental effects. Phasing out fuel subsidies would be a first step towards more cost-reflective energy pricing.

Recurrent taxes on land and structures raise relatively little revenue. The first step is to ensure local governments are able to maintain and update their property tax databases. Then the cap on rates should be raised.

The youthful population is an opportunity

Half of Indonesia's population is under 30 years old. This favourable age structure will contribute to future prosperity, if policies are put in place to take advantage of it. Reaping the benefits of this opportunity requires shifting the jobs mix to high-quality, high-productivity formal-sector jobs. Improving the health of students and workers will raise learning and productivity.

Around half of all dependent employees and 70% of all workers are estimated to still be informal (Figure C). These jobs tend to be associated with lower wages, poorer working conditions and fewer training opportunities. Disadvantaged groups are more likely to be affected, particularly those with less education.

Figure C. Informality has fallen but is still high

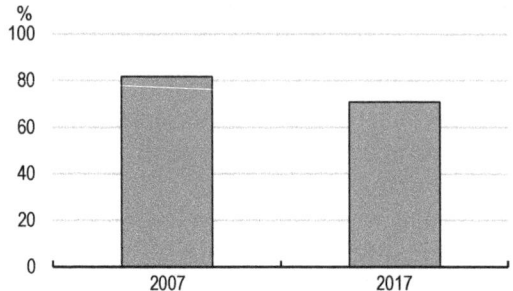

Source: Statistics Indonesia; OECD calculations.

StatLink https://doi.org/10.1787/888933832723

Stringent employment regulations, including high dismissal costs and minimum wages, curtail formal-sector employment. Easier employment regulations and a discounted minimum wage for youth could be trialled in special economic zones and, if successful, extended across the country. Improving business regulation at all levels of government would lower the barriers to formalisation. Linking the turnover tax to additional benefits such as access to business development services and book-keeping applications could encourage formalisation and increase revenue. To contain costs, eligibility for the tax should be restricted to very small firms.

Educational attainment has increased, but a scarcity of skills is holding back growth and incomes. The quality of education is still a concern. Teachers should be evaluated regularly and encouraged to undertake professional development by linking remuneration to performance. The government is focusing on developing skills by improving vocational schools. Strong employer engagement and national co-ordination are crucial for success.

Relatively little use is currently made of foreign workers to fill skill shortages. These workers could help to quickly fill acute skills shortages in high-skill jobs, boosting growth, supporting foreign investment and facilitating knowledge transfer. A list of highly skilled occupations with severe shortages could be

created, for which processes could be simplified and expedited.

Tourism can boost regional development

Growth in tourism has been remarkable. Annual visits have almost tripled over the past decade, with China becoming the largest source (Figure D). The government aims to reach 20 million foreign tourists by 2019. To unleash the full benefits for regional populations, vocational and on-the-job training should be expanded, driven by local needs. Infrastructure rollout is encouraging tourism, but gaps remain including in tourism-specific infrastructure and environmentally related infrastructure.

Figure D. Tourist arrivals have surged

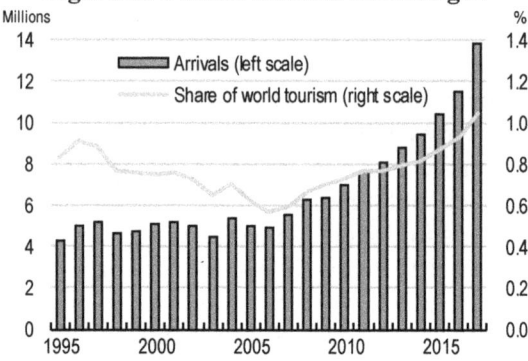

Source: CEIC; UNWTO.

StatLink https://doi.org/10.1787/888933832742

The central government is driving the tourism strategy, which helps prioritisation. However, local governments are not sufficiently involved. Greater co-ordination would ensure that tourism serves regional development needs. Targets should focus less on tourist numbers and more on revenue generated.

Tourism can create economic incentives to protect natural resources. Protected areas should be expanded and more open to visitors. User fees, along with quantitative restrictions as necessary, could control visitor numbers and help fund the maintenance of these sites.

Land clearing and peatland fires continue to generate environmental, health and economic costs. Moreover, air pollution from transportation is rising. Clearer land rights and better law enforcement would help control deforestation. Taxes, together with road pricing, could help curtail vehicle use.

MAIN FINDINGS	KEY RECOMMENDATIONS
Making the economy more resilient and inclusive	
Growth is projected to remain healthy but there is a risk of continued capital outflows. Monetary policy and fiscal policy are successfully balancing growth and stability, and the fiscal stance is broadly neutral. Reform of energy subsidies has stalled.	Deepen domestic financial markets to mitigate risks of capital outflows. Continue to act pre-emptively, including by raising interest rates as needed, to maintain price and financial stability. Improve targeting of social assistance, including by shifting towards more conditional transfers.
State-owned enterprises contribute to development but rising leverage, increasing cost pressures and losses at some firms represent fiscal risks. In some sectors they crowd out private investors.	Improve the transparency and governance of state-owned enterprises, including by strengthening their supervision and selection of board members. Give public enterprises clearer mandates with greater independence to achieve these.
Low-quality, informal jobs remain prevalent and there are many informal micro enterprises. Stringent employment regulation, high severance costs and high minimum wages discourage formal employment of low-skilled workers. Business regulations have been streamlined but are still burdensome at all levels of government.	Pilot lower levels of employment protection and discounted minimum wages for youth in special economic zones. If successful, extend them. Further simplify business regulations to encourage formalisation and collect user feedback to improve the online single submission system. Tighten eligibility for the turnover tax to very small firms and link registration to access to additional non-financial benefits.
Educational attainment is rising but still low. The quality of education remains a concern. Skills shortages are constraining growth. Better targeted government social assistance is expected to reduce student drop-out rates.	Introduce regular teacher evaluations and link teacher remuneration more closely to performance and ongoing training. Encourage greater employer engagement in vocational education and training. Create a list of highly skilled occupations with acute skills shortages, and ease restrictions on hiring foreign workers in these areas.
Raising more revenues to meet spending needs	
Tax revenues remain low, constraining public spending on infrastructure, education, health and social protection. Registration has increased, but improving compliance remains a challenge. Planned technology upgrades at the tax administration will raise demand for highly skilled civil servants. Complex regulations and frequent policy changes add to compliance costs.	Increase investment in tax administration, particularly staff, electronic services and databases. Make greater use of information technology to strengthen monitoring and facilitate tax compliance. Continue to expand and improve tax expenditure estimates and publish them annually, as planned.
A high basic tax allowance for personal income tax reduces the number of taxpayers. Higher rates are not applied until high levels of income. Different types of income are treated differently.	Freeze the basic tax allowance for individuals to broaden the tax base. Gradually lower thresholds for paying the top two rates of personal income tax. Include fringe benefits and employer allowances in taxable income.
Numerous exemptions and a high threshold for compulsory registration reduce the efficiency and effectiveness of the VAT. Sectors such as hotels, restaurants and entertainment are instead subject to sales tax at the sub-national level.	Broaden value-added tax by removing most exemptions, especially for intermediate goods, replacing local sales tax with VAT, and lowering the threshold for compulsory registration. Compensate sub-national governments for lost sales tax revenue and allow them to charge a tax on accommodation nights.
Taxes are used less than in other countries to target health and environmental outcomes. Smoking rates for men are amongst the highest in the world.	Increase and harmonise tobacco excise across products.
Recurrent taxation of immovable property raises relatively little revenue partly because of a cap set by the national government. Some district registers are out of date and many districts lack capacity to administer property taxes.	Increase training and assistance for sub-national governments to improve the quality of property tax databases, valuation methods and tax administration. Raise the cap on property tax rates.
Developing a stronger and sustainable tourism sector	
The central government is driving the tourism strategy. This helps prioritise planning and co-ordination, but local governments are not sufficiently involved. Local infrastructure is still lacking, including environmental infrastructure and tourism-specific services such as information centres.	Incorporate needed infrastructure in forthcoming destination management plans to ensure sustainable development of tourism.
Tourism is labour intensive and growing rapidly and skills shortages are increasing.	Expand vocational and on-the-job training to build tourism-related skills in the workforce, especially in areas with skills shortages.
Government medium-term objectives are mostly based on the number of tourists, which risks generating unsustainable inflows.	Give more prominence to revenue-based targets for tourism in future plans.
Natural assets are plentiful. The share of protected areas is low by international standards, and they are generally closed to the public to preserve highly sensitive zones.	Increase the coverage of protected areas, and consider opening more for tourism use, but with visitor controls including regulations, and appropriate user and concession fees.

Key Policy Insights

Income gains and government policies are lifting well-being

Indonesia is Southeast Asia's largest economy, rich in all types of natural resources as well as cultural diversity. A young and dynamic democracy, it is urbanising and modernising rapidly. In contrast with most OECD countries and many emerging economies, around half of the population is under 30 years old, and the working-age population ratio is set to rise during the next decade (United Nations, 2017).

Two decades after the 1998 Asian Financial Crisis, and one decade after the Global Financial Crisis, Indonesians' living standards are far higher than before, and their economy is more resilient. GDP per capita has risen by 70% during the past two decades (Figure 1). The end of the commodity price boom weighed on incomes and government revenues, yet GDP growth has remained around 5%, and per capita income has increased by almost 4% annually. Poverty rates have fallen in both rural and urban areas (Figure 2, Panel A). Distribution has also improved of late: the Gini coefficient on consumption has been declining since 2015. Confidence in the national government is higher than in any OECD country (Panel B). Prudent macroeconomic policies and progress in structural reforms have been recognised by credit rating agencies, and Indonesia has climbed up international rankings of competitiveness and the business environment. Since 2015 Indonesia has leapt 34 places in the World Bank's *Ease of Doing Business* ranking to 72nd.

Figure 1. Incomes have grown rapidly in the past decade

Income per capita, 2011 USD, constant PPP-adjusted exchange rates

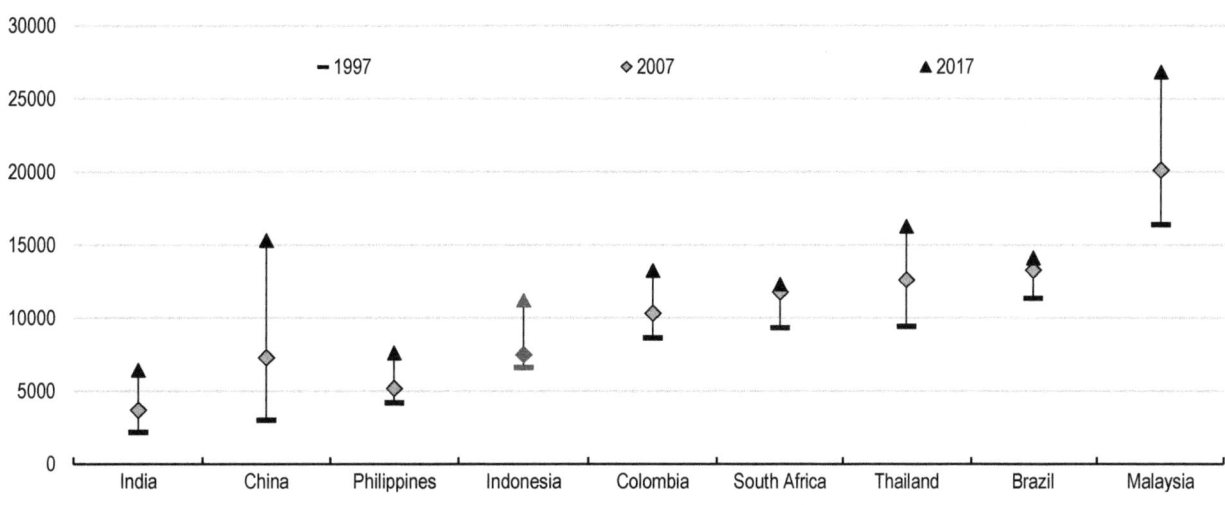

Source: Thomson Reuters.

StatLink https://doi.org/10.1787/888933832761

Nonetheless, policy makers are faced with numerous challenges as Indonesia progresses towards higher-income status. Many of the poor are trapped in precarious employment relative to other emerging economies, particularly women (Figure 3). Regional disparities in income and well-being are also huge (OECD, 2016a). Infrastructure needs are large – equivalent to 7% of GDP each year according to the government's medium-term plan for

2015-19. And there is more work to do to streamline regulations, increase regulatory certainty and fight corruption. Health spending is low relative to GDP, and the social safety net is still in its infancy. There are also risks that growth endangers environmental sustainability. The main messages of this *Survey* are:

- Shifting the job mix to high-quality, high-productivity positions in the formal sector will boost living standards and share the demographic dividend with future generations. Doing so will require tackling pervasive informality and skills deficiencies.

- Low tax revenues constrain government spending on infrastructure and social services. The key to durably raising revenue is to improve compliance and broaden tax bases.

- Tourism has the potential to diversify the economy, boost regional development and reduce inequalities. Tourist numbers are soaring but measures are needed to make this rapid growth consistent with long-run environmental sustainability.

Figure 2. Poverty is improving and trust in the national government is high

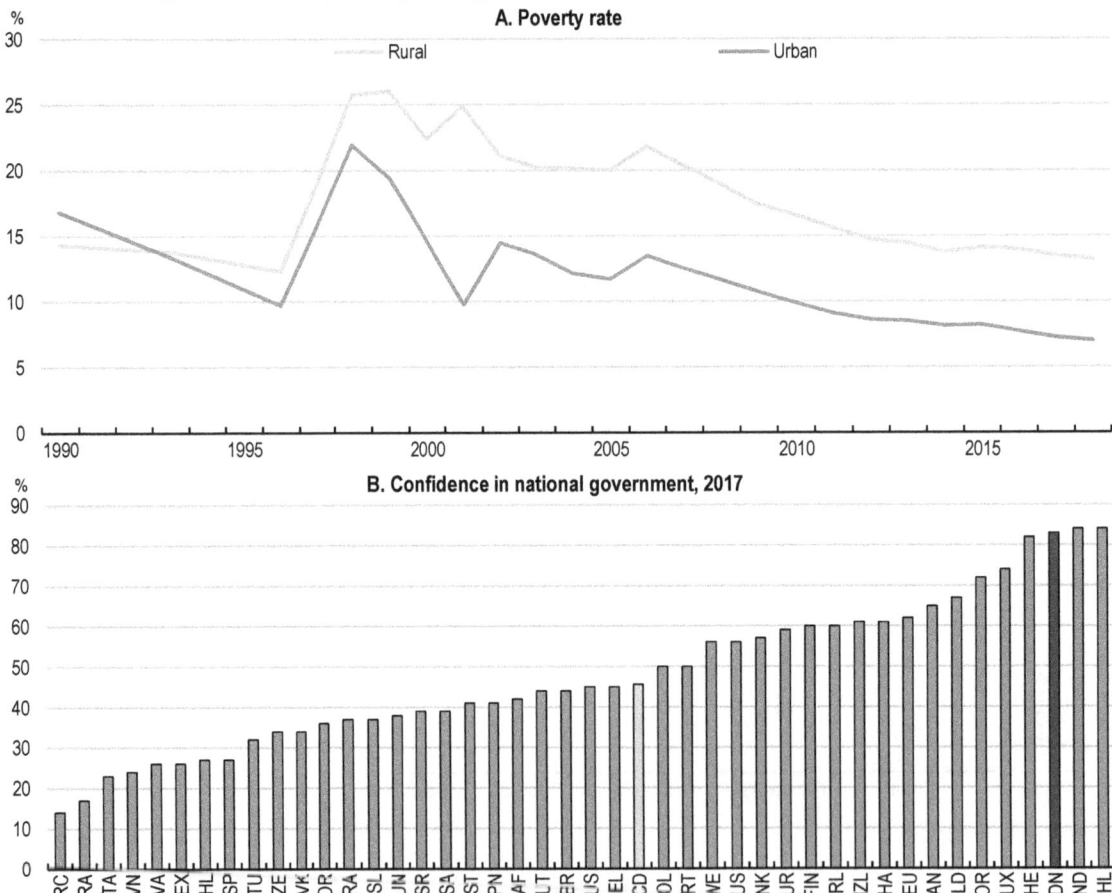

Note: The poverty rate is the percentage of the population below the poverty line, which is based on the minimum expenditure for food equivalent to 2 100 kilocalories per day, and basic housing, clothing, education and health needs.
Source: Statistics Indonesia; Gallup World Poll.

StatLink ᴍꜱᴾ https://doi.org/10.1787/888933832780

Figure 3. Many people are still in vulnerable forms of employment

Share of contributing family workers and own-account workers in employment, by gender, 2016

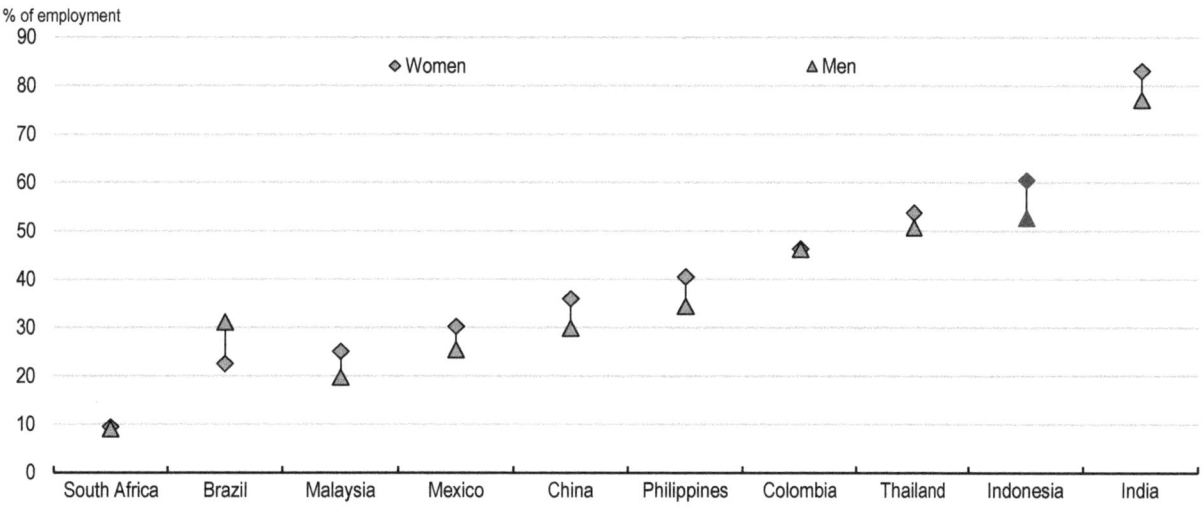

Source: World Bank, *World Development Indicators Database*.

StatLink https://doi.org/10.1787/888933832799

The economy is expanding at a healthy pace

GDP growth has remained around 5% since 2013. Supportive macroeconomic policies, greater confidence and stronger external demand boosted activity in 2017, with momentum continuing into 2018. Consumption continues to underpin spending (Figure 4, Panel A). Consumer confidence is relatively high, and unemployment has declined, supporting income gains. Infrastructure investment increased strongly, though from low levels, and capital goods imports have soared (Panel C). Services sectors have been growing robustly (Panel B). The increase in commodity prices, notably for mineral products, is supporting mining activity (Panel D). The overall business environment is friendlier, thanks to ongoing regulatory reforms. However, frequent regulatory changes add to uncertainty.

Exports are growing again, and broadly in line with growth in export markets (Figure 5, Panel A). Commodities account for 40% of total exports, down from around half at the peak of the commodity price boom (Panel C). Services, mostly tourism, and manufactures have grown in importance. The recent surge in investment-related imports, along with higher oil prices, has eroded the trade surplus of 2017 (Panel B). The primary income deficit was 3.2% of GDP in 2017. This deficit is likely to continue due to Indonesia's success in attracting foreign investment, although rising interest rates abroad will add to income. Overall, these developments led to the widening of the current account deficit to 2.6% of GDP in the first half of 2018.

In the first half of 2018 capital outflows associated with US monetary policy normalisation caused tighter financial conditions in Indonesia and other emerging economies (Figure 6). Indonesia's bond prices are particularly exposed to capital outflows because of foreign-currency risk and high foreign ownership: at March 2018 international debt securities in foreign currencies amounted to 19% of GDP, and almost 40% of local-currency government bonds were foreign-owned. In May Bank Indonesia began raising key interest rates to stem capital outflows. It followed this with further increases in June, August and

September. It has tried to partly offset the effect on financial conditions by injecting additional liquidity in domestic money markets and raising loan-to-valuation ratios for property lending.

Figure 4. The economy continues growing solidly

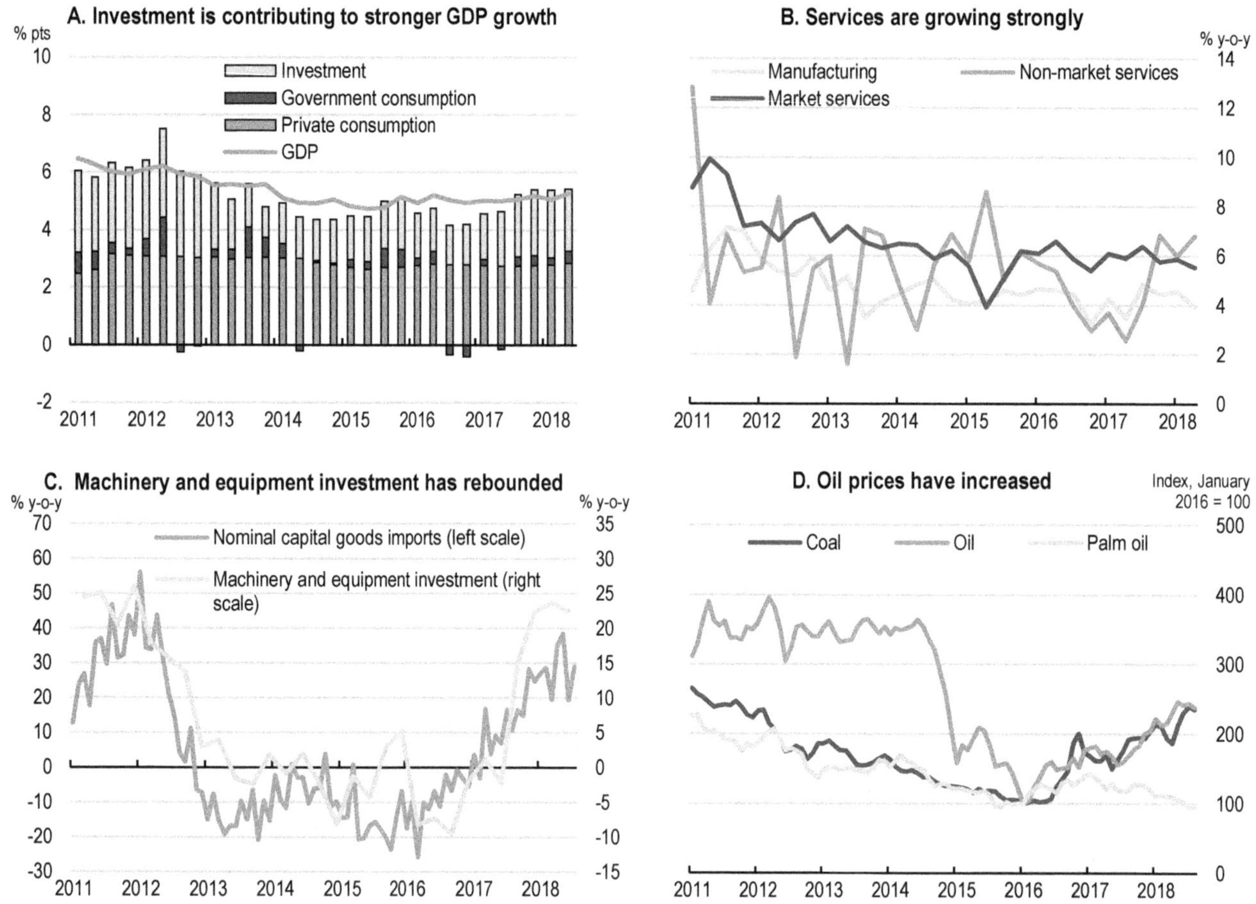

A. Investment is contributing to stronger GDP growth

B. Services are growing strongly

C. Machinery and equipment investment has rebounded

D. Oil prices have increased

Note: In Panel C, capital goods imports are adjusted for the shift in the timing of Idul Fitri and seasonality. In Panel D the coal price is for Australian coal; other series are averages where multiple prices are available.
Source: CEIC; World Bank Pink Sheet.

StatLink ᴹˢᴾ https://doi.org/10.1787/888933832818

Inflation eased to 3.1% in the third quarter of 2018, well within the official target range of 3.5% +/- 1% (Figure 7). Core inflation is subdued. Food price inflation picked up in early 2018, partly driven by some temporary shortages. The prices of some products, such as rice, are capped, and the government has decided to freeze administered energy prices for 2018-19. These measures aim to limit the pass-through of cost increases to consumers but have knock-on effects on producers and increase the budgetary cost of energy subsidies.

GDP growth is projected to reach 5.3% in 2019 (Table 1). Even with pass-through from currency depreciation, inflation is likely to remain within the target range. Income gains and low inflation will boost private consumption. Investment growth will hold up ahead of the 2019 elections, which may also induce higher government spending. Improved logistics and price competitiveness will support export growth even as trading-partner economies slow somewhat.

Figure 5. Exports are growing again

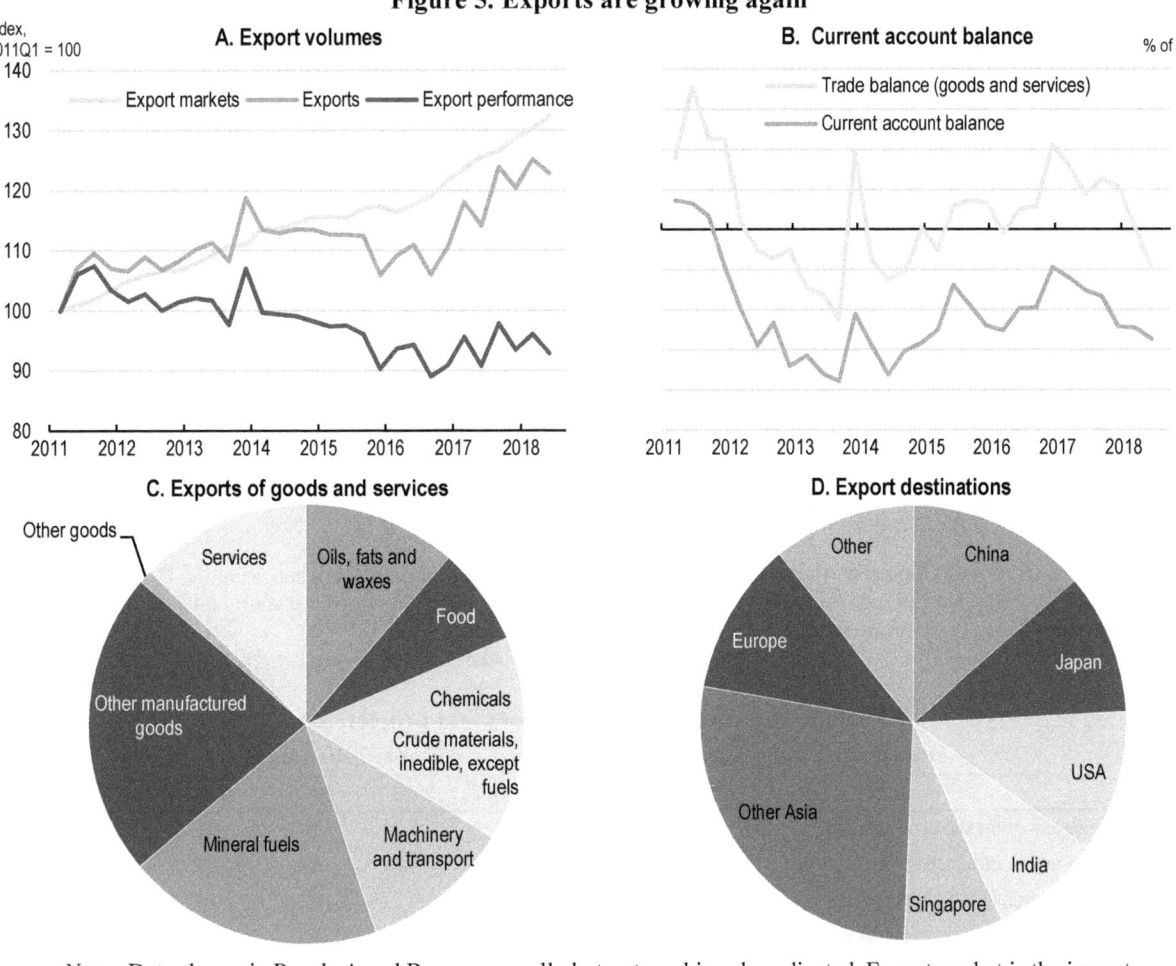

Note: Data shown in Panels A and B are seasonally but not working-day adjusted. Export market is the import volume of trading partners weighted by export shares. Export performance is the ratio between actual exports and export market. Panels C and D are for 2017. Export destination data are available only for goods.
Source: OECD, OECD Economic Outlook 103 Database; CEIC; United Nations, Comtrade Database.

StatLink https://doi.org/10.1787/888933832837

Figure 6. Financial markets moved sharply during 2018

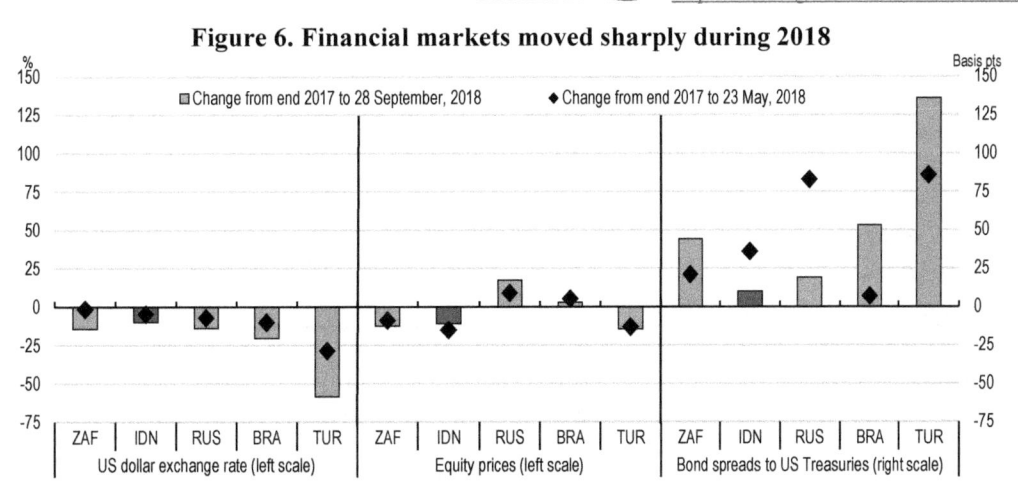

Note: Equity prices are the MSCI Index for each country. Bond spreads are the JPM EMBI+ Bond Index stripped spread (to US Treasuries) for dollar-denominated bonds.
Source: Thomson Reuters.

StatLink https://doi.org/10.1787/888933832856

Figure 7. Inflation has eased to low levels

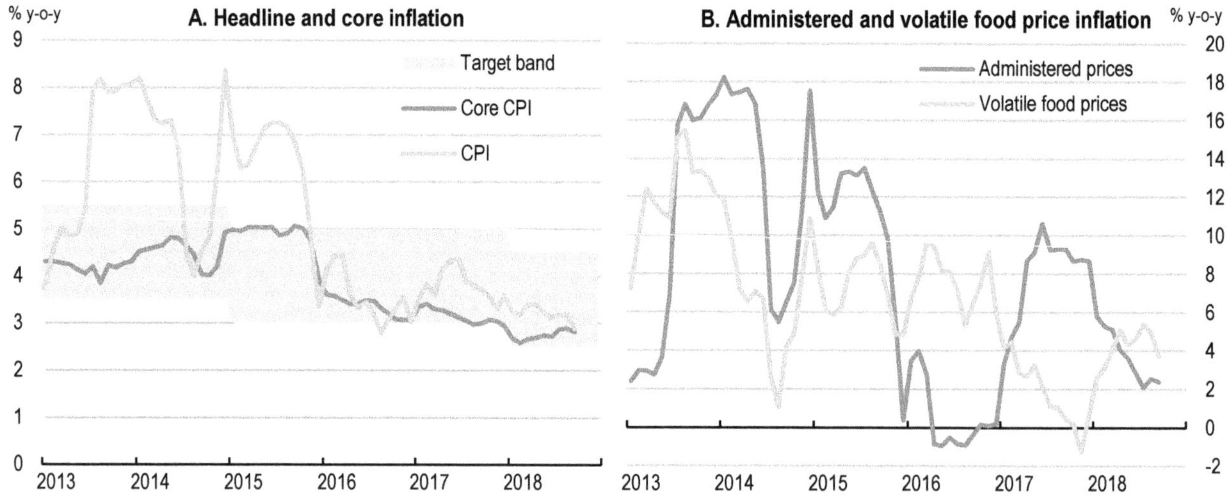

Note: CPI is the Consumer Price Index. Core inflation excludes administered and volatile food prices. Administered prices include those for cigarettes, electricity, water, some modes of transport and certain fuels.
Source: CEIC; Thomson Reuters.

StatLink https://doi.org/10.1787/888933832875

Table 1. Macroeconomic indicators and projections

Percentage change unless otherwise indicated, volumes at 2010 prices

	2015	2016	2017	2018	2019
Gross domestic product (GDP)	4.9	5.0	5.1	5.2	5.3
Private consumption	4.8	5.0	5.0	5.2	5.4
Government consumption	5.3	-0.1	2.1	4.7	3.6
Gross fixed capital formation	5.0	4.5	6.2	6.5	5.9
Stock building[1]	-0.8	0.6	-0.2	0.7	0.0
Total domestic demand	4.0	5.0	4.8	6.1	5.3
Exports of goods and services	-2.1	-1.6	9.1	5.5	5.6
Imports of goods and services	-6.2	-2.4	8.1	10.3	5.7
Net exports[1]	0.9	0.2	0.3	-0.8	0.1
Other indicators					
GDP deflator	4.0	2.5	4.2	3.8	4.1
Consumer price index	6.4	3.5	3.8	3.5	3.9
Trade balance[2,3]	0.4	0.8	1.2	-0.5	-0.4
Current account balance[2]	-2.0	-1.8	-1.7	-2.5	-2.5
Government fiscal balance[2]	-2.8	-2.4	-2.5	-2.2	-2.0
Three-month money market rate[4]	8.3	7.2	6.5	6.1	6.8
Ten-year government bond yield, average[4]	8.2	7.6	7.0	7.5	8.6

1. Contribution to changes in real GDP.
2. As a percentage of GDP.
3. National accounts basis, which can differ from official estimates on a balance-of-payments basis.
4. In per cent.
Source: OECD, *OECD Economic Outlook Database, OECD Interim Economic Outlook*, September 2018.

A key downside risk to the projections is that stemming capital outflows might require a steeper path for interest rates, slowing growth. Rising trade protectionism is a risk to exports, especially if it targets Indonesian exports directly or dents Chinese demand for

Indonesian exports. On the upside, reforms to reduce red tape together with the completion of large infrastructure investments could provide a larger boost to private investment and exports than projected. Further increases in relevant commodity prices would raise nominal export growth and government revenues more than projected. Since Indonesia is a large oil producer but also a net importer, an oil price spike would widen the current account deficit and heighten cost pressures.

External debt is low relative to the past and to other countries (Figure 8, Panels A, C and D). But foreign-currency-denominated debts are higher (Panel B). Together with current account and budget deficits, this means that major disruptions in financial markets could have a large impact, especially if accompanied by falling commodity prices, which would reduce foreign-currency earnings (Table 2). An unexpectedly sharp slowdown in China would also be costly, as could a natural disaster. However, compared to other countries the overall level of government and private debt are low and the banking sector is highly capitalised (Panels E to H).

Policy makers have taken steps to reduce external vulnerabilities, particularly after the current account deficit widened during the second quarter of 2018. Official reserves stood at USD 118 billion in August 2018 – equivalent to 6.6 months of imports and debt servicing. To maintain sufficient funds to provide insurance against a crisis, their use should be limited to containing volatility in the interim. Since 2015 hedging and liquidity requirements have been phased in for borrowers with foreign-currency debt: 25% of net foreign-currency liabilities falling due within each of the next two quarters must be hedged with a domestic bank. Around 90% of corporates have complied, but risks remain (Republic of Indonesia, 2018). Agreements with neighbouring countries to settle payments bilaterally in local currencies rather than US dollars reduce demand for dollars. In August, the "IndONIA", a new overnight benchmark interest rate, was launched to facilitate the development of derivatives products by providing a reliable reference rate. Additional measures are planned. Further developing financial markets would lower the cost of hedging and facilitate rupiah-denominated debt issuance, increasing resilience against exchange-rate swings.

The authorities have also enacted measures to try and narrow the current account deficit. These have included: expanding the supply of biodiesel containing palm oil to reduce fuel imports; increasing withholding tax rates on 1 147 imports, most of which are consumer goods (these taxes are treated as tax credits against corporate income tax liabilities); and postponing selected infrastructure projects with high import content that had not yet begun. There is a risk that restrictions on trade lead to adverse effects on growth. The depreciation of the exchange rate should help reduce demand for imports, while making exports more attractive. Continuing with earlier reforms to streamline export procedures and lower related costs would also help to reduce the current account deficit, as well as support growth.

Table 2. Possible shocks to the Indonesian economy

Vulnerability	Possible outcome
Disruptions to financial markets as major economies normalise monetary policy	The economy would slow down as the resulting rise in debt-servicing costs could expose weaknesses in the corporate sector and Bank Indonesia may need to raise rates significantly to prevent a sharp depreciation of the rupiah.
A sharp slowdown in China	Indonesia's exports would be hit directly and indirectly by lower Chinese demand. Prices for most Indonesian commodity exports would fall, reducing public revenues.
Natural disasters	Indonesia is prone to natural disasters such as extreme weather, volcanic activity and earthquakes, which can entail large fiscal, economic and social costs.

Figure 8. Credit levels are low and banks are well capitalised overall

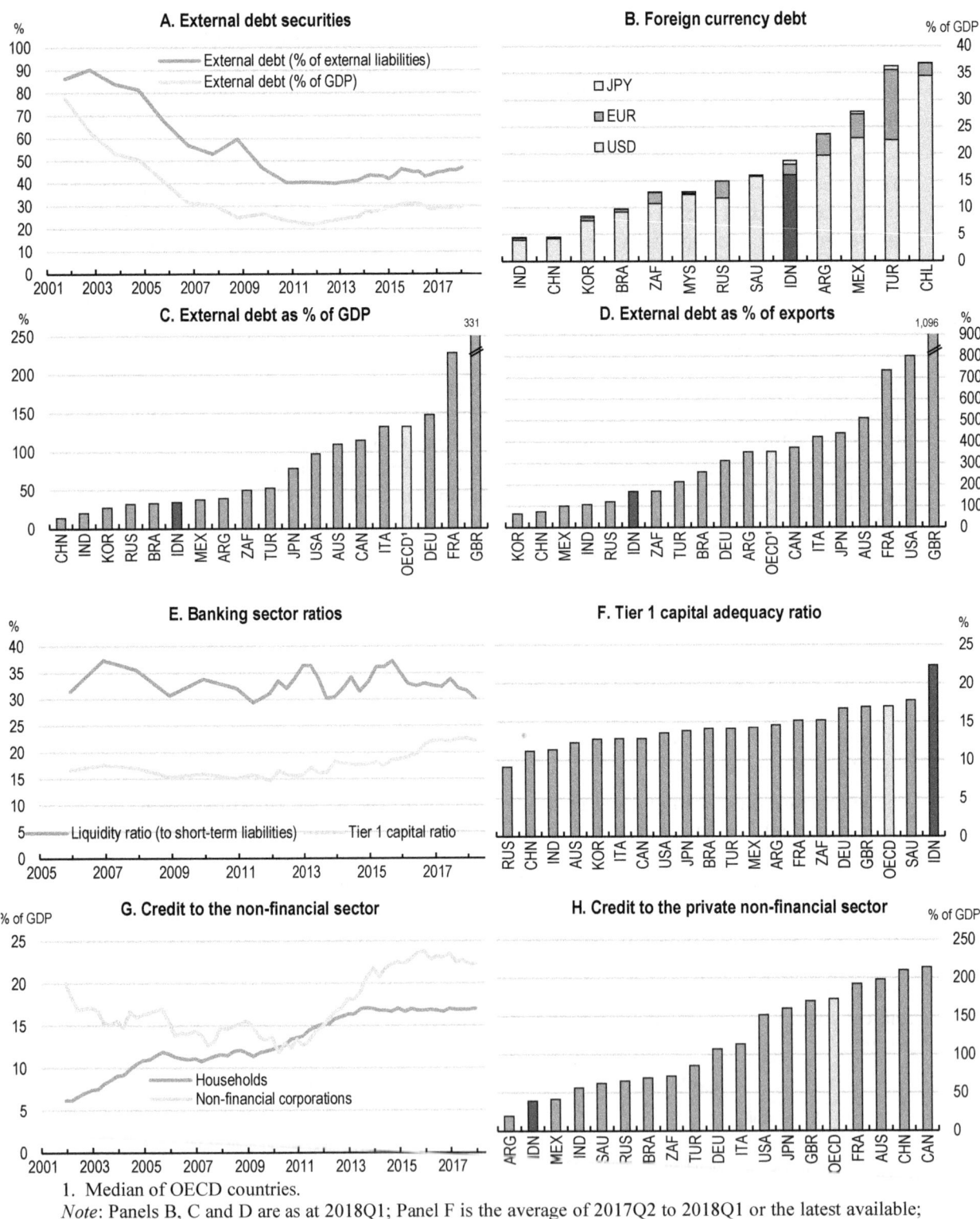

1. Median of OECD countries.

Note: Panels B, C and D are as at 2018Q1; Panel F is the average of 2017Q2 to 2018Q1 or the latest available; Panel H is the average for 2017.

Source: BIS, *Global Liquidity Indicators Database*; World Bank, *External Debt Statistics Database*; OECD, *OECD Economic Outlook Database*, *Resilience Database*; OECD calculations.

StatLink ⟶ https://doi.org/10.1787/888933832894

Monetary policy is contributing to macroeconomic stability

Diminishing inflationary pressure allowed Bank Indonesia to ease monetary policy over 2016-17 by 200 basis points to support growth (Figure 9, Panel A). Initially it responded to capital outflows in 2018 by selling foreign reserves, but in May it began raising policy rates, hiking by a total of 150 basis points by September (Panel B). Bank Indonesia's mandate is to maintain stability in the value of the rupiah, in terms of goods and services (as reflected by the inflation rate) as well as relative to other currencies. It has been given independence to undertake these tasks and pursue its inflation target. As US monetary policy normalises, interest rates will need to rise further to manage exchange-rate pressure, achieve the inflation target and maintain economic stability. Bank Indonesia has emphasised its readiness to act pre-emptively. Permitting the rupiah to depreciate gradually would reduce the steepness of the required policy tightening. Continuing to co-ordinate policy across financial regulators should help maintain investor confidence. In 2020 the inflation target range will again be lowered by ½ percentage point, reducing Bank Indonesia's room for manoeuvre.

The domestic effects of tighter monetary policy could be lessened by maintaining downward pressure on lending rates, either by reducing funding costs for banks or narrowing the spread between bank deposit and lending rates. Indeed, the spread between bank deposit and lending rates – over 500 basis points in 2017 – has been wide for many years and wider than in neighbouring countries. A range of factors contribute to the spread including higher costs of a banking network due to Indonesia's geography, under-developed money markets and inefficiencies. Competition from the growing fintech sector may help push down lending rates. More liquid money markets could lower bank funding costs. Developing money markets will help, including the recent introduction of a new benchmark overnight rate, and encouraging repurchase agreements and interest rate swaps as planned. Bank reserve requirements are being relaxed to provide greater flexibility in liquidity management and lower bank funding costs. Going forward, to increase financial stability systemically important banks will be required to hold additional capital from 2019.

Figure 9. Interest rates and reserve asset sales have been used to stabilise the rupiah

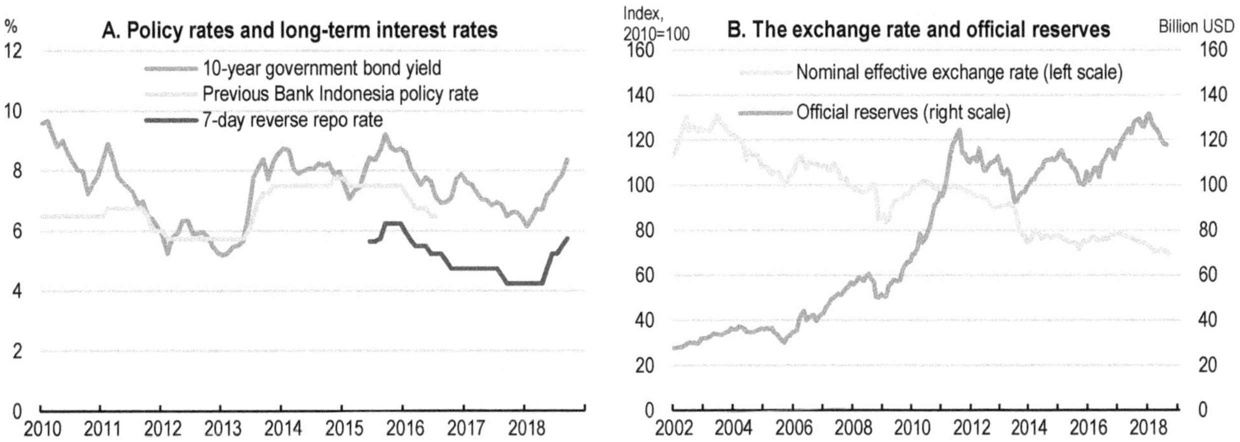

Note. As of 19 August 2016 Bank Indonesia switched to a new policy rate known as the BI 7-Day Reverse Repurchase (repo) Rate.
Source: CEIC; Thomson Reuters.

StatLink https://doi.org/10.1787/888933832913

Deepening and broadening financial markets and access

The bond market is still relatively small and dominated by government issues (Figure 10, Panel A). There is also room to improve liquidity (Panel B). Likewise, stock-market capitalisation is only 46% of GDP, which is lower than in some peers. Deeper local capital markets would help fund investment and bolster financial resilience (Table 3). This requires overcoming obstacles and challenges such as: lengthy and costly issuance procedures; a small domestic investor base; exchange-rate risks and high withholding taxes on interest income for residents from outside of tax-treaty countries, which deter foreign investors; and the need for more co-ordination among regulators and with the private sector (WEF, 2016). A national strategy for financial-market development has started to be implemented and a new overnight benchmark rate, the "IndONIA", has been launched. Streamlining procedures and regulations and aligning them with international practices should increase the supply of corporate bonds. Adopting international principles for financial products, developing reference rates and hedging products, and improving creditor protection would boost investor demand (IMF, 2018; WEF, 2016). Market participants and investors should be consulted before new regulations are implemented.

Figure 10. The local-currency bond market is still small and illiquid

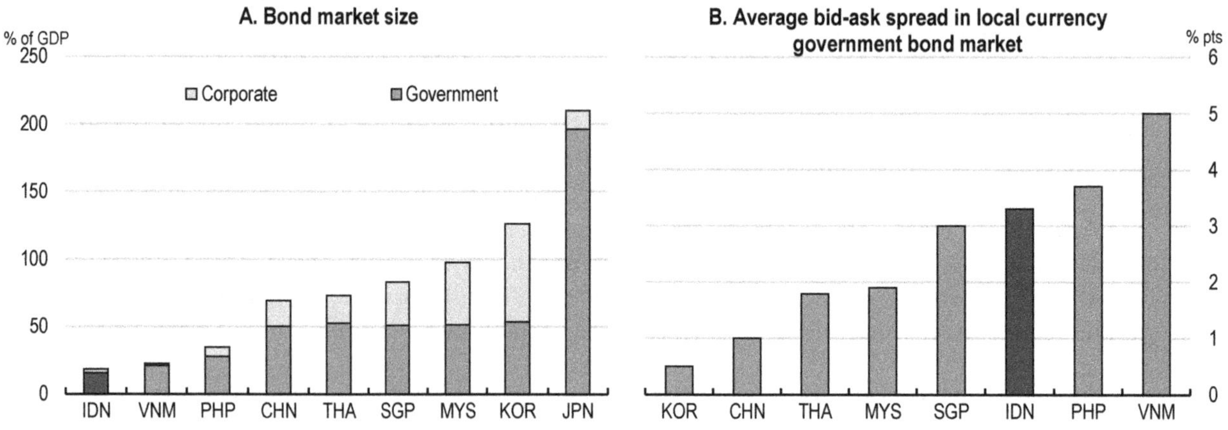

Note: Data are for 2018Q2 or latest available.
Source: Asian Development Bank, *AsianBondsOnline*

StatLink https://doi.org/10.1787/888933832932

Table 3. Past recommendations related to financial markets

Recommendations in previous *Surveys*	Action taken since the October 2016 *Survey*
Deepen and broaden financial markets by making more room for non-banks and the stock market in financing the economy.	In 2017 mechanisms for securitising state-owned enterprise infrastructure assets were implemented to help finance strategic infrastructure projects. In 2018 the authorities relaxed foreign investment restrictions in the insurance sector which is expected to increase investor demand for domestic equities and bonds.
Further develop the foreign exchange market by reducing the role of Bank Indonesia, generalising hedging and options, and enlarging the class of assets underlying the transactions.	The authorities launched the Global Master Repurchase agreement and introduced a version of the International Swap and Derivatives Association contract. The foreign exchange regulatory framework has been revised. Call spread options are now allowed for hedging.

The government also aims to deepen Islamic financial markets by promoting issuance of compliant instruments and Islamic banking. Islamic banks represent just 6% of bank assets, which is comparable to the share in Turkey but well below the 25% share in Malaysia (IFSB, 2017). Indeed, Malaysia's example illustrates the potential in Indonesia (Box 1). Growth in this segment is now outpacing that of conventional banks. Developing Islamic banking could help diversify sources of finance as well as saving. To safeguard financial stability, regulators should ensure that capital requirements are in line with those applying to conventional banks and establish the planned early warning system (IMF, 2017a). Financial education could help increase investor awareness and understanding of these new products.

Box 1. Malaysia's experience with Islamic banking

Islamic finance operates according to the principles of Islamic law, which prohibits usury and promotes risk-sharing and participatory asset-backed financing. Therefore, rather than loans, Islamic banks use non-interest-bearing instruments to fund investment and working capital. For example, they purchase the intermediate inputs or machinery on the customer's behalf and "lend" them to the customer until the loan is repaid. The bank earns a profit margin on the difference between the purchase price of the input or machinery and the price repaid by the customer. Within three decades, Malaysia has developed a competitive, liberal and globally recognised Islamic finance ecosystem that operates alongside the conventional financial system. Islamic banking assets expanded from 0.07% of domestic banking assets in 1994 to 30% by end-2017 (BNM, 2018; Caporale et al., 2016). In the first half of 2016, Malaysia accounted for 9% of global Islamic banking assets (IFSB, 2017).

Islamic banking initially began with Islamic windows set up inside conventional banks. From 2005 standalone Islamic banks were created. The investment intermediation role of Islamic banks was later strengthened through the offering of investment accounts. An "Investment Account Platform" was subsequently launched as a marketplace to match investors with projects that suit their risk appetites. New Islamic banking licences have also been issued to six foreign banks to promote Malaysia as a global Islamic financial hub.

Source: OECD (2016), *OECD Economic Surveys: Malaysia: Economic Assessment*, OECD Publishing, Paris; OECD (2014), *OECD Economic Surveys: Turkey 2014*, OECD Publishing, Paris.

Financial inclusion is improving. The share of adult Indonesians with a financial institution account rose from 36% to 48% between 2014 and 2017, as rural areas caught up (Demirgüç-Kunt et al., 2018). The authorities have adopted a range of programmes to lift financial inclusion. They have promoted digital financial services by shifting some social transfers from in-kind benefits to cash and also e-money (as part of the Cashless Society Programme). Other programmes work with different stakeholders to broaden their reach, for instance branchless banking is promoted through the "Laku Pandai" programme that provides access to simple financial services through agents (Box 2). Nonetheless, access to a saving account is still lagging other countries (Figure 11, Panel A). Cash dominates transactions, and wage-earners are typically paid in cash. The new National Payments Gateway will facilitate greater use of electronic payments. Transactional accounts with wage inflows would provide a credit record, enhancing access to finance. Insufficient funds and distance are common reasons for not having an account (Demirgüç-Kunt et al., 2018).

Programmes such as "Laku Pandai" can help address these challenges but require greater awareness and training of agents, plus improvements in telecommunications and internet infrastructure (LPEM, 2017).

Box 2. Examples of programmes to increase financial inclusion in Indonesia

The authorities have launched a range of programmes engaging with different stakeholders and focussing on different aspects of financial inclusion. For example:

- The "Laku Pandai" programme aims to provide simple financial services such as bank accounts, micro credit and micro insurance through agents – a form of "branchless banking". As of December 2017, it covered 13.6 million customers in 27 banks compared to 3.7 million in 20 banks a year before.

- "SimPel" and "Simpel B" are student savings programmes with simple accounts at conventional and Islamic banks, respectively. They are operated in conjunction with the banking sector. By March 2018, there were 11 million accounts at over 214 000 schools.

- The "Team to Accelerate Regional Financial Access" programme (TPAKD) aims to build co-ordinating forums at the local level to accelerate financial access in regional areas. The teams comprise government institutions and local stakeholders. By March 2018, there were 31 teams at the provincial level and 35 teams at the municipal level.

Source: Bank Indonesia; Financial Services Authority (OJK).

Figure 11. Some measures of financial inclusion still lag other countries

Per cent of population aged 15 years or over

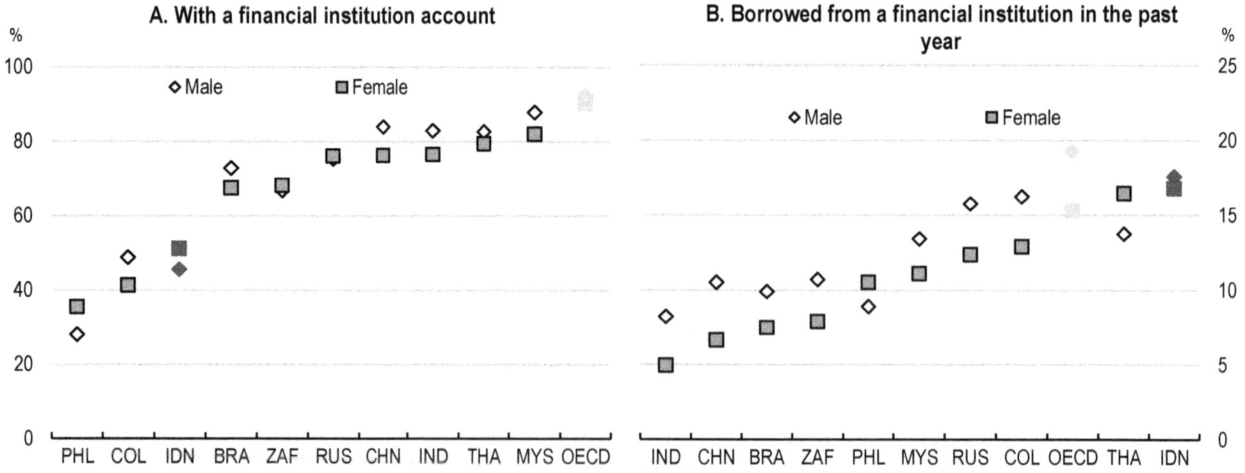

Source: World Bank, *Global Findex Database*.

StatLink https://doi.org/10.1787/888933832951

Indonesia's microfinance sector has grown in prominence, led by banks, as noted in previous *Surveys* (OECD, 2012a). Indeed, borrowing from a financial institution is more common than in some comparable countries (Figure 11, Panel B). The government has taken many measures to increase SME access to finance (OECD, 2018a). These have mostly been bank-focussed and include expanding the subsidised SME lending programme with partial guarantees (KUR) and steadily increasing the floor for bank SME lending to 20% of loans, with administrative penalties for non-compliance. A new programme ("UMi") offers short-term low-interest-rate loans to micro-enterprise borrowers who are too small to qualify for the KUR programme. Policies to promote bank lending to SMEs may have unintended consequences, such as increasing non-performing loans or reducing competition in the banking sector (OECD, 2018a). Non-performing loans under the KUR programme are currently low but should be monitored and the effect of subsidised loans on SME performance should be evaluated. The rapid expansion of peer-to-peer lending is providing SMEs with an alternative to bank finance, with over 60 domestic and foreign fintech lenders registered in June 2018. Further developing credit bureaus may also facilitate access to finance from bank and non-bank lenders alike (OECD, 2018a).

Fiscal policy is sound, but public spending is constrained by low revenues

Indonesia's fiscal stance is prudent thanks to the 2003 Fiscal Law, which caps the deficit at 3% of GDP and debt at 60% of GDP. Since 2015 the government has matched slower growth in revenues with expenditure containment to keep the deficit around 2.5% of GDP (Figure 12). To create a larger buffer *vis-à-vis* the legislated deficit ceiling, it plans to narrow the deficit slightly in 2018 and 2019 to just under 2% of GDP. Given the uncertainty in financial markets this is sensible, but the effectiveness of spending should be improved, as discussed below, to limit the drag on growth from this and tighter monetary policy. More prudent revenue forecasts have enhanced fiscal credibility and spending efficiency by avoiding cuts late in the year. The spending mix improved in 2017, with personnel outlays increasing by 2.5% while capital expenditure expanded by 23%.

Figure 12. The central government deficit has widened but remains within the legislated limit

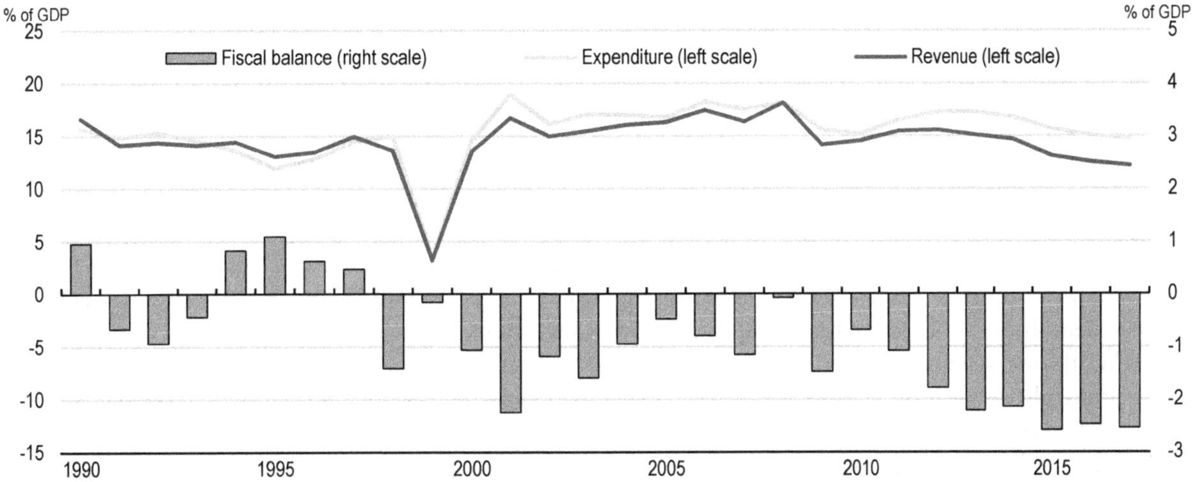

Source: CEIC; Ministry of Finance; OECD, *OECD Economic Outlook Database*.

StatLink ⬛ https://doi.org/10.1787/888933832970

Government debt is low

At 29% of GDP Indonesia's general government gross debt is low relative to other emerging economies and well below the 60%-of-GDP legal limit. Interest payments crept up to 1.6% of GDP in 2017 due to higher debt and a higher effective interest rate. The large share of foreign-currency-denominated debt means that rupiah depreciation raises financing costs (although depreciation also boosts oil-related revenues). The deficit cap, as long as it holds, means that even a large shock to interest payments would not raise debt to unsustainable levels but would crowd out other spending, even if growth remains solid (Figure 13). Otherwise, even with a larger primary deficit, debt is unlikely to rise substantially, absent extreme but low-probability shocks, such as natural disasters or bailing out a large public firm.

Figure 13. General government debt scenarios

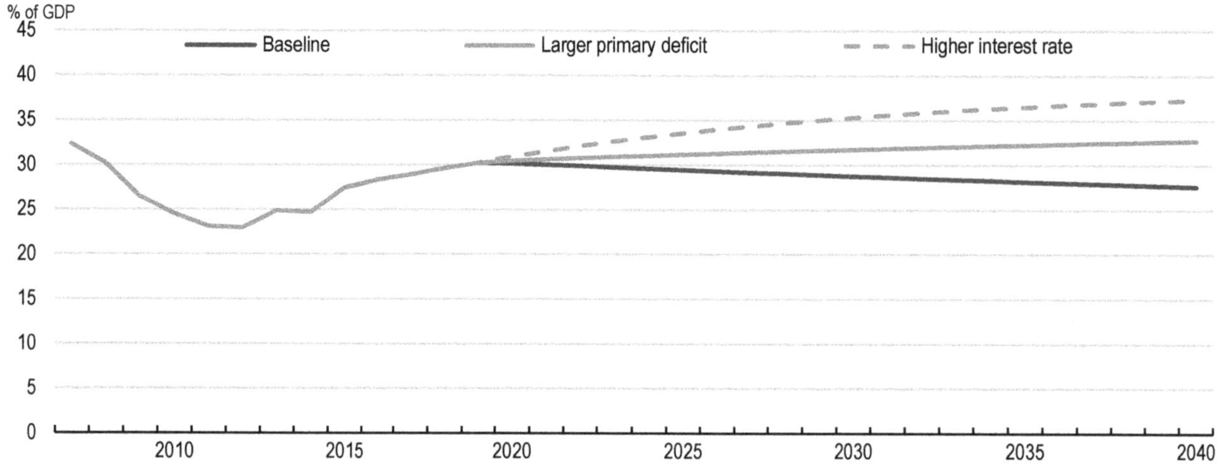

Note: In all scenarios GDP growth and inflation are in line with OECD *Economic Outlook* projections to 2019. The baseline scenario assumes constant GDP growth of 5% and inflation (in the GDP deflator) of 3.2% from 2020. The primary budget deficit is 0.5% from 2019. The effective interest rate is 6% from 2023. The "larger primary deficit" is an alternative scenario that assumes a primary deficit of 0.8% of GDP from 2019 onwards. In the "higher interest rate" scenario, the effective interest rate is assumed to rise by 150 basis points by 2021 and from 2020 the primary deficit is the difference between the 3% cap and interest payments.
Source: OECD, *OECD Economic Outlook Database*; IMF, *World Economic Outlook Database*; OECD calculations.

StatLink 🔗 https://doi.org/10.1787/888933832989

Although low relative to GDP, Indonesia's government debt appears more vulnerable to large shocks than some other emerging economies', partly due to foreign exposure but also the fact that debt-servicing costs have also tended to be relatively high (OECD, 2016a). Government debt was equivalent to around twice revenues in 2017, which is similar to many emerging economies, where raising revenues is generally more difficult. Recent research on debt limits highlights how the government could increase resilience (Box 3). While the government cannot control market volatility, it can improve regulatory quality and fight corruption at all levels, which can lower risk premia (OECD, 2018b). Exports can improve resilience by better covering debt financing. Continued improvements to logistics and finalising pending free trade agreements with the European Free Trade Association and Iran could boost exports. An agreement with Australia was concluded in August 2018. Indonesia is also considering joining the Trans-Pacific Partnership with five other ASEAN members who are not signatories, which would mitigate any trade diversion effects from being outside the agreement.

Box 3. Determinants of debt sustainability and risk premia

Recent OECD research sheds light on the non-linear relationship between a country's debt level and its risk premium, which is in turn a function of the probability of default (Fournier and Bétin, 2018). Focussing on middle-income countries, Fournier and Bétin estimate: (i) a "safe" range of debt ratios, within which the interest rate returns to equilibrium following a transient interest-rate shock without threatening fiscal sustainability; and (ii) a range of debt ratios in which a sufficiently high interest-rate shock may push the country onto a self-fulfilling path towards default. The upper limit therefore is the estimated debt limit beyond which a shock pushes a country to default.

The estimated debt levels are of course subject to some uncertainty and should be treated with caution. But the exercise highlights country-specific factors that are associated with higher "safe" debt ranges, namely: more effective government; a higher export share in GDP; higher GDP growth; lower volatility of growth; and an absence of default in neighbouring countries.

The estimated "safe" debt range is narrower in Indonesia than other middle-income countries (Figure 14). The gap with other countries is mostly due to lower-than-average export shares, even allowing for Indonesia's size, and relatively poor perceptions of government effectiveness, although the latter has improved markedly (Figure 15). This is consistent with panel regressions on the determinants of risk premia in OECD and emerging economies that highlight the role of regulatory quality, as well as the level of government debt and global financial-market volatility (OECD, 2018b).

Figure 14. Debt is low, but so is the estimated debt limit

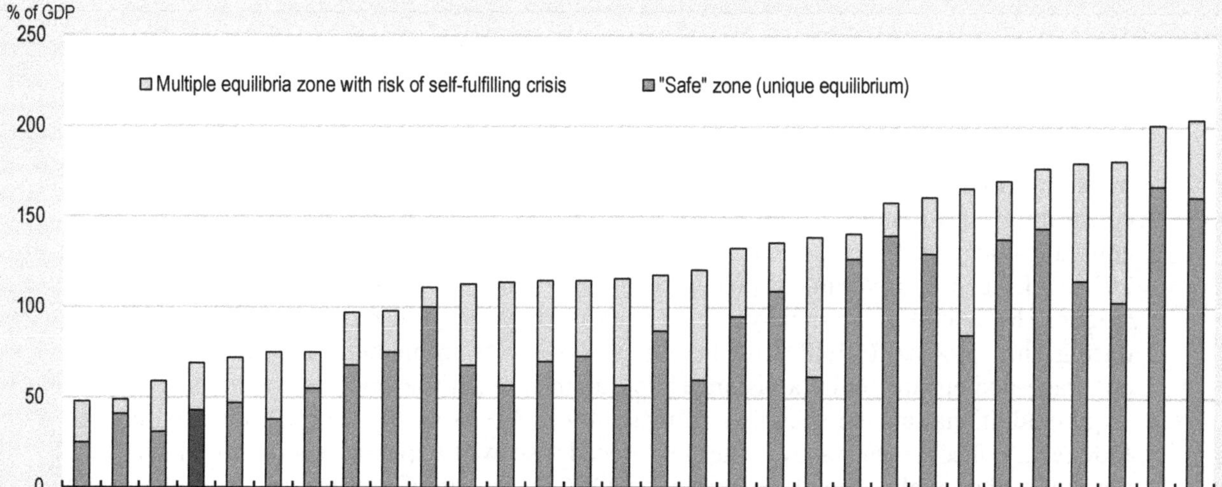

Note: The debt ranges are calibrated for a risk-neutral investor, a recovery rate after default of 50% and a risk-free interest rate of 3%. The estimates are based on smoothed data.
Source: J.-M. Fournier and M. Bétin (2018), "Limits to debt sustainability in middle-income countries", *OECD Economics Department Working Papers*, No. 1493, OECD Publishing, Paris.

StatLink ᔟᔟᔟ https://doi.org/10.1787/888933833008

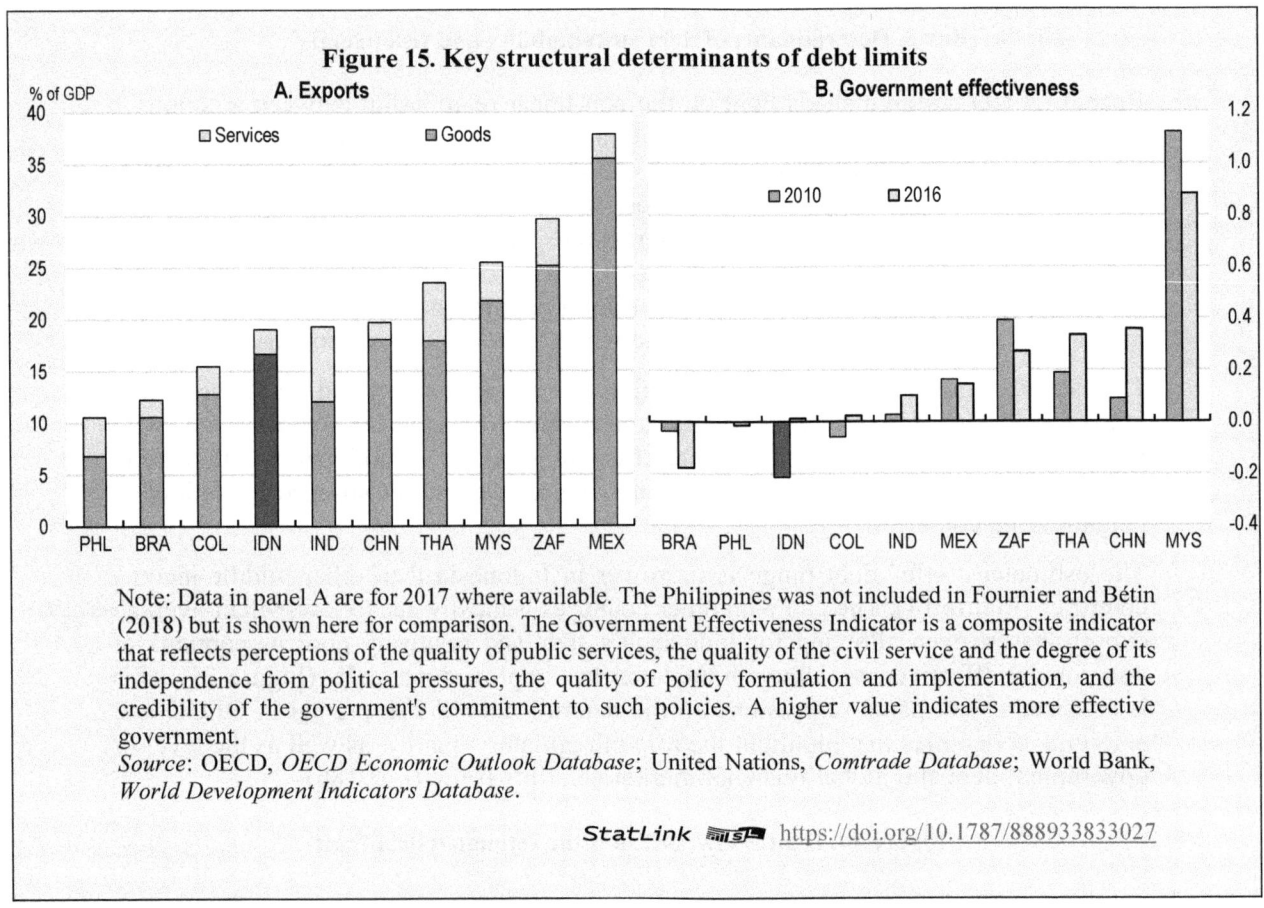

Figure 15. Key structural determinants of debt limits

Note: Data in panel A are for 2017 where available. The Philippines was not included in Fournier and Bétin (2018) but is shown here for comparison. The Government Effectiveness Indicator is a composite indicator that reflects perceptions of the quality of public services, the quality of the civil service and the degree of its independence from political pressures, the quality of policy formulation and implementation, and the credibility of the government's commitment to such policies. A higher value indicates more effective government.
Source: OECD, *OECD Economic Outlook Database*; United Nations, *Comtrade Database*; World Bank, *World Development Indicators Database*.

StatLink ᵃⁱˢᴾ https://doi.org/10.1787/888933833027

Finding funds for development-related spending is a challenge

Against this background, the biggest fiscal challenge is funding spending that will boost long-term growth and improve well-being. Indonesia's infrastructure gaps – particularly in transport, logistics and water treatment – add to costs and limit access to services, constraining development (OECD, 2016a). In 2015 the government capital stock was equivalent to just 39% of GDP, compared to 92% across emerging economies (IMF, 2017b). Likewise, government provision of health and social assistance is currently low (Figure 16). Social protection systems are expanding and will require additional funding during this process (OECD, forthcoming). To fully implement universal healthcare coverage and ensure social assistance programmes reach the poor and vulnerable would require additional annual spending equivalent to 1.4% of GDP (World Bank, 2018a). As Indonesia's income grows over the next decade, so will expectations of social services. Applying the public social spending of OECD emerging economies to Indonesia's projected demographics would imply a substantial expansion in social programmes and spending as a share of GDP in 2030 (Table 4).

Figure 16. Social spending is still relatively modest

2016 or latest available

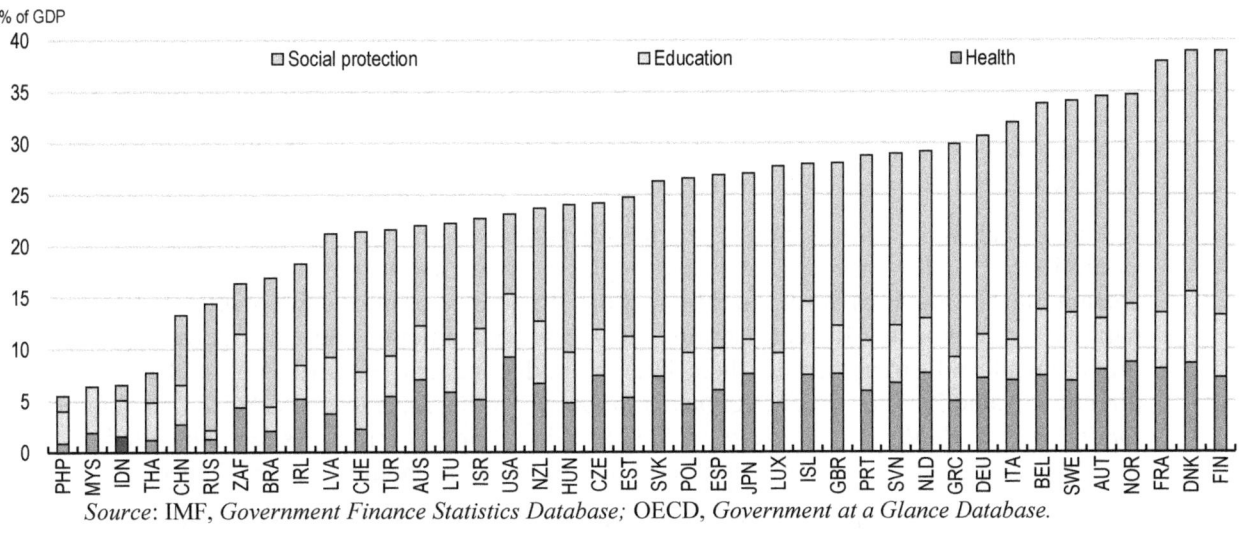

Source: IMF, *Government Finance Statistics Database;* OECD, *Government at a Glance Database.*

StatLink ⬛ https://doi.org/10.1787/888933833046

Table 4. Demands for public spending will likely increase as income rises

	Current spending (% of GDP, 2016)	Potential spending demands in 2030 based on OECD emerging market economies (% of GDP)
Health	1.5	
- All health spending		4.2
Social protection	1.4	
- Old-age pension		5.7
- Disability and sickness cash benefits		1.0
- Family benefits including early childhood education and care		2.0
- Active labour market programmes		0.2
- Unemployment benefits		0.2
Education	3.6	
- Primary, secondary and post-secondary non-tertiary education	2.5[1]	3.6
- Tertiary education	0.6[1]	1.2

Note: Estimates for family benefits, active labour market programmes, old-age pensions and education are based on spending-to-GDP ratios adjusted for projected relevant population shares in 2030. Other estimates are simple averages. The economies used for comparison are: Chile; Hungary; Mexico; Poland and Turkey.
1. In 2015.
Source: IMF, *Government Finance Statistics Database;* OECD, *Government at a Glance Database, Social Expenditure Database*; OECD (2017), *Education at a Glance 2017*; United Nations, Department of Economic and Social Affairs, Population Division (2017), *World Population Prospects: The 2017 Revision*, DVD Edition; OECD calculations.

Given the difficulty of raising revenues, increasing the efficiency of public spending – as highlighted in the previous *Survey* – remains a high priority for freeing up funds (OECD, 2016a). The energy subsidy reforms of 2014-17 contributed to a 14 percentage point fall in the share of government expenditure on energy subsidies, freeing up funds for infrastructure and better targeted social programmes. The shift from rice subsidies to e-vouchers for a wider variety of food is also in line with previous OECD recommendations

(OECD, 2016a; 2015a). Nonetheless, national accounts data indicate that total subsidies on production were still equivalent to 1% of GDP in 2017, compared to 0.6% in OECD countries. Energy subsidies are expected to increase by IDR 66 trillion (0.4% of GDP) in 2018, largely due to a larger diesel subsidy. Energy and fertiliser subsidies, which encourage overuse, should be replaced with more targeted support such as cash transfers for poor households and education and investment to raise agricultural productivity (OECD, 2016a; 2015b). Sub-national transfers are becoming better targeted, but more targeting and monitoring are still needed (Table 5). Costs associated with the expansion of health coverage will need to be controlled (OECD, forthcoming).

Agencies such as the national public procurement authority and the Corruption Eradication Commission (KPK) have crucial roles to play in reducing losses due to bribery and corruption. The previous *Survey* highlighted the importance of improving practices at sub-national governments. Recent reforms at local governments such as increasing e-procurement and strengthening their internal budgeting and controls go in the right direction (Table 5). The *OECD Recommendation on Public Integrity* and *OECD Principles for Integrity in Public Procurement* could help guide further reforms. As recommended in the previous *Survey*, the authority and resources of the KPK should be strengthened.

Table 5. Past recommendations for improving the efficiency of the public sector

Recommendations in previous *Surveys*	Action taken since the October 2016 *Survey*
Improve corruption-prevention mechanisms, while further boosting efforts to combat all its forms. Support the Corruption Eradication Commission (KPK), and provide it with more resources and authority.	In 2017 the KPK launched e-LHKPN, an online reporting system to ease the process for government officials to report their assets and GOL KPK, an app for reporting gifts. Local governments are being encouraged to adopt technology that reduces the scope for corruption, such as e-procurement, and to strengthen internal budgeting and controls. In 2018 an electronic system for licensing was launched – the Online Single Submission system. This is expected to reduce corruption.
Move ahead with the implementation of performance-based budgeting ("money follows the programme"). Improve evaluation of existing and future programmes, and reinforce links with medium-term objectives.	The "Architecture and Performance Information" (ADIK) application for ministries and institutions was implemented to improve the quality of budget allocation.
Revise the system of transfers from central to sub-national governments to remove the link with payroll. Reform the system of village transfers to account for population size and poverty prevalence for the basic allocation.	There is now a cap on the basic allocation component of the General Allocation Funds transferred to sub-national governments, which weakens the link with payroll expense. From 2018 the village transfers apportion weights to population (10%), number of poor people (50%), land area (15%) and degree of geographic difficulty (25%). Additional transfers are given to underdeveloped villages with many poor people.
Phase out all remaining energy subsidies. Phase out fertiliser subsidies in favour of the development of irrigation systems, rural infrastructure and research, and direct cash support to the poorest farmers. Replace RASKIN with food vouchers for the poorest.	During 2017 electricity subsidies were removed for non-poor households with 900 volt-ampere connections. However, energy subsidies have increased in 2018. In the 2018 Budget the government announced plans to shift Rastra (formerly RASKIN) recipients of rice to vouchers under the non-cash food aid (BPNT) programme.

State-owned enterprises (SOEs) are a key plank in the government's infrastructure and development strategy. For instance, the 2016 plan to accelerate 245 national strategic projects assumed that 30% would be financed by SOEs' investment. The 143 national-level SOEs operate in almost all sectors of the economy, ranging from manufacturing, construction and transportation to agriculture. SOEs are more pervasive across the economy than in any country in the OECD's Product Market Regulation database except China. Listed SOEs represent almost one-quarter of equity market capitalisation. SOEs' capital expenditures are targeted to reach almost 3% of GDP in 2018, more than twice their 2015 share. This was facilitated by government support, particularly capital injections in

2015-16 and a programme that encouraged them to revalue their assets. As SOEs have tapped capital markets, the leverage of some has risen dramatically (Reuters, 2018).

Financial vulnerabilities are rising at some SOEs. Rapid investment and higher leverage exposes SOEs involved with infrastructure projects to cash-flow difficulties, particularly if interest rates increase or projects are delayed. Measures to contain retail electricity and fuel prices are generating financial pressures for those firms. For example, the price of low-octane fuel ("premium") has not been changed since 2016 despite the increase in the international oil price. In total 14 SOEs made losses in 2017, fewer than in 2016. State-owned banks' exposures to SMEs and the construction sector have risen rapidly. On-balance-sheet loans and guarantees to SOEs are relatively small. Recognised contingent liabilities were only 0.01% of GDP in 2017, as these are confined to government-guaranteed loans. But the potential need for capital injections represents an indirect fiscal risk. Despite ongoing efforts to improve corporate governance, lack of transparency remains a concern (IFC, 2018).

Given these risks, monitoring SOEs and ensuring good governance are crucial. Plans to consolidate many SOEs into six sectoral holding companies are intended to improve efficiency but will probably make their financial situation more opaque. While all incorporated SOEs are required produce externally audited financial reports, these should be made publicly available and easily accessible to facilitate monitoring. Listing more SOEs would also improve corporate governance. An ownership policy could guide this process. Better disclosure could also help address concerns about integrity. Board members should be appointed in transparent nomination processes with limited political interference (IFC, 2018). Supervision by line ministries should be strengthened. Boards should also have clear mandates with sufficient independence to achieve them, as recommended in the *OECD Guidelines on Corporate Governance of State-owned Enterprises*. Greater attention should be given to the implicit risks from SOE losses and rising debt. Supervisors should be vigilant regarding credit quality of new loans from public banks.

Greater private-sector involvement in infrastructure projects would reduce the pressure on SOEs, but the private sector is being crowded out (World Bank, 2017). The government has increased the use of public-private partnerships (PPPs): in 2017 there were 11 PPPs underway, totalling USD 15.4 billion (World Bank, 2018b). Well-designed PPP projects with appropriately managed risks can harness the efficiency and expertise of the private sector (OECD, 2016a). However, prospective investors face legal and regulatory uncertainty and a lack of viable projects due to deficiencies in the project cycle (World Bank, 2017). SOEs sometimes act as "private" bidders which may also deter private investors (OECD, 2012b).

Several instruments have been created to attract more private sector interest in PPPs: "viability gap funding" (to subsidise capital costs); government guarantees (to cover government-related performance risks); "project development facilities" (to help prepare documentation such as feasibility studies); and "availability payments" (to increase certainty of cash flows by providing periodic payments for infrastructure services that comply with pre-agreed criteria). A stronger PPP unit and a more prominent role for the Ministry of Finance would help to manage PPP-related risks (OECD, 2016a; 2012b). But fundamental issues such as property rights, shallow capital markets and conflicting regulations should also be addressed. More generally, alternatives such as concessioning, asset recycling, asset securitisation and foreign direct investment should be promoted, including by revisiting the negative investment list (OECD, 2016b).

Raising revenues to meet spending needs

Falling non-tax revenues have weighed on overall revenue growth in recent years, largely due to lower receipts from resources such as oil. Consequently, the ratio of general government revenue to GDP declined to 14% in 2016 (Figure 17, Panel A). Tax revenues (12% of GDP according to the OECD's definition) are particularly low relative to other countries at a similar income level, including Malaysia and the Philippines (Panel B). Higher commodity prices and improvements in compliance are expected to raise revenue-to-GDP ratios somewhat in 2018. Tax reforms that durably raise medium-term revenues would reduce exposure to commodity cycles and could push Indonesia into a higher-tax, higher-growth equilibrium (Gaspar, Jaramillo and Wingender, 2016). This depends on both raising compliance and improving tax design, as highlighted in the OECD's 2012 *Economic Survey* (OECD, 2012a). Over 2012-16, the number of registered taxpayers rose by almost 12 million, but registration levels remain low by international standards (Table 6). Accordingly the government's tax reform agenda includes actions to raise compliance, including through strengthening the tax administration and simplifying tax design.

Figure 17. Fiscal revenues have been low

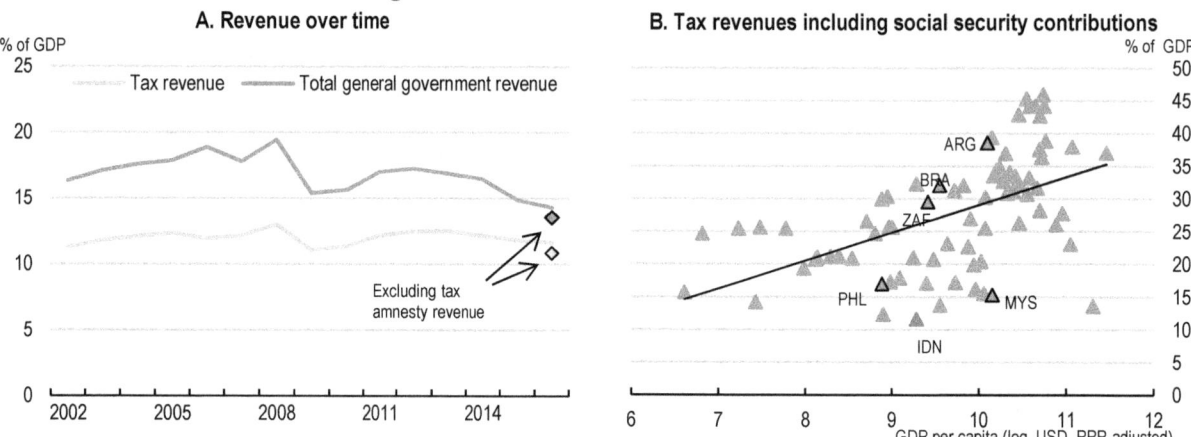

Note: Tax revenue data are based on the OECD's definition of tax revenues and can differ from national definitions. In Panel A the diamonds exclude revenue equivalent to 0.8% of GDP raised during the tax amnesty for individuals and firms that began in July 2016. Data for Indonesia do not include social security contributions; those that would be classified as tax revenue are estimated to total less than 0.5% of GDP. In Panel B data are for 2016 or latest available.
Source: OECD, *Revenue Statistics Database*, *OECD Economic Outlook Database*; World Bank, *World Development Indicators Database*; IMF, *World Economic Outlook Database*; World Bank (2018), *Indonesia Economic Quarterly: Towards Inclusive Growth*, World Bank, Jakarta.

StatLink https://doi.org/10.1787/888933833065

Upgrading tax administration and increasing enforcement are priorities

The main tax administration is the Directorate General of Taxes (DGT), which sits within the Ministry of Finance but has offices around the country. Restructuring the administration and developing its human resources are part of the tax reform agenda. Spending on staff has been low in the past but by 2016 had risen to be comparable with other non-member countries (Table 6). It rose further in 2017. The number of employees is low relative to the number of adults, although it is higher relative to the number of taxpayers. However, the administration has been expanding its workforce and investing in training existing staff. Nonetheless, auditors, analysts and IT professionals are in short supply. Further training will be crucial in strengthening the administration and enabling staff to adapt to new technologies and challenges. Hiring and reallocation are needed but hampered by public-sector staffing regulations. Giving the DGT temporary authority to make more transformative staffing changes (with oversight) could accelerate the pace of change.

Table 6. Tax administration performance and resources

	Indonesia	Non-OECD average	OECD emerging market economies	OECD average
Indicators of performance				
Registered personal income taxpayers (% of population 15+ years)	Between 17.8 and 35.7[1]	56.1	73.6	87.6
On-time filing (%)				
- Personal income taxpayers	60.6	78.6	63.5	90.6
- Corporate income taxpayers	57.6	71.9	59.8	84.5
On-time payment – value-added tax (%)	86.0	90.4	-	93.3
Indicators of resources				
Citizens (15 + years) per staff member	4 893	3 030	1 917	1 269
Active personal income taxpayers per staff member	446	562	1 065	635
Total budget as % GDP	0.08	0.12	0.14	0.19
Staff costs as % total recurrent budget	61.0	64.3	74.9	72.6
Training costs as % total recurrent budget	0.4	0.3	1.2	0.5
IT budget as % total recurrent budget	3.3	11.0	3.8	13.4

Note: Data are for 2015 except for data for Indonesia on registered PIT taxpayers and staff costs, which are for 2016. The number of countries covered varies with response rates to the questionnaire, up to 55 countries. OECD emerging market economies is the average of Chile, Hungary, Mexico, Poland and Turkey; the average is not shown where there is only data for one country.
1. Calculated from data provided by the Directorate General of Taxes. Registered taxpayers are at end 2016. Note that married individuals typically pay tax at the household level; the lower bound is calculated by adjusting the number of taxpayers for the share that file tax jointly and the upper bound assumes that every taxpayer represents a two-taxpayer household.
Source: OECD (2017), *Tax Administration 2017: Comparative Information on OECD and Other Advanced and Emerging Economies*, OECD Publishing, Paris; Directorate General of Taxes; United Nations, Department of Economic and Social Affairs, Population Division (2017), *World Population Prospects: The 2017 Revision*, DVD Edition; OECD calculations.

Information systems are ageing but are being modernised as part of the reform agenda. This can promote compliance by lowering costs for taxpayers and raising the probability of detection. E-filing rates for income tax have risen to 82% in 2017, but experience from Brazil and Mexico shows 100% is attainable. Filing and payment can be made easier through pre-filled returns and reminders, for example. The 2016-17 tax amnesty and Automatic Exchange of Information from September 2018 add to the vast quantity of data to protect and process; detecting non-compliance is critical to reinforce the success of the amnesty. In 2018 the government plans to begin procurement of a "core tax administration" system that will capture all business processes including compliance system management and taxpayer account management. The procurement process should be open and implementation risks carefully managed.

Complexity and uncertainty add to compliance costs and increase opportunities for tax avoidance. The burden of paying tax appears more costly, in terms of time, than in other emerging economies, notwithstanding improvements in recent years (World Bank / PwC, 2018). The tax regime is still perceived as more contradictory and less consistently enforced than in most regional comparators even though it is perceived to have improved (Deloitte, 2017). Policy changes are frequent, which is partly due to changing circumstances but also because insufficient consultation leads to further changes. Simplifying the tax code, as planned, and reducing the frequency of changes would ease compliance costs. Broader public consultations on draft legislation would improve the quality of legislation. To build an evidence base for future reform, the tax reform team could be tasked with consulting stakeholders and the public on policy reforms and publishing reports on these, as the Davis Tax Committee did in South Africa (OECD, 2015c). Planned changes to the tax administration's website are expected to make it more user-friendly. Clear and simple explanations of current obligations and online calculators, for example, would assist taxpayers in complying. Greater use of risk-based auditing would improve efficiency and perceptions of fairness.

Taxes can be broader and more inclusive

Around half of all tax revenue is raised from income taxes and a further 30% from value-added tax. Other taxes include tobacco excise, trade taxes and local government taxes. Overall, the structure is similar to that of other emerging market economies but the level of revenues raised from key tax bases – corporate income, labour and goods and services – is lower (Figure 18). This suggests that higher revenues from all major taxes should be possible.

With low incomes and high rates of informality, the current personal income tax net includes few individuals and raises little revenue. Due to large increases in the basic tax allowance, Indonesian workers start paying a marginal tax rate of 5% when their gross income is around twice the average employee's earnings (or more if they have dependents). Social security contributions apply to all workers but are relatively low (and not included in Figure 18). Compared to other large emerging economies, marginal tax rates at medium-to-high incomes are low (Figure 19). This also limits the progressivity of the system: in 2016 an individual hit the 30% marginal tax rate only when their gross income was more than 20 times average earnings. Holding the basic tax allowance constant over time would see more workers gradually join the system. Lowering the top two brackets would make the system more progressive and raise more revenue. The administration would need to monitor the effects of these changes on compliance to ensure they do not increase informality or avoidance.

Figure 18. Most components of tax revenue are lower than in other countries

As a percentage of GDP, 2016 or latest

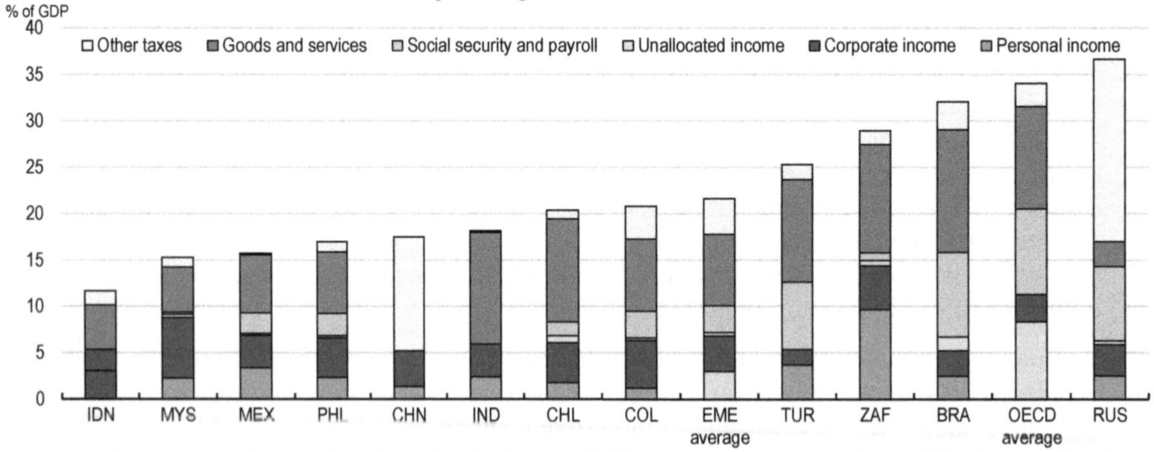

Note: Tax revenue data are based on the OECD's definition of tax revenues and can differ from national definitions. Data for Indonesia do not include social security contributions; those that would be classified as tax revenue are estimated to total less than 0.5% of GDP. Data for Indonesia for 2016 include the effects of the tax amnesty, which added 0.8% of GDP to revenue in 2016.
Source: OECD, *Revenue Statistics Database*; CEIC; Ministry of Finance (2016), *Indian Public Finance Statistics: 2015-2016*.

StatLink ᵐˢᵖ https://doi.org/10.1787/888933833084

Figure 19. Top personal income tax rates bite at high levels of income

Statutory marginal personal income tax rates by income level, 2016

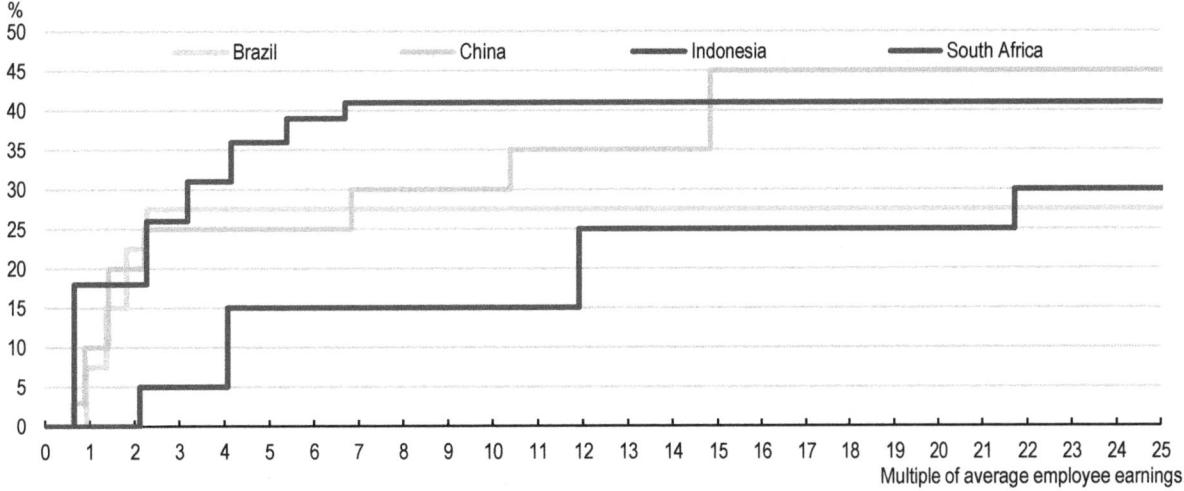

Note: Rates shown are statutory rates. They take into account the basic tax allowance but do not include other tax allowances that reduce effective tax rates. Earnings are a harmonised measure of average monthly earnings of all employees.
Source: ILO, *ILOSTAT Database*; EY (2016), *Worldwide Personal Tax and Immigration Guide 2016-17*; OECD calculations.

StatLink ᯔᰚᴸ https://doi.org/10.1787/888933833103

Unequal treatment of different forms of income reduces the tax base and complicates the system. In particular, fringe benefits and allowances paid by employers are untaxed under the personal income tax system (but employers may not deduct them as expenses). This is regressive, as such benefits are more likely to accrue to those on higher incomes and so should be taxable income. Discussions are underway to recognise these benefits as personal taxable income and in turn recognise them as expenses for corporate income tax. Individuals' investment income is also taxed at different rates depending on the source. This can distort saving decisions and create tax planning opportunities. The 10% tax rate on real estate rental income is far below the 20% rate on bank interest, creating a strong incentive to invest in real estate. The rate schedule should be reviewed to reduce such disparities.

Indonesia's statutory corporate income tax rate of 25% is roughly in line with G20 and OECD averages. In recent years tax incentives have been expanded to attract investment. In April 2018 the government widened the eligibility for tax holidays to 17 specified "pioneer" industries (including oil and gas refining, machinery manufacturing and economic infrastructure) and simplified the application process. The holidays range from 5 to 20 years, depending on investment size. There are also tax holidays and other incentives in designated zones and tax allowances for 145 business segments. Experience from other countries suggests that tax holidays are often ineffective in raising investment because the broader issues hampering investment remain or foreign investment displaces domestic investment (IMF / OECD / UN / World Bank, 2015; IADB, 2013). Moreover, tax holidays (and special economic zones) create tax planning opportunities, distort competition and create the potential for policy capture and corruption (OECD, 2018c; 2012a; IADB, 2013).

Rethinking tax incentives could broaden the tax base and be more effective in promoting investment. The publication in late September 2018 of detailed tax expenditure estimates for 2016-17 increases transparency and is a welcome first step in evaluating the incentives. The tax expenditure report should continue to be improved and be published annually, as planned. Because many countries in the region offer tax holidays, Indonesia could lead a co-ordinated approach within ASEAN. It would be preferable to shift away from tax holidays to cost-based incentives (tax deductions or credits) linked to investment in capital or skills. Those incentives would better target new investment but would require ensuring sufficient administrative capacity to oversee them. All incentives should be monitored carefully to detect abuse and subject to a sunset clause to guarantee regular reviews. Investor concerns related to the regulatory environment would be better addressed directly rather than through the tax system.

A turnover tax for small businesses aims to encourage formalisation of small firms. Businesses in eligible sectors with annual turnover below IDR 4.8 billion (around USD 323 000 in September 2018) can opt into the scheme and pay a rate of 0.5%, which was halved from 1% in July 2018. The threshold for compulsory value-added tax (VAT) registration is also IDR 4.8 billion. By 2017 the turnover tax regime had already attracted 1.5 million registrants, of which 205 000 were incorporated and 1.3 million were individuals. However, the sheer number of SMEs in Indonesia means that increasing registration remains a challenge (Table 7). The regime's cost has not yet been included in the tax expenditure report. Access to the turnover tax is limited to three years for incorporated firms, and to seven years for individuals. The time limit aims to avoid creating disincentives to grow but it will disadvantage firms that do not have the capacity to comply with the standard tax system.

Regional tax offices are increasingly offering services for SMEs. Linking the turnover tax to additional benefits such as access to business development services, book-keeping assistance and applications, and simplified administrative procedures could encourage formalisation. To contain costs, eligibility for the tax should be restricted to very small firms. Such comprehensive programmes increased registration in Mexico, Brazil and Colombia. Micro enterprises should be allowed to remain on the simplified scheme.

Table 7. Micro enterprises dominate the business landscape

	Cut-off values for each category (IDR)		By number		By employment	
	Net assets (excluding premises)	Annual revenue	Thousand	% of total	Thousand	% of total
Micro enterprises	50 million	300 million	23 864	89.3	41 032	58.4
Small enterprises	500 million	2.5 billion	2 399	9.0	12 609	17.9
Medium enterprises	10 billion	50 billion	412	1.5	8 132	11.6
Large enterprises			35	0.1	8 547	12.2
Total			26 711		70 320	

Note: Data are for establishments in 2016 and exclude the agriculture, forestry and fisheries sector, government administration, defence and social security sector, and household activities as employers or own production sector. Unregistered businesses are included.
Source: Statistics Indonesia, *Economic Census 2016.*

Taxes on goods and services could be more efficient

Value-added tax (VAT) revenues have been increasing in recent years. This is welcome, given that base's potential to be a comparatively efficient source of revenue (Akgun, Cournède and Fournier, 2017; Acosta-Ormaechea and Yoo, 2012). There is a single rate of 10%, but numerous exemptions and a high threshold for registration reduce the VAT's efficiency and effectiveness considerably. In addition to exemptions for specific basic foods and common exemptions (such as education), there are exemptions for "strategic" intermediate inputs, services subject to local sales taxes (hotels, restaurants, entertainment, parking), certain resource-related products, and services supplied to local shipping firms. Exemptions weaken the efficiency of VAT, because the tax cascades, (OECD/KIPF, 2014) and self-enforcement, because the purchaser has no incentive to demand a VAT invoice. The high threshold for registration significantly reduces the share of firms participating in the system and therefore reinforcing compliance.

A comprehensive VAT reform could broaden its base and increase its effectiveness. Exemptions for services that are subject to the 10% local sales taxes (such as hotels and restaurants) and intermediate inputs should be removed to harness the self-enforcement properties of VAT. The corresponding local sales taxes should be eliminated and local governments compensated for lost revenue via transfers. While changing the local sales tax would likely be difficult because it would require changing the laws related to decentralisation, it would benefit the firms in these sectors because they could claim back the VAT paid on inputs. Local governments could be permitted to charge a small accommodation tax, which would incentivise them to develop tourism. Because the exemptions for basic food items generally benefit lower-income households (with the exception of meat), these could be zero-rated until the social protection system is able to provide similar targeting (Figure 20).

The VAT legislation is currently under review. A package of reforms that: (i) replaced most exemptions with the standard rate; (ii) replaced exemptions on basic necessities with a zero rating; and (iii) reduced the threshold for compulsory registration to be in line with international norms, would broaden the tax base. It should be accompanied by strengthened administration of the VAT. IMF estimates imply that removing exemptions may lead to an initial fiscal cost of 0.1% of GDP because inputs could be claimed back (IMF, 2017c). But the reform would bring more firms into the VAT system which should raise revenues and the broader base would lay the foundation for efficiently raising more revenue in the future via a higher VAT rate.

Figure 20. VAT exemptions for food generally benefit poorer households

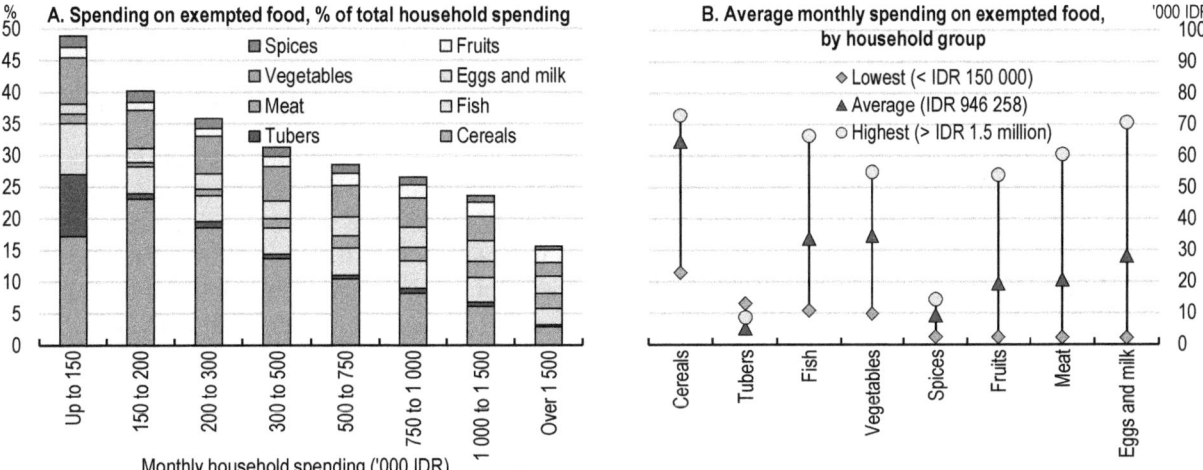

Note: Data are for 2016. Salt and soybeans are also exempt from VAT but are not shown here. In Panel B food items are ordered by the spending of the poorest households.
Source: Statistics Indonesia.

StatLink ⟶ https://doi.org/10.1787/888933833122

Excise taxes can be efficient tools for curbing behaviours with high social or long-term costs, such as smoking (WHO, 2017). Indonesia has particularly high smoking rates among men (but among the lowest for women) and is one of the few countries with a rising smoking rate (Figure 21 Panel A) (OECD, 2017a). Given smoking's well-recognised health costs and the future financial burden on the health system, reducing smoking should be a priority. The most popular packet of cigarettes was taxed at a rate of 57% in 2016, which is the maximum tariff allowed under the excise law but below the WHO guideline of 70% and other countries' rates (Panel B). Taxes vary across products; for instance, excise is lower on hand-rolled cigarettes. Excises should be increased, rates harmonised across products and awareness of health costs raised.

Figure 21. Tobacco use is high, and taxes are relatively low

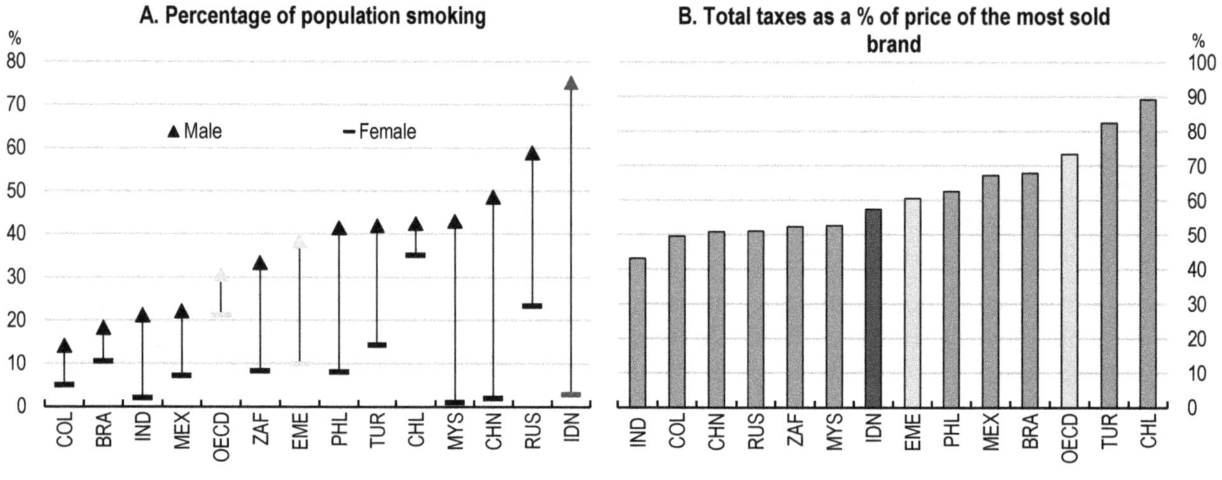

A. Percentage of population smoking

B. Total taxes as a % of price of the most sold brand

Note: "EME" is an unweighted average of the emerging market economies shown. Data in panel A are for 2015 and in panel B for 2016.
Source: World Health Organisation (2017), *WHO Report on the Global Tobacco Epidemic 2017*, Appendix IX and X.

StatLink ⟶ https://doi.org/10.1787/888933833141

The government is considering a tax on sugar-sweetened beverages to help combat rising rates of diabetes and other non-communicable diseases. Such taxes reduce consumption and, if set sufficiently high, can have positive health outcomes (Thavorncharoensap, 2017). If introduced, it should be part of a broader campaign to counter lifestyle-related diseases.

Environmentally-related taxes can be efficient tools for reducing emissions of pollutants and road congestion. OECD estimates suggest that such taxes are equivalent to less than 1% of GDP in Indonesia. Compared to OECD countries, Indonesia raises sizeable revenue from motor vehicle taxes but little from energy use (Table 8) (OECD, 2018d). There is substantial scope to adjust motor vehicle taxes so that environmental impacts influence purchasing decisions. The World Bank and Ministry of Finance estimated that converting the luxury goods sales tax on vehicles to a specific tax and changing the rates according to environmental impacts could raise the equivalent of 0.6% of GDP (World Bank, 2018a). The annual motor vehicle levy could be converted to a flat tax that varies based on car types and their emissions, rather than being linked to value, which declines over time. A gradual shift to more cost-reflective pricing of energy would help users internalise costs associated with its use. A first step would be to phase out subsidies, as discussed above.

Table 8. Key environmentally-related taxes

Tax	Tax base	Level of government	Maximum rate allowed	Revenue as % of GDP, 2016
Vehicles				
Motor vehicle taxes (annual registration fee, transfers)	Value of motor vehicles	Sub-national	5% for annual tax, 10% for transfers	0.5
Luxury goods sales tax	Imports and domestic motor vehicles	Central	200%	0.01
Energy use				
Motor vehicle fuel tax	Fuel consumption of motor vehicles excluding VAT	Sub-national	5%, 7% in some regions	0.1
Street lighting tax	Electricity consumption of households and businesses	Sub-national	1.5%, 3%, 10%	0.1

Note. Import tariffs on motor vehicles are not included.
Source: A. Nasution (2016), "Government decentralization program in Indonesia", *ADBI Working Paper Series*, No. 601; Ministry of Finance; OECD calculations.

Property tax could yield medium-term revenue gains

Property taxes are levied by central and sub-national governments. OECD estimates suggest that they are equivalent to around 0.4% of GDP, which is low in international comparison (Figure 22). Most revenue comes from recurrent tax on immovable property (land, buildings and other structures), and most of this is from natural resources-related properties, rather than residential or commercial real estate. There are also transactions-based property taxes. Although part of the recurrent tax on immovable property is decentralised, notably taxation of residential and commercial land and buildings, national legislation sets out a minimum exemption and a maximum rate of 0.3%. But these taxes have also been found to be far below their revenue-maximising level, given current legislation (von Haldenwang et al., 2015).

Figure 22. Property taxes raise little revenue

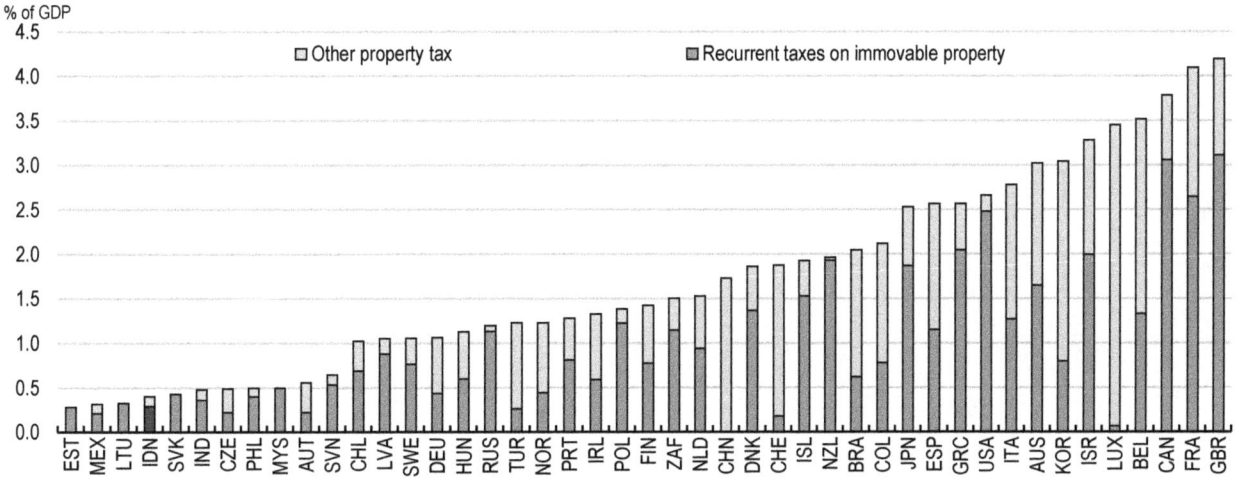

Note: Data are for 2016 or latest. Data for Indonesia are from national sources. OECD is an unweighted average of OECD member countries. Data for China, India and Russia are for 2009, 2009-10 and 2010, respectively and taken from Prakash (2013).
Source: OECD, *Revenue Statistics Database*; Ministry of Finance; P. Prakash (2013), "Property taxes across G20 countries: can India get it right?", *Oxfam India Working Papers Series*, XV, January; OECD calculations.

StatLink ᔆᓚ https://doi.org/10.1787/888933833160

There are strong arguments for raising more revenue from recurrent tax on immovable property. It can in principle raise revenue for local governments (thereby strengthening their accountability) in a more economically efficient way than other taxes and can contribute to greater progressivity (Akgun, Cournède and Fournier, 2017; Arnold et al., 2011). The latter is especially relevant given estimates that Indonesians' wealth is concentrated in real estate (Credit Suisse, 2017). In Russia and South Africa, this tax raises revenue of around 1% of GDP (Figure 22). However, before rates are raised, it is important that local government property tax databases are up-to-date and that local administrations are able to update and maintain them. This will likely require further training by the central government, including in using available information systems, and assistance in improving the administration of taxes.

Reaping the demographic dividend

Indonesia's youthful demographics are both an opportunity and a challenge. Half of the population is under 30 years old, and the working-age population is growing by around 2 million annually. Unlike in much of the world, the working-age population is projected to increase to 68% of the Indonesian population by 2030 (Figure 23). This alone boosts estimated potential GDP per capita growth by 0.3 percentage points annually until 2030 (Box 4). The challenge is to shift the job mix to high-quality, high-productivity jobs in the formal sector, which will grow incomes and government revenues, thereby enabling better services to be provided for current and future generations. This challenge is recognised in, for example, government plans such as the "Making Indonesia 4.0" roadmap, which aims to expand the manufacturing sector and raise labour productivity.

Figure 23. Indonesia's working-age population is rising in the near term

Population aged 15-64 years as a percentage of the total population

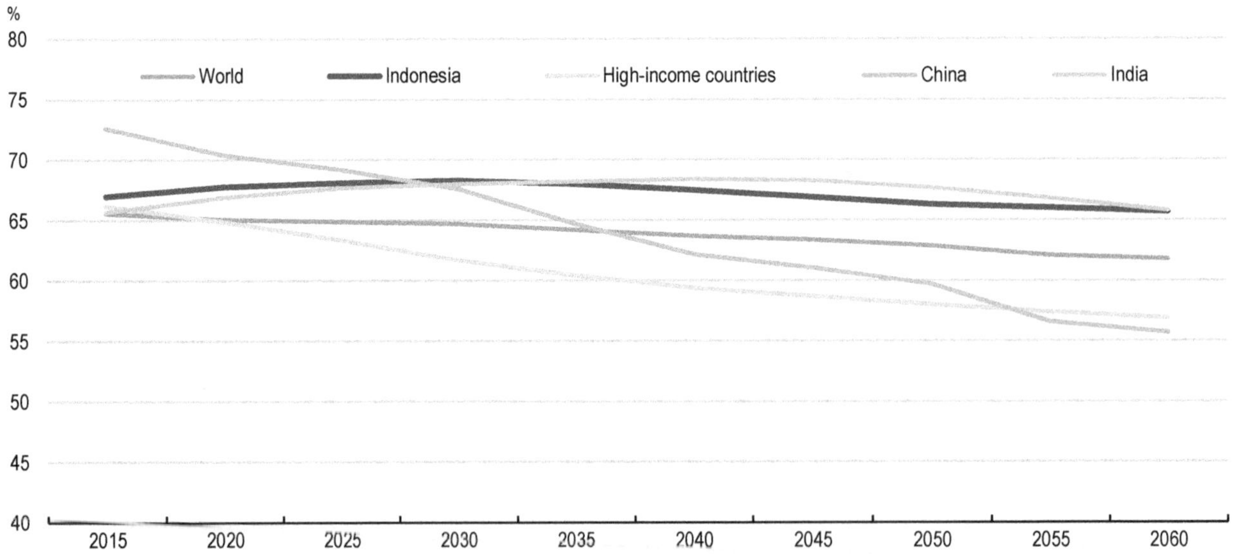

Source: United Nations, Department of Economic and Social Affairs, Population Division (2017), *World Population Prospects: The 2017 Revision*, DVD Edition.

StatLink ⭐ https://doi.org/10.1787/888933833179

Box 4. Long-run scenarios for Indonesia's economy

The OECD's long-term scenarios shed light on the forces driving growth over the coming decades (Guillemette and Turner, 2018). The baseline scenario assumes current trends continue, with some catch-up in variables such as educational attainment, gender employment gaps and total factor productivity. Gains in Indonesia's GDP per capita are projected to slow after 2030, as the direct benefits of the demographic dividend pass and then as cohort effects that raise employment fade (Figure 24). Indonesia would probably become the world's fourth-largest economy during the 2030s.

Figure 24. Decomposition of real GDP per capita growth to 2060

Baseline scenario, contribution in percentage points

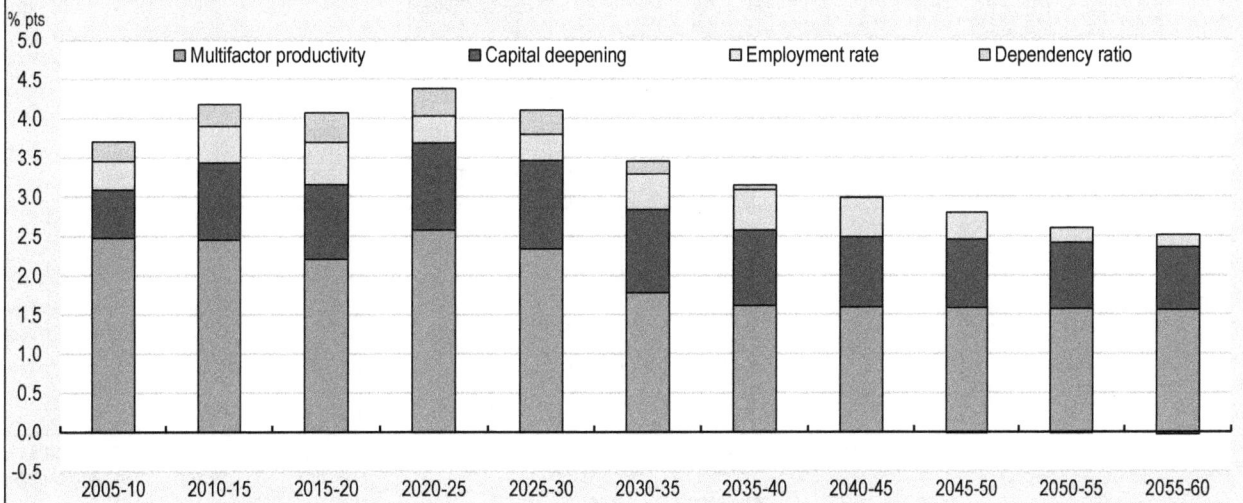

Note: Educational attainment increases as recent gains across cohorts are extended into the future, which translates into an average increase of 2.7 years at school. The gender employment gap narrows from 30 to 22 percentage points.
Source: OECD estimations based on Y. Guillemette and D. Turner (2018), "The Long View: Scenarios for the World Economy to 2060", *OECD Economic Policy Papers*, No. 22, OECD Publishing, Paris.

StatLink ⬛ https://doi.org/10.1787/888933833198

Most workers are still informally employed

Informality remains pervasive: 93% of Indonesian firms are estimated to be operating informally (Rothenberg et al., 2016). New OECD analysis suggests that around 70% of workers are employed informally, close to the share in Peru but much higher than in Brazil (35%) (Figure 25, Panel A). This is around 10 percentage points lower than a decade ago (Panel B). The least educated are most likely to be working informally; women, youth and over 55-year-olds also appear more affected (Panel C). Informality is highest in the agriculture, construction and transport and storage sectors. The rate of informality outside of agriculture is estimated to be around 60%. Across countries, informal jobs are typically of lower quality, with lower productivity and therefore lower wages, fewer training opportunities and poorer working conditions (OECD, 2015d; La Porta and Shleifer, 2014).

Figure 25. Informality rates vary by worker type

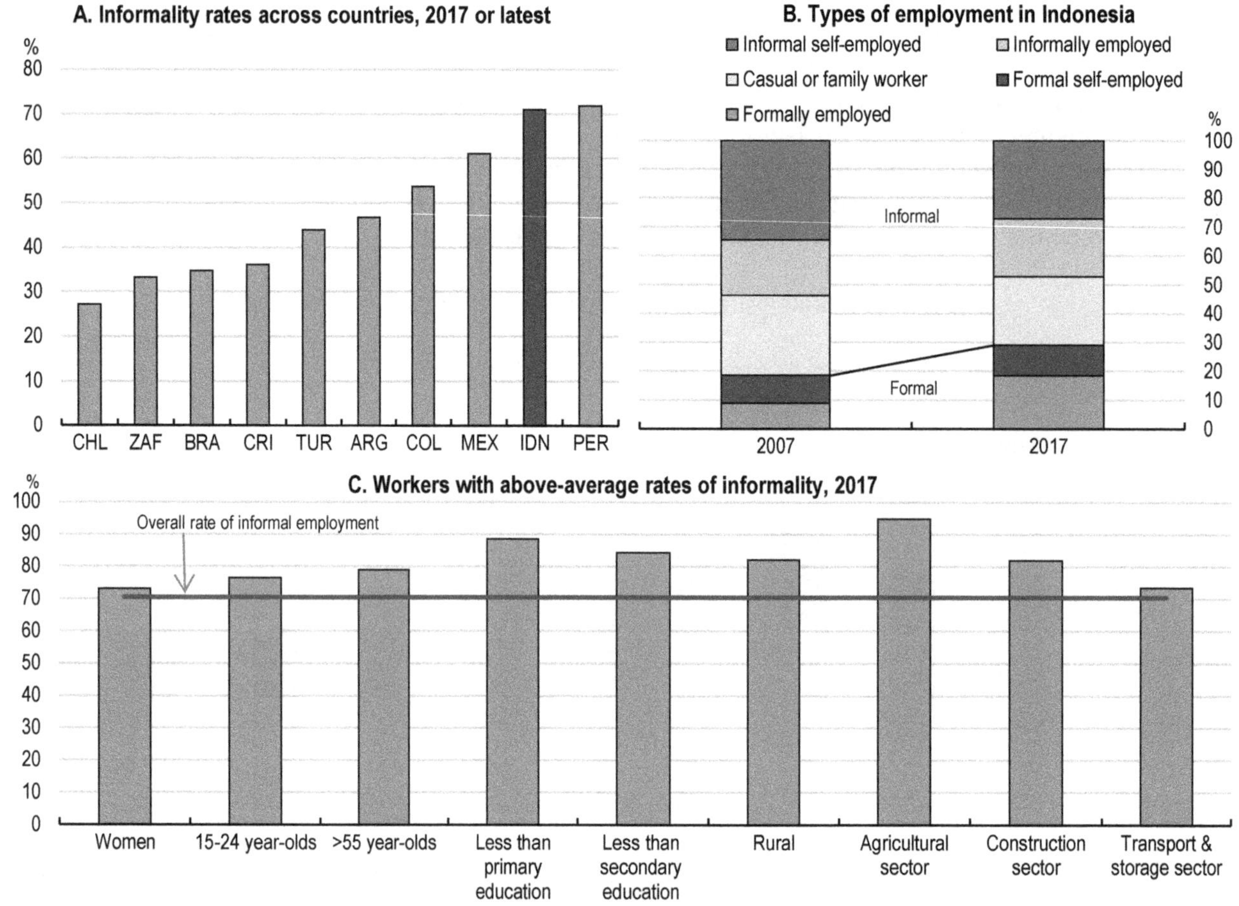

A. Informality rates across countries, 2017 or latest

B. Types of employment in Indonesia

C. Workers with above-average rates of informality, 2017

Note: Estimates are based on the ILO definition of informality and may differ from national sources due to definitional differences. In general informality is defined as employees without social security and self-employed who do not pay social security contributions or whose business is not registered (depending on data availability). For Indonesia, informality is based on the ILO definition for employees and the Statistics Indonesia proxy for identifying informal self-employed workers (based on employment type and occupation) due to data availability for the self-employed. The estimate of informality in Indonesia published by Statistics Indonesia is based on employment status. By this estimate informal employment is 58% of total.
Source: OECD calculations based on the EPH for Argentina, the PNAD for Brazil, the CASEN for Chile, the GEIH for Colombia, the ECE for Costa Rica, the SAKERNAS for Indonesia, the ENOE for Mexico, the ENAHO for Peru, the QLFS for South Africa and the HLFS for Turkey.

StatLink ᵐˢᴾ https://doi.org/10.1787/888933833217

Informality results from many interrelated factors, including: barriers to formally hiring employees; disincentives for firms or workers to operate in the formal sector and a perceived lack of benefits from doing so; and a lack of skills, as highlighted in previous *Surveys* (OECD, 2015a). Strict employment regulations and high costs discourage the hiring of low-skilled employees and add to temporary employment instead, which is associated with less training (Figure 26) (Allen, 2016). Minimum wages are high relative to the median wage and severance pay is also high in international comparison but in practice compliance rates are low (*ibid*). Severance pay aims to compensate for the lack of unemployment insurance, but workers are likely to draw on their pension savings. The OECD's Employment Protection Legislation indicators highlight that allowed dismissals are comparatively narrow and more procedurally difficult than elsewhere. Administrative burdens deter business formalisation, despite recent progress. It still takes 22 days to start a business, compared to 76 in 2013, according to the *Doing Business* indicators, and ongoing compliance costs are burdensome.

Figure 26. Regulations governing employment and product markets are strict

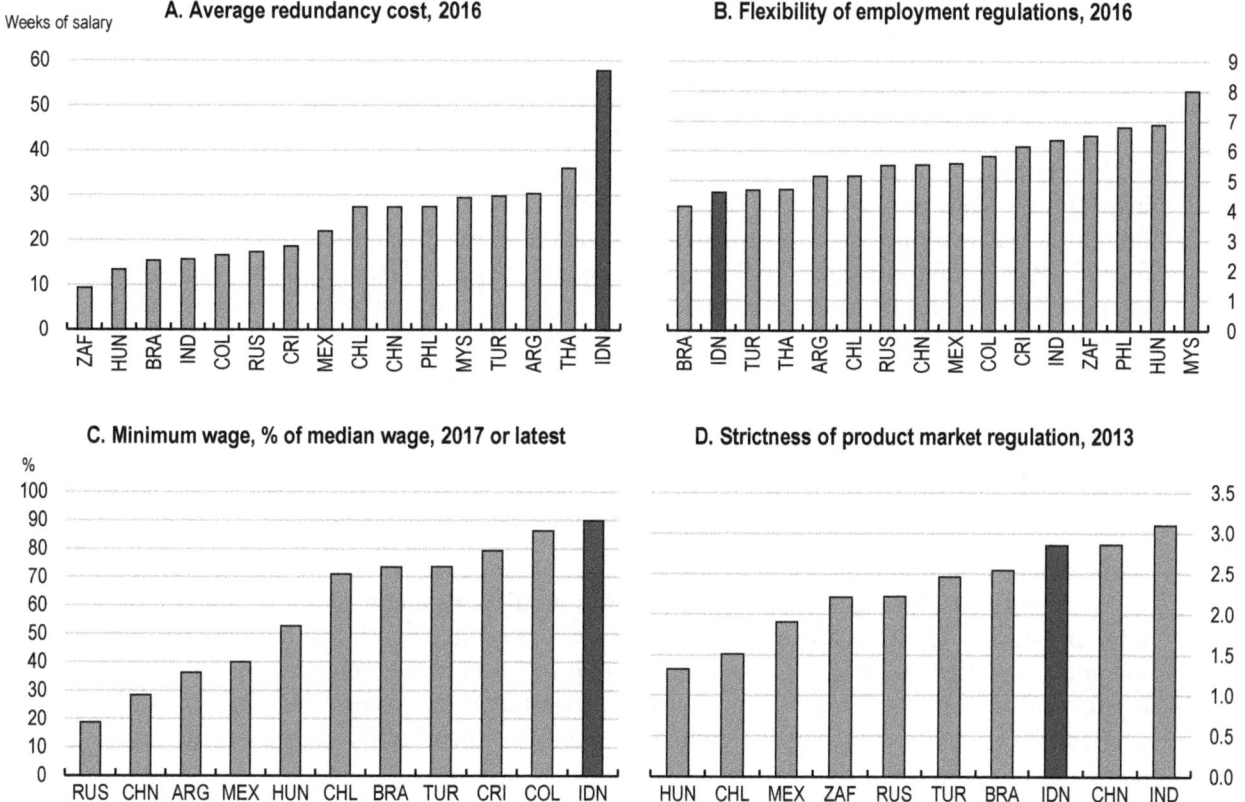

Note: Average redundancy cost is the cost of advance notice requirements, severance payment and penalties due. Flexibility of employment regulation is from the Economic Freedom Indices calculated by the Fraser Institute and ranges from 0 (low economic freedom) to 10 (high economic freedom). Product market regulation ranges from 0 (less regulated) to 6 (more stringent).
Source: World Economic Forum (2018), *Global Competitiveness Report 2017-2018*; Fraser Institute, *Economic Freedom of the World Index*; OECD, *Going for Growth Database, Labour Database, Product Market Regulation Database*; Statistics Indonesia, *SAKERNAS*; OECD calculations.

StatLink 🔗 http://dx.doi.org/10.1787/888933833236

Lower but better-enforced employment protection would better serve workers and reduce disincentives to hiring formal workers. Easier employment regulations could be piloted in the special economic zones, with effects monitored closely before extending the policies nationwide. In particular, the procedures and circumstances for dismissal could be eased and high severance pay replaced by unemployment insurance with individual accounts (OECD, 2016a). Around half of the OECD member countries set discounted minimum wages for groups of workers, such as young people, that are most likely to be disadvantaged by high minimum wages (OECD, 2015e). Discounted minimum wages for youth should be introduced, as previously recommended, and could be trialled in special economic zones

(OECD, 2016a). Although social security contributions are relatively low, the compliance burden for small firms could be eased by allowing quarterly payments.

Labour and product-market reforms could significantly increase formality and, through labour productivity, GDP per capita (Box 5). But the benefits of formality should be also promoted and the trade-off for formalising made more attractive. For instance, the turnover tax (discussed above) should be better targeted and registration linked to greater access to benefits like training and assistance with account-keeping, as in Mexico. In Colombia, financial and non-financial assistance to micro-enterprises has helped to increase formality (tax reforms to reduce high social security contributions were also important) (ILO, 2014; OECD, 2017b). An Online Single Submission system for licensing has been launched; it should be fully implemented and user feedback should be collected and used to make further improvements. In Colombia compliance was reinforced through more labour inspections. Raising the probability of inspection could help increase compliance in Indonesia but it should be accompanied by other policies to improve the trade-off with formalisation to avoid pushing workers into unemployment. The government hopes that the possibility of public health insurance (including for family members) will increase the attractiveness of formalising and from 2019, registration will be compulsory for self-employed workers. Promoting the benefits of insurance more widely, along with improvements in access to services, may help attract these workers. Colombia's experience demonstrates that informality can be reduced with a persistent and multi-faceted approach.

Box 5. Regulations, informal employment and productivity

Simulations with a small macro-structural model (Chalaux, Kopoin and Mourougane, forthcoming) shed light on relationships between regulations and informality and, in turn, GDP per capita. These relationships are estimated in two steps: to informality and then to income. The OECD's indicators of employment protection legislation and product market regulation allow cross-country comparisons of hypothetical reforms. The benefits in this case result from a productivity differential between the formal and informal sectors.

The simulations suggest that easing employment protection legislation to the OECD average level gradually over 10 years could shrink Indonesia's informal sector by about 40 percentage points and raise GDP per capita by 8-32% over 10 years, depending on the assumed productivity differential between sectors (Figure 27). Indonesia would benefit more than other emerging economies due to the combination of strict employment regulation and relatively high informality. Lowering product market regulation from its 2013 level to the OECD average could lower informality by almost 25 percentage points and raise GDP per capita by another 4-16%; reforms to ease licensing procedures made since 2013 should already be contributing to growth via this channel.

The simulations are illustrative only and depend on the size of the reform, but the assumed productivity differential appears conservative: Rothenberg et al. (2016) suggest that the labour productivity of the median micro enterprise in Indonesia is only 4.5% of a large formal firm's productivity, and the median small firm's is 13%.

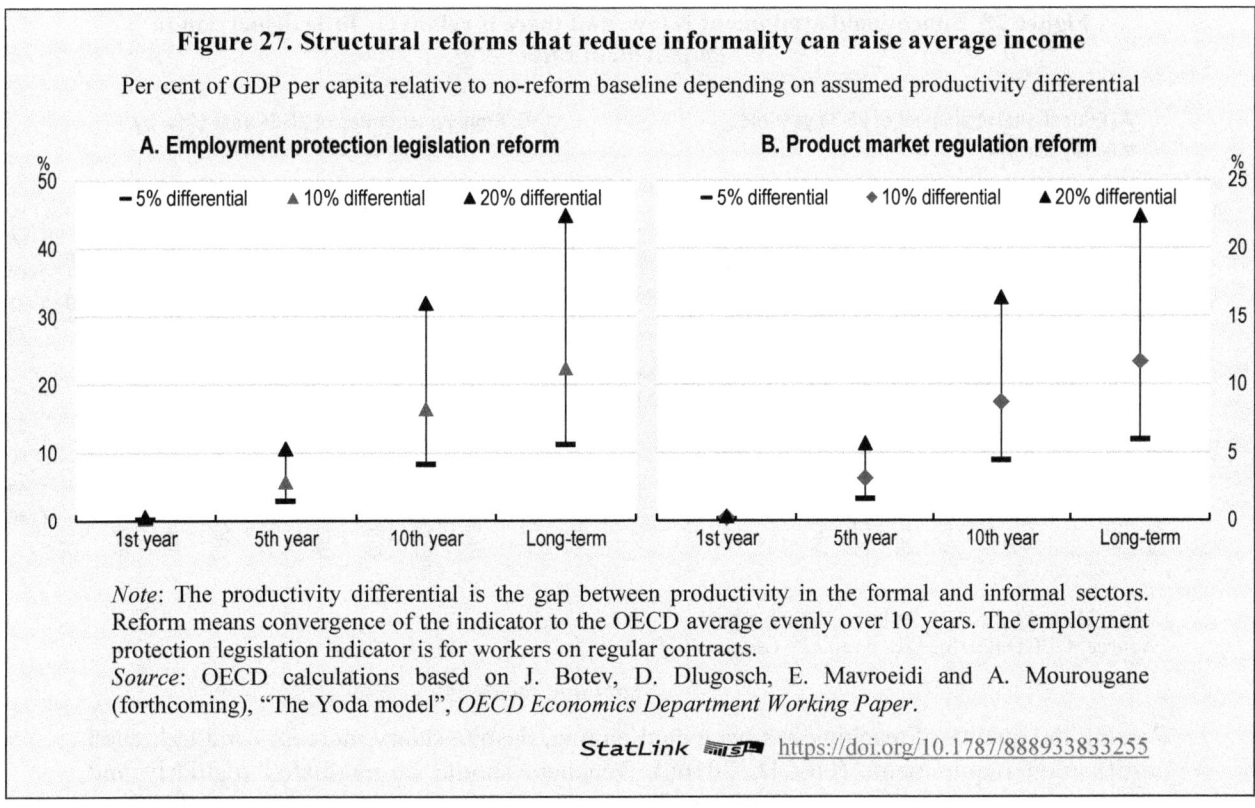

Figure 27. Structural reforms that reduce informality can raise average income

Per cent of GDP per capita relative to no-reform baseline depending on assumed productivity differential

Note: The productivity differential is the gap between productivity in the formal and informal sectors. Reform means convergence of the indicator to the OECD average evenly over 10 years. The employment protection legislation indicator is for workers on regular contracts.

Source: OECD calculations based on J. Botev, D. Dlugosch, E. Mavroeidi and A. Mourougane (forthcoming), "The Yoda model", *OECD Economics Department Working Paper*.

StatLink https://doi.org/10.1787/888933833255

Low skills are holding back growth

Indonesia is approaching universal completion of primary school and graduation rates from lower secondary school have risen rapidly. But a relatively low share of 25-34 year-olds has completed upper secondary school or higher (Figure 28, Panel A). School-to-work transitions are weak, and there does not appear to be much reward for completing upper-secondary education, with employment rates of that group close to those with lower attainment (Panel B). And unemployment rates of medium and high-skilled 20-29 year-olds are 6 percentage points higher than for the low-skilled. One explanation is the poor quality of education (OECD, 2016a; OECD/ADB, 2015). The results of a 2016 national test led to similar conclusions to the 2015 PISA results, which indicated that around three-quarters of 15 year-olds do not have basic skills in mathematics and less than one-third have basic reading proficiency (OECD, 2016c). This contributes to informality as workers do not have the skills for higher paying formal sector jobs. Although one-fifth of government outlays is mandated to be spent on education, it is clearly not as efficient as it should be. Teachers lack necessary competencies, as well as support, and teacher absenteeism remains a problem (OECD, 2016a).

Figure 28. Educational attainment is low, and there is relatively little dispersion in employment rates

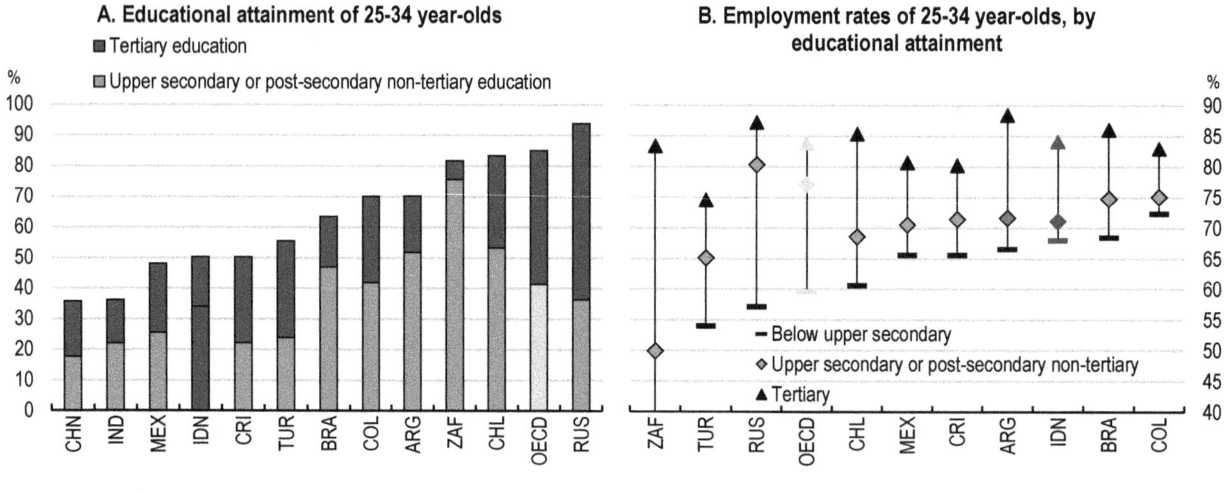

A. Educational attainment of 25-34 year-olds
- Tertiary education
- Upper secondary or post-secondary non-tertiary education

B. Employment rates of 25-34 year-olds, by educational attainment
- Below upper secondary
- Upper secondary or post-secondary non-tertiary
- Tertiary

Note: Data are for 2017, or latest available year.
Source: OECD (2018), *Education at a Glance 2018*.

StatLink https://doi.org/10.1787/888933833274

Raising the quality of teaching has been challenging, despite salary increases and tightened certification requirements (OECD, 2016a). Teachers should be evaluated regularly and encouraged to undertake professional development by linking remuneration more closely to performance and ongoing training. There are advantages in using multiple evaluators; Chile uses the principal, peer evaluators (from another school), externally accredited evaluators, and a municipal evaluation commission composed of peer evaluators (OECD, 2013). School principals should also ensure performance is regularly monitored, and teachers given feedback on what they can do to improve, for example through the creation of individual teacher development plans (OECD/ADB, 2015). Building capacity to undertake appraisals is therefore also important. Better pay has made teaching more attractive; this should be used to strengthen selection into teacher training programmes so that over time retiring teachers are replaced by increasingly committed and competent teachers. Stronger school management could also raise outcomes. The expansion of the "Smart Indonesia" programme that provides financial support to poor students who stay in school aims to reduce drop-out rates. Second-chance programmes have been re-established, as previously recommended, and should be promoted so students can re-enter formal education as their circumstances change (OECD/ADB, 2015).

Following a 2016 Presidential Decree, the government is focussing on lifting the quality of vocational education and training (VET) at upper secondary school. This is linked to the government's agenda to expand sectors such as manufacturing and tourism. Improving VET will require strong employer engagement – a critical component of successful VET systems – and co-ordination across ministries (OECD/ADB, 2015). Indeed, greater efforts are being made to engage more with industry representatives and companies. Under a new pilot programme three companies will work with 20 VET schools. As successful models for employer engagement in training and work placements are found, they should be expanded. A tax incentive for providing training is planned. New regulations opening the education sector to foreign-owned institutions could also raise the quantity and quality of supply.

An estimated 4 million additional skilled workers will be needed annually until 2030 to meet expected demand as the economy grows (Ministry of Manpower, 2017). Disincentives for investing in staff – such as fears that trained staff will leave – should be addressed via co-ordination by sectoral business groups. Training could be further encouraged through tax incentives, with appropriate monitoring. Foreign workers can fill high-priority skills gaps quickly. They transfer knowledge to local workers, contribute to a training fund and may pay higher taxes than locals. However, they are little used as regulations have been restrictive and cumbersome: at end 2017 there were 85 974 licenced foreign workers in Indonesia (BPKS Ketenagakerjaan, 2018). In 2018 the regulation relating to employing foreign workers was changed to ease the process. It is important that it be implemented effectively. The Ministry of Manpower should maintain a list of highly skilled occupations with acute shortages, as is done in several OECD countries, and ease restrictions on hiring foreign workers for these occupations accordingly.

Improving health outcomes will reinforce learning and work

Education and subsequent employment outcomes also depend on childhood health. Stunting is a major issue in Indonesia, affecting 30% of children in 2017 (Jahari, 2018; OECD, 2016a). Along with malnutrition, it has lasting effects on well-being by impairing cognitive function and school performance. The central government is now working with 100 districts to reduce stunting. More generally, the unified database of vulnerable households forms the basis of most programme targeting. Policy makers should continue to improve social assistance that targets the poorest households and promote breastfeeding (OECD, 2016a). At the same time, the prevalence of lifestyle-related non-communicable diseases is rising; cardiovascular and respiratory diseases, diabetes and related complications caused half of all deaths in 2014 (Fountaine et al., 2016). These disease burdens weigh on health outcomes, as well as productivity and incomes, and will add to health costs.

The ongoing expansion of public health insurance, with the aim of universal coverage by 2019, is an opportunity to boost early detection and prevention. Although the number of clinics and hospitals has expanded, long waiting times at affiliated centres and distance to medical centres remain barriers to take-up of health insurance as well as seeking early care. However, ensuring access to services will likely require extra funding, which will strain the system's finances further, so cost containment measures will be crucial (Dartanto, 2017; OECD, forthcoming).

Simulations of structural reforms

Simulations using the OECD's long-term model show that increasing average educational attainment by two years (compared to the baseline) could add 6% to GDP per capita by 2060, or almost 0.2% additional growth per year (Table 9). But the GDP gains from ensuring all current students graduate with basic skills (indicated by a PISA score of 420) would be even larger, at around 60% by 2095, or 0.6% per year (at compounded rates) (OECD, Hanushek and Woessmann, 2015). Facilitating adult education and training would increase the stock of skills faster. Through higher rates of formality this could increase incomes, and consequently tax revenues.

Table 9. Structural reforms to close gaps can yield large long-term gains

Average additional annual GDP growth over 2020-2060 relative to baseline

Reform	Detail	%
Every current student acquiring basic skills	Raises PISA score of current students to 420, implying Indonesia's average PISA scores are around Thailand's	0.6[1]
Higher educational attainment	Raises average years of schooling of population by 2 years in addition to the increase of 2.7 years in the baseline.	0.2[2]
Improved rule of law	Improvement in rule of law index to the OECD median country, equivalent to an increase of 1.8 point in the index	0.7[2]
Narrower gender gap in employment	Difference in employment rates narrows by an additional 7 percentage points compared to the baseline (8 percentage points)	0.1[2]
Less stringent employment protection legislation	The OECD Employment Protection Legislation indicator gradually declines to the OECD average	0.4 – 1.2[3]
More competition-friendly product market regulation	The OECD Product Market Regulation indicator gradually declines to the OECD average	0.2 - 0.7[3]

1. Estimates are based on OECD/Hanushek/Woessman (2015). These estimates are the average annual growth boost over 2015 to 2095.
2. Estimates are based on the OECD's long-term scenarios described in Guillemette (2018).
3. Estimates are based on Chalaux, Kopoin and Mourougane (forthcoming). The range shows the estimate assuming the productivity differential between the formal and informal sector is 5% and 20%. The calculation is over 30 years.
Source: OECD calculations.

Complementing higher education with reforms that narrow gender gaps in employment rates and improve the rule of law could raise GDP growth by a further 0.8 percentage points annually. The estimated effect of reforms to labour and product markets regulations via channels typically estimated for OECD countries is modest but the effect is much larger when the effects of informality are accounted for (Table 9). Although these figures are only illustrative, they highlight the huge potential gains from bringing policy settings closer to those in OECD countries.

Using tourism to diversify the economy and support regional development

Two challenges for increasing the resilience and inclusiveness of Indonesia's economic growth are the reliance on commodities for foreign currency earnings and the concentration of activity in Java. Java's economy generates 55% of Indonesia's GDP, and regional differences in income per capita are larger than in other large emerging economies (Figure 29). While it is not a silver bullet, tourism can help address both these challenges.

Tourism's potential is high but not fully exploited

The number of visitors to Indonesia has nearly tripled over the past decade to 14 million by 2017, accelerating to average growth of nearly 14% annually in the past three years (Figure 30, Panel A). This is thanks to global growth in tourism – 4% annually – and also gains in market share following infrastructure development and more aggressive promotion. However, growth can be volatile due to the seasonal nature of tourism and because Indonesia is particularly vulnerable to natural disasters. Most visitors originate from Asia, especially from China, now the top source. Arrivals are geographically concentrated: Bali – less than 0.5% of Indonesia's land mass – received almost half and Jakarta about a fifth (Panel B). More recently, tourism to other destinations – such as Borobudur and Lake Toba – has grown. The potential for job creation in many regions is large, as the sector is highly labour intensive. Likewise, the job mix in tourism implies that its expansion could raise the employment rate of women.

Figure 29. Regional income inequality is high in Indonesia

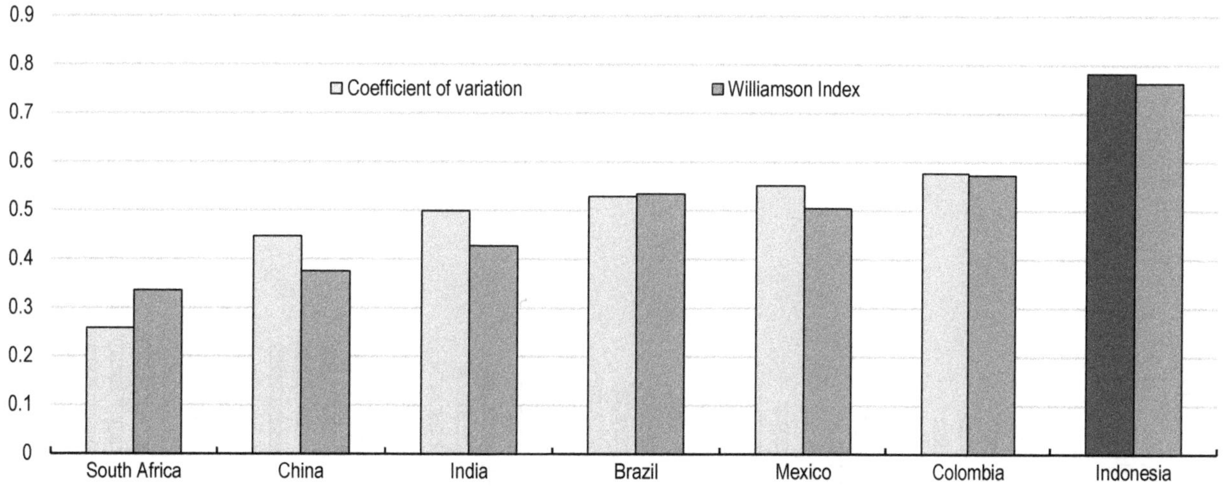

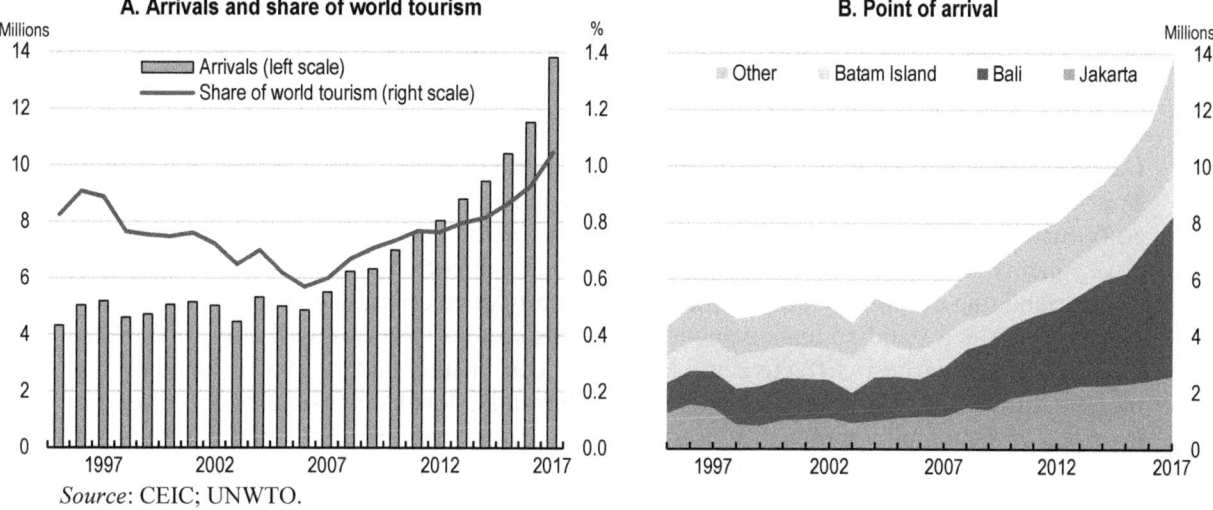

Note: The coefficient of variation is unweighted. The Williamson index is a similar measure of variance that weights regions by their share of the national population. Regional GDP per capita data are for 2016 for Indonesia, 2015 for Colombia and Mexico, 2014 for Brazil and 2013 for China and India.
Source: Statistics Indonesia; OECD, *OECD Regional Database*; OECD calculations.

StatLink https://doi.org/10.1787/888933833293

Figure 30. Indonesia is attracting more visitors

Source: CEIC; UNWTO.

StatLink https://doi.org/10.1787/888933833312

Most countries reap far higher revenues from tourism relative to GDP (Figure 31). Together with the expanding Asian middle-class, this points to an opportunity to attract more visitors, especially high-spending tourists. The Travel and Tourism Competitiveness Index highlights Indonesia's natural and cultural resources and price competitiveness as strengths relative to regional competitors (WEF, 2017). The same index reveals large gaps in various types of infrastructure, including transport, tourist services and ICT.

Figure 31. Earnings from tourism are still low

Foreign tourists' expenditure, % of GDP, 2016

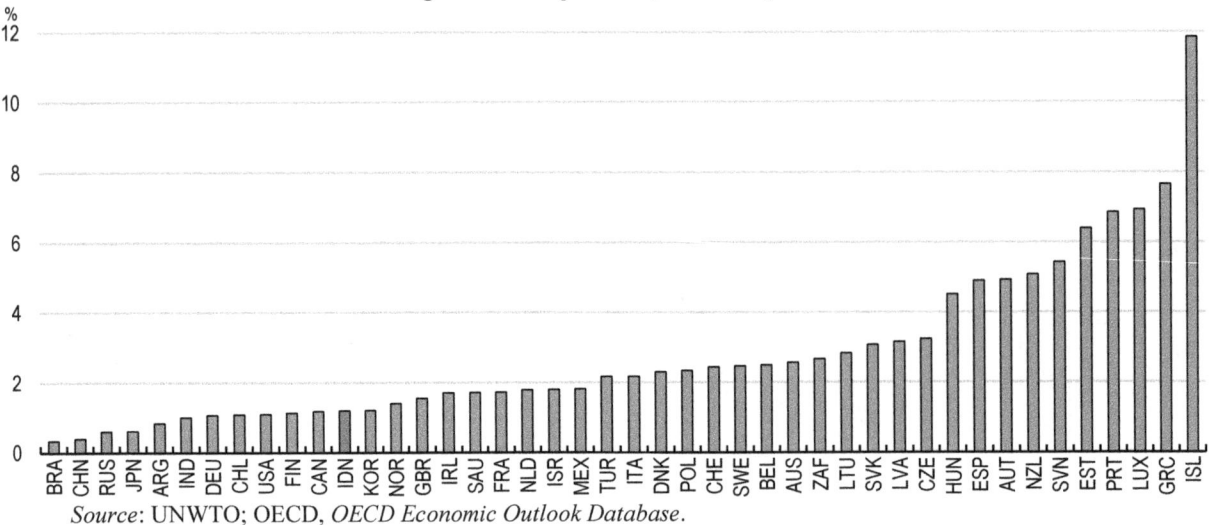

Source: UNWTO; OECD, *OECD Economic Outlook Database*.

StatLink ⫘ https://doi.org/10.1787/888933833331

Government plans foresee 20 million visitors by 2019. Tourism is prioritised in the 2015-19 medium-term development plan, which includes the development of 10 destinations – "10 new Balis". The strategy emphasises closing infrastructure gaps and concentrates investment in four locations. Four destinations have also been designated special economic zones. To improve marketing the Ministry of Tourism's budget was quadrupled in 2015, to 1% of total public spending (although it was cut in 2017 by 30%). This boosted the reach and quality of its promotional campaign. The Ministry also monitors social media at the destination level through a comprehensive digital tool to better target its marketing efforts.

Despite the medium-term plan and the associated tourism strategy, gaps in planning remain. Tourism affects numerous industries and depends on many public institutions, which makes co-ordination difficult. A lack of capacity is a challenge, especially in sub-national governments. Led by the central government and supported by the World Bank and Switzerland, the 10 priority destinations are gradually developing destination management plans (DMPs) – a standard management tool in this sector – but they will only be finalised in 2019, at the earliest. Effective use of DMPs can ensure that growth is inclusive by incorporating local characteristics and needs. Currently, local governments are often not involved in the planning process; indeed, special economic zones partly aim to circumvent excessively complicated local regulations.

Destination management organisations, comprising local government and private agents, are effective ways of managing transport, land use and the local effects of tourism (OECD, 2018e). Different forms are possible, to wit the independent agency for Langkawi island in Malaysia (LADA, 2018), or integration in the provincial government in the case of Bohol island in the Philippines (UNWTO and Griffith University, 2017). In Indonesia for example, there is a local authority for Lake Toba and a state-owned enterprise for Mandalika; however, they lack close relationships to local government or community representatives. The government should establish these in key destinations where they are missing, in partnership with local stakeholders, and encourage existing organisations to involve local stakeholders. Local governments also need more data to improve planning, monitoring and evaluation.

Tackling the infrastructure gap is crucial for scaling up tourism

The expansion of air transport infrastructure has facilitated the recent rapid growth of tourism. But capacity at the two main airports (in Jakarta and in Denpasar, Bali) is now fully utilised. Their quality is also weak relative to those in neighbouring countries. For example, Jakarta's airport has a user rating of 65% compared to 80% for Bangkok and 94% for Singapore (Flightradar24, 2018). This suggests investment is needed to improve existing airports and build new ones. The government is planning to contract out the operation of some airports, which could improve their efficiency. In addition seven new airports were recently built and eight additional ones are planned by 2019, which should expand tourism to new regions. Given the government's revenue constraints, private-sector participation should be encouraged. Cost-benefit analysis should be systematic for project selection, which is not currently the case (World Bank, 2018c). It should incorporate operation, maintenance and disposal costs as well as environmental and social impacts.

While transport is key, other infrastructure is also essential for continued growth in tourist inflows and spending. Better reach and reliability of 4G technology would enable visitors to use their smartphones more easily, including for e-payments. In addition, broadening internet availability would help local firm creation and growth and reduce the wide gap between urban and rural Internet users (72% versus 48%) (APJII, 2017). Environmental infrastructure such as waste, water, sanitation and sewerage facilities is still lacking; for example, the lack of potable tap water increases the use of plastic bottles in Jakarta.

Foreign investors can help plug some of the investment gaps that hamper tourism where the returns are sufficiently high to make projects viable. However, restrictions are significant in the transport sector, and to a lesser extent for hotels and restaurants, notably due to foreign equity limitations and restrictions on foreign personnel (Figure 32). Foreign land ownership restrictions also constrain the development of hotel and restaurants although a right to build can be issued to foreign companies for 30 years (renewable for 20 years). Easing those restrictions would facilitate private investment.

Figure 32. Restrictions on foreign direct investment across emerging market economies

FDI Regulatory Restrictiveness Index from 0 (open) to 1 (closed), 2017

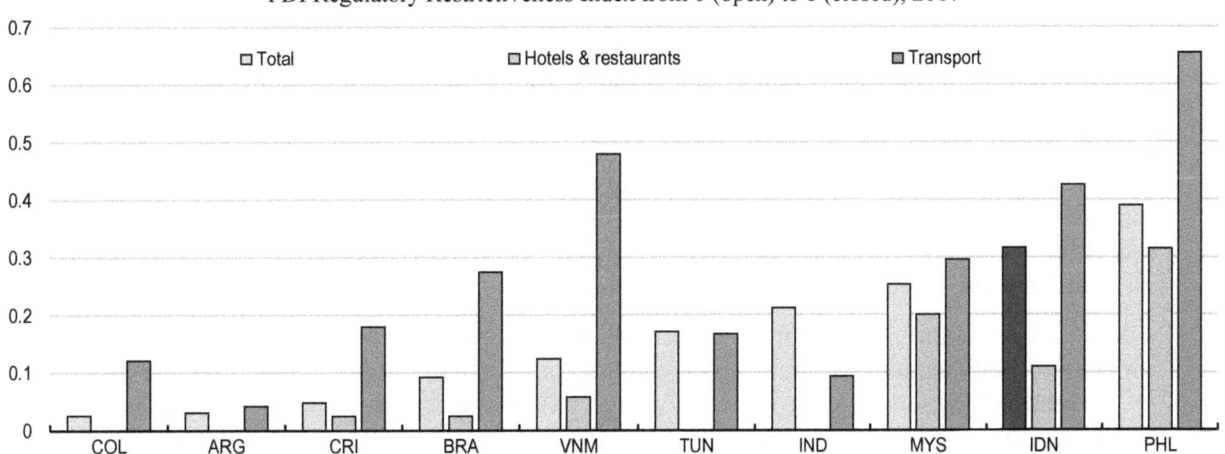

Note: The FDI Regulatory Restrictiveness Index measures statutory restrictions on foreign direct investment across 22 economic sectors. It gauges the restrictiveness of a country's FDI rules by looking at the four main types of restrictions on FDI: 1) foreign equity limitations; 2) discriminatory screening or approval mechanisms; 3) restrictions on the employment of foreigners as key personnel; and 4) other operational restrictions, e.g. on branching and on capital repatriation or on land ownership by foreign-owned enterprises.
Source: OECD, *FDI Regulatory Restrictiveness Index Database*.
StatLink ⟋⟋⟋ https://doi.org/10.1787/888933833350

Given Indonesia's highly decentralised government framework, the role of local governments in developing local opportunities should be promoted. Local initiatives are more effective in realising the potential of experience-based tourism and the creative economy (OECD, 2014). The community-led development of Banyuwangi is a successful example for other destinations (Kompas, 2016). Destinations are often missing tourist information centres that in other countries promote local businesses and provide services like Internet access. The availability of central government transfers for local governments to use for tourism-related projects is welcome: in 2018 "special allocation funds" of IDR 632 billion (USD 43 million) were allocated for 319 local government tourism-related projects, up from only 58 projects in 2016. However, as recommended in the previous *Survey*, monitoring of such projects should be stepped up. Allowing local governments to levy an accommodation tax on tourists would provide local areas with a direct benefit from increased tourism and provide additional funds for infrastructure that supports this sector.

Facilitating firm creation and growth to foster local development

The tourism sector is mostly composed of small firms. A business-friendly environment can help local populations to seize opportunities to start and grow companies. Although Indonesia's regulatory environment has improved significantly over recent years – recognised in its Ease of Doing Business ranking – its ranking of 72nd indicates that there is still substantial scope for further improvement. Starting a business and enforcing contracts are especially difficult. An online single-submission system for licensing and permits has been launched but is not fully implemented yet.

Raising basic competencies, as discussed above, will facilitate the creation and growth of formal-sector firms. The tourism industry relies on specialised workers, such as chefs, hotel managers and tour guides, who are usually trained through vocational education and training. Several higher-education institutions specialise in tourism, but the supply of training will need to expand to meet growing needs. The government is now developing vocational higher-education institutions in more regions but should also better monitor private schools, which are the major provider of education and training in tourism. On-the-job training could be developed through more work placements. Closer and more local interaction between education institutions and employers would help in designing appropriate curricula. Colleges' focus should be flexible enough to respond to changing needs. Adult training programmes could help ensure that existing workers, including women outside the labour force, can benefit from tourism's growth. Skills shortages are currently difficult to monitor but are evidenced in some areas such as in Lombok where the authorities are now establishing a new vocational higher-education institution. Forthcoming destination management plans should assess current and future skills shortages. Easing procedures for recruiting foreign workers, as currently envisaged, would help mitigate existing shortages and facilitate knowledge transfer to local personnel.

Like in other countries, the tourism sector has been an early adopter of digitalisation. The process of digitalisation, particularly relevant for tourism, can promote greater competition, create jobs and, by reducing the barrier of geographic distance, make growth more inclusive (OECD, 2017c). Digital platforms can provide opportunities for small businesses specialising in local services, such as accommodation and transportation. The Indonesia Travel X-Change, launched in 2016 to ease business-to-business connections, provides a booking and online payment system. However, it is still being developed and manages only 2 270 rooms (Nurdin, 2018). The platform should be finalised quickly and advertised more widely. Online delivery of training could help reach many people at lower cost than traditional programmes. Online applications for filing income tax and VAT and for paying local licence fees can reduce compliance costs.

Policies need to manage the sustainable development of tourism

Indonesia's exceptional natural assets are key attractions for tourists, but its environmental sustainability is lower than in regional competitors, reflecting insufficient wastewater treatment, deforestation and a large number of threatened species (WEF, 2017). The recent growth in tourists adds to pressure on infrastructure that is already insufficient, such as sanitation, waste and water-treatment facilities. This especially affects some remote regions, but also Bali (OECD, 2016a; Bali, 2015). Moreover, tourists' consumption tends to be higher. The government's plan is ambitious and counts on rapid growth in a limited number of destinations, which highlights the need to have the acceptance of the local population.

Shifting towards revenue-based targets, and relying less on tourist numbers, in planning would help focus on less but higher-quality tourism, and mitigate the environmental impact. Iceland's experience highlights the importance of planning supporting infrastructure. There, tourist numbers quadrupled between 2010 and 2016, but investment failed to catch up, rapidly creating social and environmental strains (OECD, 2017d). Environmentally related infrastructure needs should be systematically incorporated in tourism planning, and infrastructure development plans should consider tourism projections. Risks of "white elephants" due to projection errors could be mitigated by designing scalable projects. Destination management plans would help identify these local needs. The creation of five sustainable tourism observatories with UNWTO can improve monitoring of the environmental impacts of tourism.

Recognising the high opportunity cost of exploiting natural resources and the economic value of tourism to these areas could reduce deforestation and preserve landscapes. Protected areas cover a relatively small share of Indonesia's land compared to Brazil and Costa Rica, which are also rich in biodiversity (Figure 33). Eleven biosphere reserves have been created to better link preservation of biodiversity and local communities. More areas could be protected, but at the same time, a higher share could be used for sustainable tourism. User fees, combined with quantitative restrictions in highly sensitive areas, are an effective way of controlling the number of visitors to avoid over-exploitation and providing funds for maintenance and preservation (Eagles, McCool and Haynes, 2002). Raising awareness and involvement of the local population would expand what is on offer for tourists and enhance tourism's economic benefits, thereby boosting local approval, which is also crucial for sustainability. For example, Costa Rica has successfully implemented small-scale ecotourism projects in rural zones. These projects provide revenues and employment to the local community and have helped to preserve the local environment (OECD, 2016d). Costa Rica also uses a "Social Progress Index" in tourist destinations to assess and promote sustainable social and environmental development (Stern, Wares and Epner, 2017; ITC, 2017).

Figure 33. Protected areas in Indonesia are mostly highly restrictive

Terrestrial protected areas by classification, in % of total land

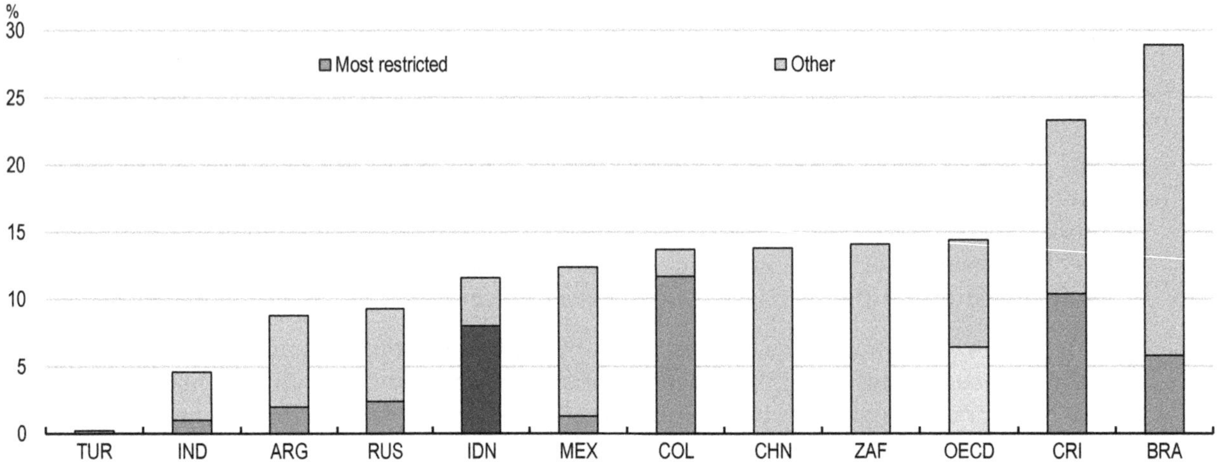

Note: The most restricted protected areas corresponds to the International Union for Conservation of Nature categories 1 and 2 which cover strict nature reserves and wilderness areas managed mainly for science or wilderness protection, and national parks managed mainly for ecosystem protection.
Source: A. Mackie et al. (2017), "Indicators on Terrestrial and Marine Protected Areas: Methodology and Results for OECD and G20 countries", *OECD Environmental Working Papers*, No. 126, OECD Publishing, Paris.

StatLink 🖳 https://doi.org/10.1787/888933833369

Adjusting to a greener growth path

Natural-resource-based production (minerals, energy, agriculture, forestry and fishing) accounted for one-fifth of value added in 2017. Indonesia is one of 17 "mega diverse" countries rich in biodiversity, having, for example, 18% of the world's coral reefs (CBD, 2018; UNEP-WCMC, 2014). Previous *Surveys* emphasised the importance of sound management of these resources to ensure sustainable growth over the long run (OECD, 2016a; 2015a). The *Indonesia Biodiversity Strategy and Action Plan 2015-20* aims to improve co-ordination and set priorities to preserve Indonesia's wealth of biodiversity. The upcoming *Green Growth Policy Review* of Indonesia will provide timely policy advice on managing Indonesia's unique natural resources.

Deforestation and pollution threaten sustainability

Indonesia's forest cover has declined at a decelerating rate in the past decade (Figure 34). However, the change during 2005-15 was the world's largest after Brazil's. Illegal forest and peatland fires used to clear land, notably for oil palm and timber plantations, also generate pollution and health costs. A moratorium on new concessions for plantations and logging of primary forests and peatlands has been in place since 2011 but has not been fully effective (Austin et al., 2017; Busch et al., 2015). In 2018 the President signed a three-year moratorium on new licences for oil palm plantations. More clarity over land rights and better law enforcement would help control deforestation (Table 10). The 2015 "One Map" initiative to establish a cadastre and resolve conflicting property rights is also crucial; co-operation across institutions should intensify to finalise it by 2019 as planned. Better forest management would help preserve biodiversity and also raise revenues; only one-third of potential revenues from forest use were collected over 2003-14 (KPK, 2015). Protecting more forest areas and using satellite imagery to assist enforcement could also reduce deforestation, as in Brazil (OECD, 2018f).

Figure 34. Deforestation in Indonesia is the second largest in the world

Change in forest area for ten largest sources of deforestation

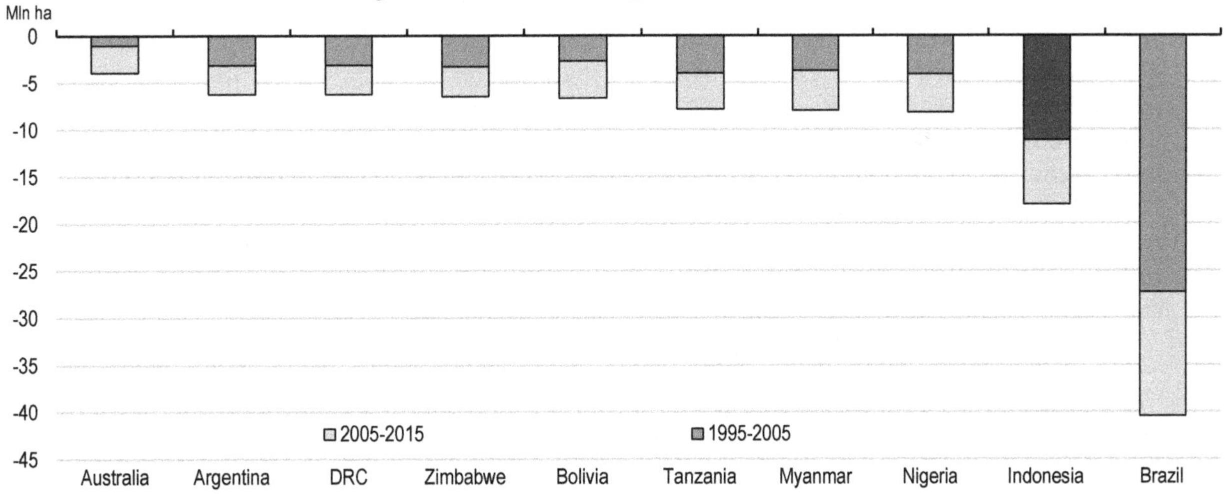

Note: The ten countries have the largest loss of forest area in million hectares.
Source: FAO, *FAOSTAT Database*.

StatLink ⬛ https://doi.org/10.1787/888933833388

Table 10. Past recommendations related to environmental sustainability

Recommendations in previous *Surveys*	Action taken since the October 2016 *Survey*
Phase out all remaining energy subsidies. To meet rising power needs, invest in low-carbon generating capacity, including renewables and geothermal sources.	During 2017 electricity subsidies were removed for non-poor households with 900 volt-ampere connections. However, energy subsidies have increased in 2018.
Tighten and strengthen enforcement of laws on forest clearing. Improve productivity in the palm oil and timber industries.	In December 2016 the President signed a regulation (PP No. 57/2016) to better protect peatland by imposing a moratorium on clearing, banning draining and allowing the restoration of degraded land. In September 2018 the President signed a three-year moratorium on new licences for oil palm plantations.

Air pollution has increased sharply in recent years, with the year-to-year severity driven by forest and peat fires (Figure 35, Panel C). Transport, especially by road, is a major driver of the surge in NO_x and CO_2 emissions, while coal-fired power generation is driving up SO_x emissions (Yudha, 2017). The number of vehicles in use almost tripled over 2005-15 (OICA, 2018). Jakarta has become the third-most congested city in the world (TomTom, 2018). Licence plate-based restrictions are in force in Jakarta, and toll roads are common. In addition to the environmentally-related tax reforms discussed above, further use of road pricing should be considered in large cities. Emissions standards for heavily polluting industries, such as coal-fired power plants, should be raised to international norms.

Marine pollution is a growing concern. Indonesia is the second-largest contributor to sea-borne plastic pollution, and its coral reefs are the most plastic-ridden in the Asia-Pacific (Lamb et al., 2018; Jambeck et al., 2015). Marine pollution is largely driven by improper disposal of municipal waste, only half of which is collected (according to the Ministry of Environment). Public education can help fight pollution, complemented by better co-ordination and capacity for waste management at local government level.

Transitioning to a low-carbon and energy-efficient economy

Growth in CO_2 emissions had decoupled from GDP growth during the 2000s, but that trend stopped recently (Figure 35, Panel B). The government's objective of reducing greenhouse gas (GHG) emissions by 29% from a business-as-usual scenario by 2030 (Republic of Indonesia, 2016) is challenging because of deforestation and peat fires and rising energy consumption. The Low Carbon Development Plan launched in 2017 in preparation for the next medium-term plan focuses on using the agriculture, forestry, waste, transport and marine sectors to reduce GHG emissions. Coal accounts for over half the energy supply, and this share will undoubtedly increase. But the potential of geothermal and hydroelectricity is huge. Renewables account for 12% of electricity supply, implying that massive investment is needed to reach the targeted 23% by 2030 (IISD, 2018). Removing foreign equity restrictions in renewables generation could boost investment, as would more cost-reflective pricing. The 2017 regulation imposing locally based tariffs limits investment incentives in some regions (like Java) and should also be reviewed (Allen and Overy, 2017).

Figure 35. Some environmental indicators have deteriorated recently

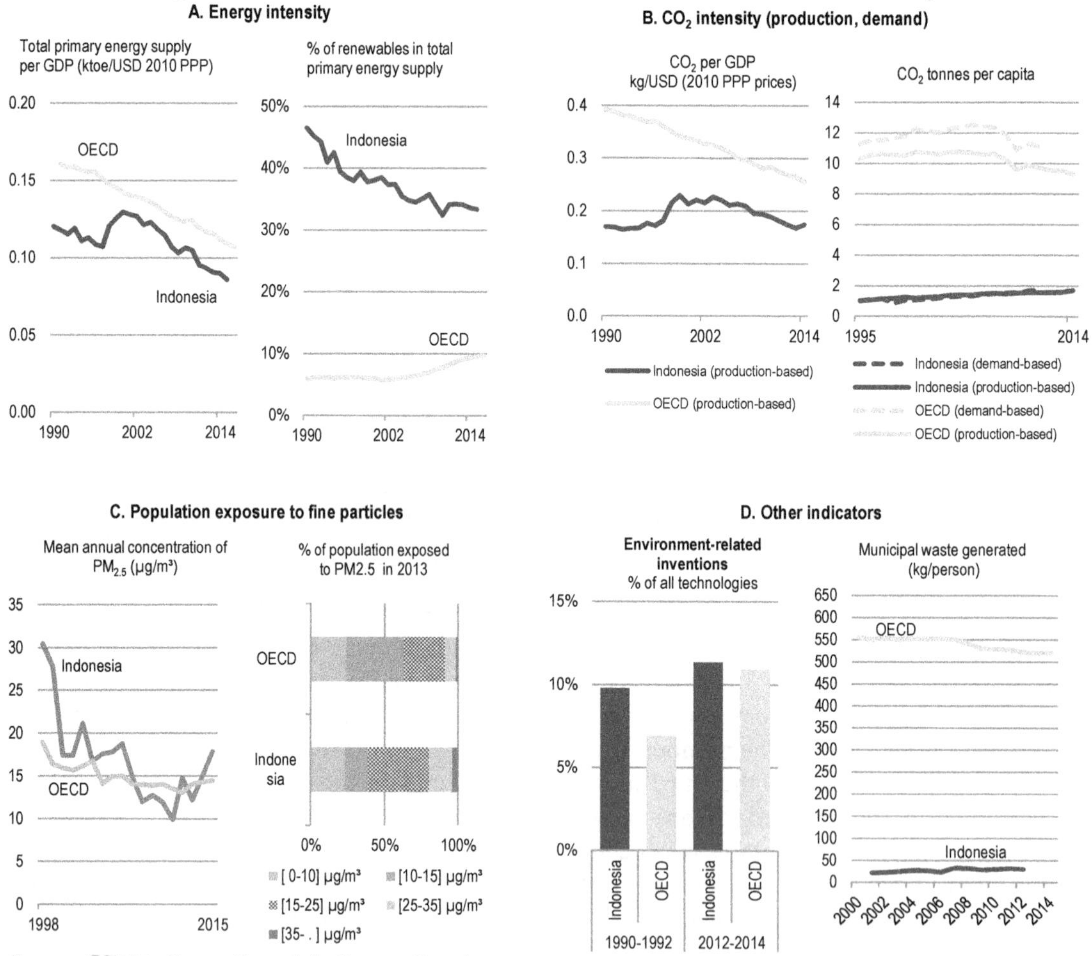

Source: OECD, Green Growth Indicators Database.

StatLink ⫘⫘⊡ http://dx.doi.org/10.1787/888933833407

As discussed above, Indonesia has one of the lowest tax rates on energy among OECD and G20 countries (OECD, 2018d). Phasing out energy subsidies would help make the implicit price of emissions positive. Following that an explicit carbon tax should be introduced, initially at a low level.

Bibliography

Akgun, O., B. Cournède and J. Fournier (2017), "The effects of the tax mix on inequality and growth", *OECD Economics Department Working Papers*, No. 1447, OECD Publishing, Paris, http://dx.doi.org/10.1787/c57eaa14-en.

Allen and Overy (2017), *Indonesia Power Sector: New Regulation on Tariff and Tendering for Renewable Energy Projects*, www.jdsupra.com/legalnews/indonesia-power-sector-new-regulation-41003/.

Allen, E. (2016), "Analysis of trends and challenges in the Indonesian labor market", *ADB Papers on Indonesia*, No. 16, Asian Development Bank, Manila.

APJII (2017), *Penetration and Behavior of Indonesian Internet User 2017*, Indonesia Internet Service Provider Association, https://blog.apjii.or.id/index.php/2018/02/19/survei-apjii-penetrasi-internet-indonesia-jangkau-547-persen-populasi-di-2017/.

Arnold, J., B. Brys, C. Heady, Å. Johansson, C. Schwellnus and L. Vartia et al. (2011), "Tax policy for economic recovery and growth", *The Economic Journal*, Vol. 121/550, pp. F59-F80.

Austin, K., A. Mosnier, J. Pirker, I. McCallum, S. Fritz and P. Kasibhatla (2017), "Shifting patterns of oil palm driven deforestation in Indonesia and implications for zero-deforestation commitments", *Land Use Policy*, Vol. 69, pp. 41-48.

Bali (2015), *Sustainable Tourism on Bali?*, www.bali.com/news_Sustainable-Tourism-on-Bali-_161.html.

BNM (2018), *Financial Stability and Payment Systems Report 2017*, Bank Negara Malaysia, Kuala Lumpur, www.bnm.gov.my/index.php?ch=en_publication&pg=en_fspr&ac=23&en.

BPJS Ketenagakerjaan (2018), *Hingga Akhir 2017, Sebanyak 33.000 Pekerja Asing Jadi Peserta BPJS Ketenagakerjaan* [Until the end of 2017, a total of 33,000 foreign workers became BPJS participants in employment], Press release, 30 April.www.bpjsketenagakerjaan.go.id/berita/19121/Hingga-Akhir-2017,-Sebanyak-33.000-Pekerja-Asing-Jadi-Peserta-BPJS-Ketenagakerjaan

Busch, J. et al. (2015), "Reductions in emissions from deforestation from Indonesia's moratorium on new oil palm, timber, and logging concessions", *Proceedings of the National Academy of Sciences of the United States of America*, Vol. 112/5, pp. 1328-33.

Caporale, G., A. Catik, M. Helmi, F. Ali and M. Tajik (2016), "The bank lending channel in a dual banking system: evidence from Malaysia", *DIW Berlin Discussion Papers*, No. 1557, German Institute for Economic Research, Berlin.

CBD (2018), *Indonesia - Country Profile*, www.cbd.int/countries/profile/default.shtml?country=id.

Chalaux, T., A. Kopoin and A. Mourougane (forthcoming), "A formal look at regulations and labour market informality in emerging-market economies", *OECD Economics Department Working Paper*, OECD Publishing, Paris.

CNBC Indonesia (2018), *Distribusikan BBM Bersubsidi, Pertamina Rugi Rp 5,5 T* [Distribution of Subsidised Fuel, Pertamina Loss Rp 5.5 T], www.cnbcindonesia.com/news/20180410154429-4-10431/distribusikan-bbm-bersubsidi-pertamina-rugi-rp-55-t.

Credit Suisse (2017), *Credit Suisse Global Wealth Databook 2017*, Credit Suisse Research Institute

Dartanto, T. (2017), *Universal Health Coverage in Indonesia: Informality, Fiscal Risks and Fiscal Space for Financing UHC*, Presentation at IMF-JICA Conference on "Regional Development: Fiscal Risks, Fiscal Space and the Sustainable Development Goals".

Deloitte (2017), *Shifting Sands: Risk and Reform in Uncertain Times - 2017 Asia Pacific Tax Complexity Survey.*

Demirgüç-Kunt, A., L. Klapper, D. Singer, S. Ansar and J. Hess (2018), *The Global Findex Database 2017: Measuring Financial Inclusion and the Fintech Revolution*, World Bank, Washington DC.

Eagles, P., S. McCool and C. Haynes (2002), *Sustainable Tourism in Protected Areas – Guidelines for Planning and Management*, World Commission on Protected Areas, United Nations Environment Programme, World Tourism Organisation and IUCN.

Fenochietto, R. and C. Pessino (2013), "Understanding countries' tax effort", *IMF Working Papers*, No. 13/244, International Monetary Fund, Washington DC.

Flightradar24 (2018), www.flightradar24.com/data/ (accessed on 9 March 2018).

Fountaine, T., J. Lembong, R. Nair and C. Süssmuth Dyckerhoff (2016), *Tackling Indonesia's Diabetes Challenge: Eight Approaches from Around the World*, McKinsey & Company and Center for Healthcare Research and Innovation.

Fournier, J. and M. Bétin (2018), "Limits to debt sustainability in middle-income countries", *OECD Economics Department Working Papers*, No. 1493, OECD Publishing, Paris, https://doi.org/10.1787/deed4df6-en.

Gaspar, V., L. Jaramillo and P. Wingender (2016), "Tax capacity and growth: is there a tipping point?", *IMF Working Papers*, No. 2016/234, International Monetary Fund, Washington DC.

Guillemette, Y. and D. Turner (2018), "The long view: scenarios for the world economy to 2060", *OECD Economic Policy Papers*, No. 22, OECD Publishing, Paris, http://dx.doi.org/10.1787/b4f4e03e-en.

IADB (2013), *More than Revenue: Taxation as a Development Tool*, Palgrave Macmillan US, New York.

IFC (2018), *The Indonesia Corporate Governance Manual*, 2nd edition, International Finance Corporation, Jakarta.

IFSB (2017), *Islamic Financial Services Industry Stability Report 2017*, Islamic Financial Services Board, Kuala Lumpur.

IISD (2018), *Missing the 23 Per Cent Target: Roadblocks to the Development of Renewable Energy in Indonesia*, International Institute for Sustainable Development, Winnipeg.

ILO (2014), *Trends in informal employment in Colombia: 2009-2013*, International Labor Organisation, Geneva.

IMF (2018), "Indonesia: Selected issues", *IMF Country Report*, No. 18/33, International Monetary Fund, Washington DC.

IMF (2017a), *Indonesia: Financial System Stability Assessment*, International Monetary Fund, Washington DC.

IMF (2017b), *IMF Investment and Capital Stock Dataset*, 2017, International Monetary Fund, Washington DC.

IMF (2017c), "Indonesia: Selected Issues", *IMF Country Report*, No. 17/48, International Monetary Fund, Washington DC.

IMF / OECD / UN / World Bank (2015), *Options for Low Income Countries' Effective and Efficient Use of Tax Incentives for Investment,* A report to the G-20 Development Working Group by the IMF,

OECD, UN and World Bank, www.oecd.org/tax/tax-global/options-for-low-income-countries-effective-and-efficient-use-of-tax-incentives-for-investment.pdf.

ITC (2017), *Social Progress Index in Tourist Destinations of Costa Rica*, http://cf.cdn.unwto.org/sites/all/files/docpdf/presentation-socialprogresindexintouristdestinationsofcostarica-institutocostarricensedeturismo.pdf.

Jahari, A. (2018), *Penurunan Masalah Balita Stunting* [Decrease in toddler stunting problems], Presentation at the National Health Working Meeting, 6-8 March.

Jambeck, J. et al. (2015), "Plastic waste inputs from land into the ocean", *Science*, Vol. 347/6223, pp. 768-71.

Kompas (2016), *Empat Strategi Banyuwangi Raih Penghargaan Pariwisata PBB* [Four Banyuwangi's Strategies Receive UN Tourism Awards], https://travel.kompas.com/read/2016/01/22/104123127/Empat.Strategi.Banyuwangi.Raih.Penghargaan.Pariwisata.PBB.

KPK (2015), *Preventing State Losses in Indonesia's Forestry Sector: An Analysis of Non-tax Forest Revenue Collection and Timber Production Administration*, Corruption Eradication Commission, Jakarta.

La Porta, R. and A. Shleifer (2014), "Informality and development", *Journal of Economic Perspectives*, Vol. 28/3, pp. 109-126.

LADA (2018), *Langkawi Development Authority*, www.lada.gov.my/en/.

Lamb, J. et al. (2018), "Plastic waste associated with disease on coral reefs", *Science*, Vol. 359/6374, pp. 460-462.

LPEM (2017), *Layanan Keuangan Digital dan Laku Pandai: Inclusivitas, Kendala, dan Potensi* [Digital Financial Services and Smart Behaviour: Inclusivity, Constraints, and Potential], *Policy Brief*, Universitas Indonesia, Jakarta.

Ministry of Manpower (2017), *Pentingnya Peran Swasta Dalam Upaya Peningkatan Kompetensi Tenaga Kerja* [The Importance of Private Role in Efforts to Increase the Competence of Labor], Press release, http://kemnaker.go.id/berita/berita-kemnaker/pentingnya-peran-swasta-dalam-upaya-peningkatan-kompetensi (accessed on 27 May 2018).

Nurdin, H. (2018), *Indonesia Tourism Exchange*, http://pemasaranpariwisata.com/2018/02/26/indonesia-tourism-exchange/.

OECD (2018a), *SME and Entrepreneurship Policy in Indonesia 2018*, OECD Studies on SMEs and Entrepreneurship, OECD Publishing, Paris, https://doi.org/10.1787/9789264306264-en.

OECD (2018b), *OECD Economic Surveys: Turkey 2018*, OECD Publishing, Paris, http://dx.doi.org/10.1787/eco_surveys-tur-2018-en.

OECD (2018c), *OECD Investment Policy Reviews: Southeast Asia*, OECD Publishing, Paris, www.oecd.org/daf/inv/investment-policy/Southeast-Asia-Investment-Policy-Review-2018.pdf.

OECD (2018d), *Taxing Energy Use 2018: Companion to the Taxing Energy Use Database*, OECD Publishing, Paris, http://dx.doi.org/10.1787/9789264289635-en.

OECD (2018e), *OECD Tourism Trends and Policies 2018*, OECD Publishing, Paris, http://dx.doi.org/10.1787/tour-2018-en.

OECD (2018f), *OECD Economic Surveys: Brazil 2018*, OECD Publishing, Paris, http://dx.doi.org/10.1787/eco_surveys-bra-2018-en.

OECD (2017a), *Health at a Glance 2017: OECD Indicators*, OECD Publishing, Paris, https://doi.org/10.1787/health_glance-2017-en.

OECD (2017b), *OECD Economic Surveys: Colombia 2017*, OECD Publishing, Paris, http://dx.doi.org/10.1787/eco_surveys-col-2017-en.

OECD (2017c), *Key Issues for Digital Transformation in the G20*, OECD Publishing, Paris, http://www.oecd.org/G20/key-issues-for-digital-transformation-in-the-G20.pdf.

OECD (2017d), *OECD Economic Surveys: Iceland 2017*, OECD Publishing, Paris, http://dx.doi.org/10.1787/eco_surveys-isl-2017-en.

OECD (2016a), *OECD Economic Surveys: Indonesia 2016*, OECD Publishing, Paris, http://dx.doi.org/10.1787/eco_surveys-idn-2016-en.

OECD (2016b), *G20/OECD Support Note on Diversification of Financial Instruments for Infrastructure*, OECD Publishing, Paris, http://www.oecd.org/daf/fin/private-pensions/G20-OECD-Support-Note-on-Diversification-of-Financial-Instruments-for-Infrastructure.pdf.

OECD (2016c), *PISA 2015 Results (Volume I): Excellence and Equity in Education*, PISA, OECD Publishing, Paris, http://dx.doi.org/10.1787/9789264266490-en.

OECD (2016d), *OECD Economic Surveys: Costa Rica 2016: Economic Assessment*, OECD Publishing, Paris, http://dx.doi.org/10.1787/eco_surveys-cri-2016-en.

OECD (2015a), *OECD Economic Surveys: Indonesia 2015*, OECD Publishing, Paris, http://dx.doi.org/10.1787/eco_surveys-idn-2015-en.

OECD (2015b), *Managing Food Insecurity Risk: Analytical Framework and Application to Indonesia*, OECD Publishing, Paris, http://dx.doi.org/10.1787/9789264233874-en.

OECD (2015c), *OECD Economic Surveys: South Africa 2015*, OECD Publishing, Paris, http://dx.doi.org/10.1787/eco_surveys-zaf-2015-en.

OECD (2015d), "Enhancing job quality in emerging economies", in *OECD Employment Outlook 2015*, OECD Publishing, Paris, http://dx.doi.org/10.1787/empl_outlook-2015-9-en.

OECD (2015e), *Minimum Wages After the Crisis: Making Them Pay*, www.oecd.org/social/Focus-on-Minimum-Wages-after-the-crisis-2015.pdf.

OECD (2014), *Tourism and the Creative Economy*, OECD Studies on Tourism, OECD Publishing, Paris, http://dx.doi.org/10.1787/9789264207875-en.

OECD (2013), *Teachers for the 21st Century: Using Evaluation to Improve Teaching*, International Summit on the Teaching Profession, OECD Publishing, Paris, http://doi.org/10.1787/9789264193864-en.

OECD (2012a), *OECD Economic Surveys: Indonesia 2012*, OECD Publishing, Paris, http://dx.doi.org/10.1787/eco_surveys-idn-2012-en.

OECD (2012b), *OECD Reviews of Regulatory Reform: Indonesia 2012: Strengthening Co-ordination and Connecting Markets*, OECD Reviews of Regulatory Reform, OECD Publishing, Paris, http://dx.doi.org/10.1787/9789264173637-en.

OECD (forthcoming), *Social Protection System Review of Indonesia*, OECD Publishing, Paris.

OECD/ADB (2015), *Education in Indonesia: Rising to the Challenge*, Reviews of National Policies for Education, OECD Publishing, Paris, http://dx.doi.org/10.1787/9789264230750-en.

OECD/KIPF (2014), "The distributional effects of consumption taxes in OECD countries", *OECD Tax Policy Studies*, No. 22, OECD Publishing, Paris, http://dx.doi.org/10.1787/9789264224520-en.

OECD, E. Hanushek and L. Woessmann (2015), *Universal Basic Skills: What Countries Stand to Gain*, OECD Publishing, Paris, https://doi.org/10.1787/9789264234833-en.

OICA (2018), *Vehicles in Use 2005-15, International Organisation of Motor Vehicle Manufacturers*, www.oica.net/category/vehicles-in-use/ (accessed on 21 December 2017).

Republic of Indonesia (2018), *Stability at the Forefront with Unwavering Reforms Commitment - August 2018*, Investor Relations Unit - Republic of Indonesia, Jakarta.

Republic of Indonesia (2016), *First Nationally Determined Contribution*, http://www4.unfccc.int/ndcregistry/PublishedDocuments/Indonesia%20First/First%20NDC%20Indonesia_submitted%20to%20UNFCCC%20Set_November%20%202016.pdf.

Reuters (2018), *S&P Cautions on Worsening Balance Sheets at Indonesian State Firms*, www.reuters.com/article/us-indonesia-s-p-infrastructure/sp-cautions-on-worsening-balance-sheets-at-indonesian-state-firms-idUSKCN1GP0QW.

Rothenberg, A. et al. (2016), "Rethinking Indonesia's informal sector", *World Development*, Vol. 80, pp. 96-113.

Stern, S., A. Wares and T. Epner (2017), *Social Progress Index 2017 - Methodology Report*, www.socialprogressindex.com/assets/downloads/resources/en/English-2017-Social-Progress-Index-Methodology-Report_embargo-until-June-21-2017.pdf.

Thavorncharoensap, M. (2017), "Effectiveness of obesity prevention and control", *ADBI Working Paper*, No. 654, Asian Development Bank Institute, Manila.

Thomas, A., I. Joumard, T. Hanappi and M. Harding (2017), "Taxation and investment in India", *OECD Economics Department Working Papers*, No. 1397, OECD Publishing, Paris, http://dx.doi.org/10.1787/4258e11a-en.

TomTom (2018), *TomTom Traffic Index*, www.tomtom.com/en_gb/trafficindex/list?citySize=LARGE&continent=ALL&country=ALL (accessed on 15 March 2018).

UNEP-WCMC (2014), *Review of Corals from Indonesia* (coral species subject to EU decisions where identification to genus level is acceptable for trade purposes).

United Nations, Department of Economic and Social Affairs, Population Division (2017), *World Population Prospects: The 2017 Revision*, DVD Edition.

UNWTO and Griffith University (2017), *Managing Growth and Sustainable Tourism Governance in Asia and the Pacific*, World Tourism Organisation.

von Haldenwang, C. et al. (2015), "The Devolution of the Land and Building Tax in Indonesia", *Studies Deutsches Institut für Entwicklungspolitik*, No. 89, German Development Institute, Bonn.

WEF (2017), *The Travel and Tourism Competitiveness Report 2017: Paving the Way for a More Sustainable and Inclusive Future*, World Economic Forum, Geneva.

WEF (2016), *Accelerating Capital Markets Development in Emerging Economies: Country Case Studies*, World Economic Forum, Geneva.

WHO (2017), *WHO Report on the Global Tobacco Epidemic 2017*, World Health Organization, Geneva.

World Bank (2018a), *Indonesia Economic Quarterly: Towards Inclusive Growth*, World Bank, Jakarta.

World Bank (2018b), *Indonesia Snapshots - Private Participation in Infrastructure (PPI)*, https://ppi.worldbank.org/snapshots/country/indonesia (accessed on 05 May 2018).

World Bank (2018c), *Indonesia – Public Expenditure and Financial Accountability (PEFA): Assessment Report 2017*, World Bank.

World Bank (2017), *Indonesia Economic Quarterly: Closing the Gap*, World Bank, Jakarta.

World Bank / PwC (2018), *Paying Taxes 2018*, www.pwc.com/payingtaxes.

Yudha, S. (2017), *Air Pollution and its Implications for Indonesia: Challenges and Imperatives for Change*, http://pubdocs.worldbank.org/en/183201496935944434/200417-AirQualityAsia-Air-Pollution.pdf.

Annex. Progress in structural reform

This Annex reviews actions taken on recommendations from previous Economic Surveys that are not covered in tables within the main body of the Key Policy Insights. Recommendations that are new to this Survey are listed at the end of the Executive Summary and the relevant chapters.

Recommendations in previous Surveys	Actions taken since October 2016
A. Promoting inclusive and sustainable economic growth	
Direct more public resources to improving education access and outcomes. Continue regular teacher assessments and professional development, and link teacher salaries more closely to qualifications and performance.	The 2019 State Budget targets 20.1 million students to be reached by the "Smart Indonesia" programme, which provides financial support to poor students who stay in school.
Raise public spending on infrastructure. Focus on transportation and logistics to support industry, as well as natural disaster prevention and water treatment.	The 16th economic policy package, released in July 2017, focused on reducing logistics costs. It includes the development of regional distribution centres, and aims to speed up processing of imports and exports by simplifying and reducing documentation.
Avoid protectionist measures that inhibit openness to trade and foreign investment with uncertain development payoff.	In 2018 the authorities relaxed foreign investment restrictions in the insurance sector and decided to allow foreign universities to open branches in Indonesia in co-operation with local private universities. The regulation relating to employing foreign workers was also changed to ease procedures. .
To meet rising power needs, invest in low-carbon generating capacity, including renewables and geothermal sources.	In 2017 the government signed 68 power purchase agreements with private companies who will build renewable energy power plants.
Introduce a sub-minimum wage for youth directly linked to the general minimum wage.	No action taken.
Reduce impediments to hiring and dismissal. Reduce onerous severance payments, and ease dismissal procedures in the formal labour market. In return, introduce unemployment benefits coupled with individual unemployment savings accounts.	No action taken.
Improve the enforcement of intellectual property rights.	No action taken.
Remove formal education from the negative investment list.	In January 2018 the government decided to allow foreign universities to open branches in Indonesia in co-operation with local private universities.
Encourage tertiary education financing through establishing a student loan system.	In collaboration with the Ministry of Research, Technology and Higher Education, the state-owned bank BRI launched a student loan programme in March 2018 named "Briguna Flexi Pendidikan". It is targeted at master and doctorate students who already have a fixed income.
Provide incentives for investment in skills. Create a national training fund to consolidate resources allocated to training and direct them to their most cost-efficient use.	No action taken.
B. Reducing poverty and inequality	
Increase, and further improve targeting of, spending on poverty alleviation and health measures.	Conditional cash transfers continue to expand with the Family Hope Programme (PKH) granted to the 10 million poorest families by the end of 2017. The unified database of vulnerable households is being used to improve targeting.
Expand existing programmes to tackle stunting, including by encouraging breastfeeding.	In August 2017, the government launched the Accelerated Stunting Reduction Strategy which focuses efforts in 10 priority districts. The President committed in 2018 to reduce the stunting ratio to 28% by 2019 from 30% in 2017.
Liberalise the importation of food. Refocus National Logistics Agency (BULOG) activities on managing emergency supplies.	No action taken.
Increase financial inclusiveness by further developing branchless banking, drawing lessons from such countries as India, Mexico, the Philippines and Kenya.	As of December 2017, the Laku Pandai programme which aims to expand branchless banking covered 13.6 million customers in 27 banks compared to 3.7 million in 20 banks a year before.
Tackle labour market informality by reducing rigidities in the formal sector, and by enhancing the effectiveness of the tax-transfer system for poverty alleviation and paying other social benefits.	The coverage of the unified database of vulnerable households has continued to improve.
Streamline social assistance, and integrate social security payments with the income tax system. Boost funding for the most efficient measures, such as conditional cash transfers. Continue efforts to create a unified database of beneficiaries.	Conditional cash transfers continue to expand with the Family Hope Programme (PKH) granted to the 10 million poorest families by the end of 2017. The coverage of the unified database of vulnerable households has continued to improve.

Recommendations in previous Surveys	Actions taken since October 2016
C. Making the most of natural resources while preserving the environment	
Refocus the mineral ore export ban based on an evaluation of the costs and benefits of onshore processing for each mineral. Provide infrastructure and electricity to the new smelters.	The export ban was relaxed in January 2017 for firms that get a new mining licence. The new licences impose divestment of up to 51% and the obligation to build a smelter within five years.
Increase agricultural productivity by providing technical assistance and training, including through agreements between smallholders and large estates. Increase farmers' access to credit by accelerating land titling.	In 2017 the Ministry of Agrarian Affairs and Spatial Planning had mapped 5.3 million plots of land as part of a Land Certification Programme. By June 2018 2.3 million land certificates had been issued.
D. Enhancing regional development	
Work with the sub-national governments to move the regulation of business to best practice.	An online single submission system was launched in 2018; after it is fully implemented it will centralise all licensing procedures of all levels of government.
Experiment with different incentives in special economic zones, including more flexible labour regulation, with a view to extending proven good practices to the whole economy.	No action taken.
Expand assistance to help regions to improve budget planning and implementation capacity. In the interim, make greater use of special allocation funds to prioritise sub-national spending.	Performance-based budgeting has been developed in several provinces such as West Sumatra, West Java, Riau and Yogyakarta in 2017 and Gorontalo in 2018.
Do more to encourage sub-national governments to develop their own sources of revenue, such as by offering matching grants. Modify the transfer formula so that it does not penalise jurisdictions that exploit more fully their own fiscal capacity.	In the 2017 budget the proportion of the general allocation fund (DAU) basic allocation covering personnel costs was reduced. In the 2018 budget, the proportion of the village funds basic allocation (equal across villages) was reduced and more weight put on poor villages, the size of the area, the population and the construction cost index.
Make explicit villages' service delivery responsibilities, and develop audit mechanisms to oversee their budgets.	No action taken.

Thematic chapters

Chapter 1. Raising more public revenue in a growth- and equity-friendly way

Indonesia's government needs more revenue to fund spending that can boost GDP growth, raise well-being and reduce poverty. The tax-to-GDP ratio is low relative to other emerging market economies. The difficulty is to raise revenues without denting growth or worsening inequality. Successive reforms have modernised the tax administration and increased the number of taxpayers. Nonetheless, raising compliance is an ongoing challenge. Investing in the tax administration, particularly human resources and information systems, rightly remains a government priority. This will help ease compliance costs and strengthen enforcement, raising revenue. There is also scope to improve the design of various taxes. Broadening the bases of income and consumption taxes would raise more revenue and reduce distortions. Expanding property taxation, if appropriately implemented, could provide additional funds for local governments, which have substantial responsibilities in Indonesia's decentralised system of delivering government services. Taxes can also be used more extensively to discourage activities and behaviours with negative health and environmental externalities. Strengthening property rights and fighting illegal extraction would increase revenues from Indonesia's natural resource wealth.

Indonesia's government aims to raise the tax-to-GDP ratio by around 2 percentage points in coming years. This would finance much-needed spending on infrastructure, human capital and social protection, which would spur growth, reduce poverty and raise well-being. The 2012 OECD *Economic Survey* of Indonesia highlighted significant scope to improve the tax system by broadening tax bases, removing distortionary exemptions and improving tax administration (OECD, 2012). It also proposed ways of increasing revenues from natural resources through more efficient taxation. Six years later, this chapter revisits options for tax policy, given that raising the tax-to-GDP ratio has proved difficult. The chapter begins with an overview of government revenue. It then assesses the administration of the tax system and ways of enhancing tax compliance, which is a pre-condition for a sustainable increase in the revenue-to-GDP ratio. In light of the research on the effects of taxes on growth and inequality it then looks at ways of growing revenues from key taxes: on incomes, consumption and property. It finishes by considering raising revenues from Indonesia's vast natural resource wealth.

Main characteristics of the Indonesian tax system

Tax revenues have remained low

Total government revenue across all levels of government was equivalent to 14% of GDP in 2016 (Figure 1.1, Panel A). The decline in the ratio to GDP over 2012-16 was driven by falling oil and gas receipts, which have been growing again since 2017 thanks to higher prices. Tax revenues amount to only 12% of GDP (according to the OECD's definition), little changed since the early 2000s, despite efforts of successive governments. This is low relative to other countries at similar income levels (Panel B). A higher ratio would provide funds for government priorities and reduce dependence on volatile oil revenues.

Figure 1.1. Fiscal revenues have been low

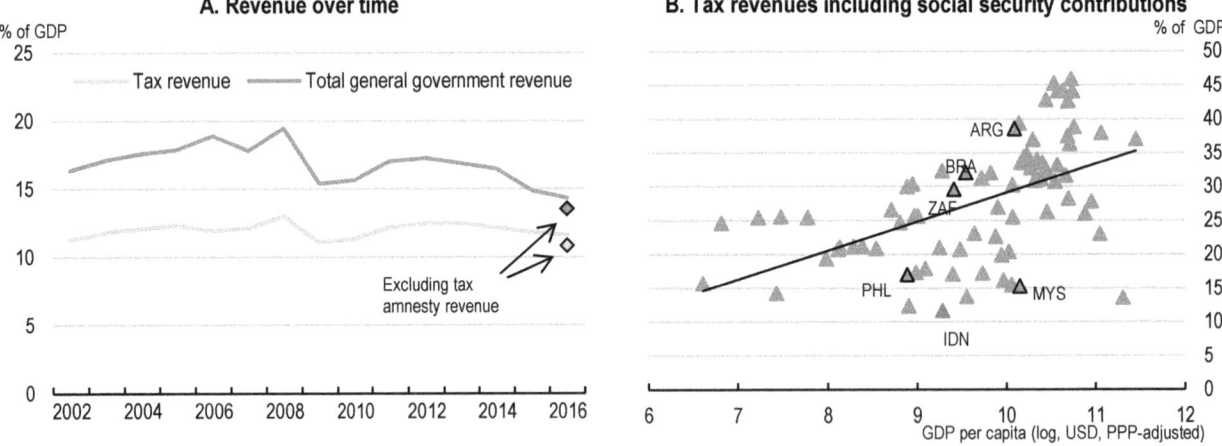

Note: Tax revenue data are based on the OECD's definition of tax revenues and can differ from national definitions. In Panel A the diamonds exclude revenue raised during the tax amnesty for individuals and firms that began in July 2016 (0.8% of GDP). Data for Indonesia do not include social security contributions; those that would be classified as tax revenue are estimated to total less than 0.5% of GDP. In Panel B data are for 2016 or latest available.
Source: OECD, *Revenue Statistics Database*, *OECD Economic Outlook Database*; World Bank, *World Development Indicators Database*; IMF, *World Economic Outlook Database*; World Bank (2018), *Indonesia Economic Quarterly: Towards Inclusive Growth*, World Bank, Jakarta.

StatLink ⟐ᵐˢᴸ https://doi.org/10.1787/888933833065

Cross-country research suggests that historically when countries have raised their tax revenue above a "tipping point" of around 13% of GDP, GDP per capita has been 0.7 percentage points higher each year for the following decade (Gaspar, Jaramillo and Wingender, 2016a). This can happen if social norms improve tax compliance, and in turn higher tax revenues strengthen the government's accountability, which in turn supports growth. This result is closely related to the evidence that state capacity – better enforced property rights, growth in the formal sector and other improvements in fiscal and economic institutions – also support growth and tax revenues (Gaspar, Jaramillo and Wingender, 2016b; Besley and Persson, 2014). Overall, it suggests Indonesia can move to a better equilibrium.

One way to shed light on Indonesia's low tax-to-GDP ratio is to estimate the predicted level of tax revenues given the economy's features and compare it with actual revenue collected (following OECD (2015a)). The difference gives an indication of "tax effort" and its evolution over time as well as structural factors weighing on revenues. Indonesia's GDP per capita, agriculture's share of the economy and openness to trade imply an expected tax-to-GDP ratio of around 22%, 10 percentage points above the current ratio, while income alone predicts 25% (Figure 1.2; Box 1.1). Indonesia's high share of agriculture and low openness to trade reduce its predicted tax ratio, which means that structural transformation can be expected to support higher tax revenues. But the consistently large gap between actual and predicted revenues points to the huge effort that is still required. The gap is likely to be linked to widespread informality (with 70% of employment and half of all dependent employees estimated to be informal), as well as tax evasion and narrow tax bases, which were all highlighted in the 2012 *Survey* (OECD, 2012). Increasing the tax ratio will likely involve raising voluntary compliance, through greater willingness and strengthened administration, along with reforms to broaden bases.

Figure 1.2. Revenues could be considerably higher

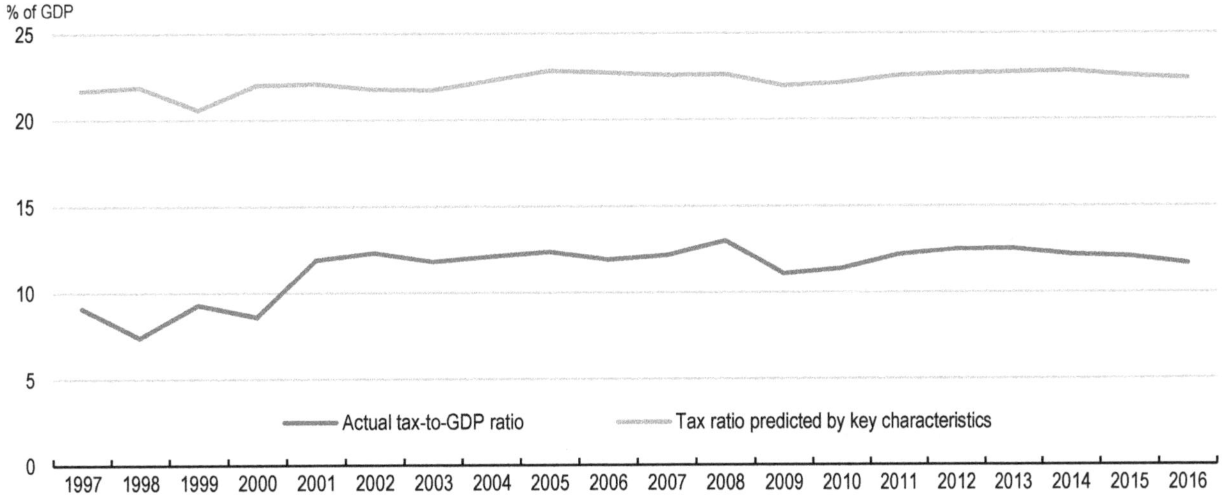

Note: The predicted ratio is based on a fixed-effects regression using: the log of GDP per capita (in constant prices); the log of trade openness; and agricultural value-added as a share of GDP. See Box 1.1 and Annex A for details of the specifications.
Source: OECD calculations based on OECD, *Revenue Statistics Database*, B. Égert, P. Gal and I. Wanner (2017), "Structural policy indicators database for economic research (SPIDER)", *OECD Economics Department Working Papers*, No. 1429, OECD Publishing, Paris; World Bank, *World Development Indicators Database*.

StatLink ⬛ᵐˢ᷄ https://doi.org/10.1787/888933833426

Box 1.1. Tax capacity and tax effort

The potential tax revenue that an economy can generate depends on its structural features as well as its institutions. Higher levels of income per capita, greater trade openness and a lower agricultural value added share are all associated with higher tax revenues, as are public expenditure on education, less corruption and less inequality (Fenochietto and Pessino, 2013). Institutional factors such as the tax administration's resources and governance quality also influence revenue-raising potential (Besley and Persson, 2014; Akgun, Bartolini and Cournède, 2017). Tax effort and the tax design will then determine actual revenue.

Similar to OECD (2015a), the following equation is estimated for 77 countries covered by the OECD's *Revenue Statistics Database* (shown in Figure 1.1, Panel A), over 1997-2016, subject to data availability:

$$\frac{Tax}{GDP_{it}} = \alpha + \beta_1 \ln(GDP\ per\ capita)_{it} + \beta_2 \ln(openness)_{it}$$
$$+ \beta_3 Agriculture's\ share\ of\ GDP_{it} + c_i + \varepsilon_{it}$$

Predicted tax ratios and corresponding gaps depend somewhat on the model used (Annex A). Using GDP per capita alone, the predicted ratio for Indonesia is 25%, while the ratio is 22% using the model shown. These are consistent with earlier estimates of a maximum ratio of 28% based on stochastic frontier analysis (Fenochietto and Pessino, 2013). Over the period, Indonesia's revenues have been 10 percentage points below their predicted level; by contrast, South Africa has attained its predicted ratio on average, while Brazil has exceeded its by 7 percentage points.

Since 2002 there have been four successive phases of reforms focussed on raising tax effort by modernising tax administration and building administrative capacity. Reforms have sought to modernise processes and the administrative system, improve human-resource capacity, enhance the tax office's integrity, expand the number of taxpayers and reduce tax evasion. The 2015-19 medium-term plan prioritises administration and legislative reform. Over 2017-2020 reform is focussed on improving: services for taxpayers; business processes and databases; risk management; and organisation and human resource management. In 2017 a tax reform team including experts from outside the government was created to advise the Minister on reforms and their implementation. Increasing consultation and transparency during this process could help build stakeholder support for difficult reforms and enhance credibility. The reform team could be tasked with consulting stakeholders and the public on policy reforms and publishing reports on these. An example is the "Davis Tax Committee" in South Africa, which was created in 2013 to review the country's tax policy by conducting research and public consultations and has produced reports in 14 areas of revenue policy. OECD countries have used similar committees.

Most tax revenues are from income and consumption taxes raised by the central government

Around half of all tax revenue is raised from income taxes and a further 40% from taxes on goods and services (Figure 1.3). Overall, the share of revenues from key tax bases – corporate income, labour and goods and services – is similar to an average emerging-market economy but the level of revenues relative to the size of the economy is lower. The single-largest source of revenue is the value-added tax (VAT) – which is considered to be a less harmful tax for growth than income tax (Akgun, Cournède and Fournier, 2017; Acosta-Ormaechea and Yoo, 2012; Arnold et al., 2011). Taxes on labour (personal income tax and social security contributions) were around one-quarter of tax revenue in Indonesia and other emerging economies, whereas OECD countries rely more heavily on these taxes. The low share partly reflects the difficulties of taxing individual incomes in economies with a sizeable informal sector. Corporate income tax, which is more harmful from a growth perspective, has declined in importance since the 2012 *Survey* (from almost 30% of revenue to 20% in 2016), partly due to the commodity price cycle.

Despite a high degree of decentralisation in spending policy, taxation is relatively centralised. Sub-national governments raise little tax revenue directly, even though they are responsible for half of all spending (Figure 1.4) (OECD, 2016a). Provinces raise more of their own revenue than districts; capacity is heterogeneous but weaker at lower levels of government (*ibid.*). Legislative changes in 2000 increased sub-national governments' tax-raising powers, but these were partly unwound in 2009 and a prescribed list of taxes was established to address concerns that a proliferation of taxes and user charges was harming the business environment (National Legal Development Board, 2013). Consequently, funding for services continues to be through central government transfers and, to a lesser extent, equalisation funds that share revenues from natural resources across governments. Further decentralisation is still constrained by lower levels of administrative capacity at the local level (OECD, 2016a). Indeed, after some taxes were transferred from districts to provinces, the total share of sub-national tax in total tax revenue increased from 7% in 2009 to 10% in 2017. Ultimately, additional revenue should be raised by sub-national governments to strengthen local responsibility and accountability, taking into account administrative constraints and principles of local taxation (OECD, 2016a). Options are discussed in the tax design sections below.

Figure 1.3. Most tax revenue is from income and consumption taxes

Tax revenue by type, % of total tax revenue, 2016 or latest

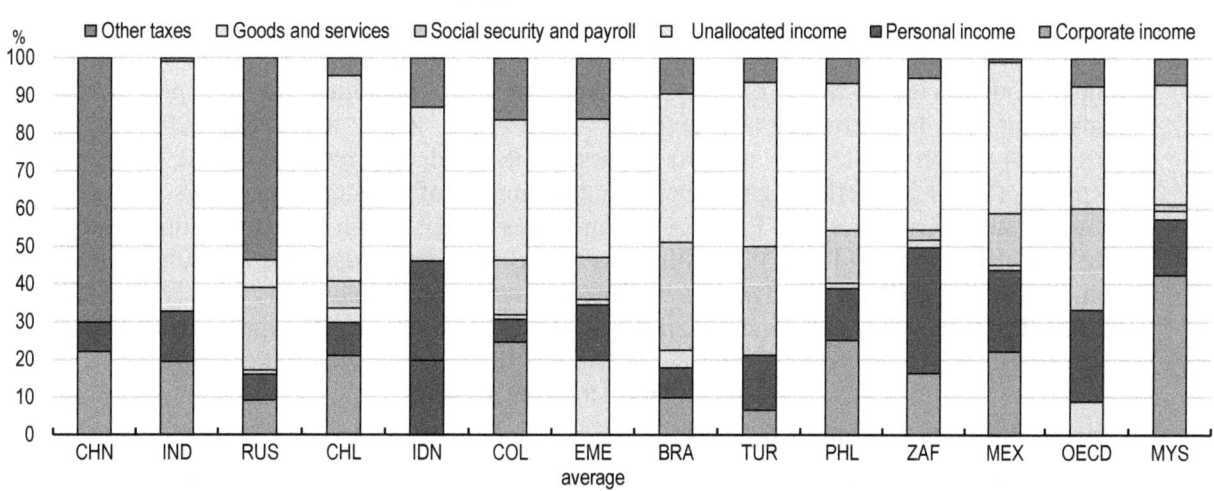

Note: EME average is the unweighted average of countries shown. The OECD average is unweighted. "Other taxes" include property taxes and local government taxes that could not be allocated to revenue types. Countries are ordered by the share of income taxes and social security contributions and payroll taxes in tax revenues. Social security contributions are not included for Indonesia but these are estimated to amount to less than 0.5% of GDP.
Source: OECD, *Revenue Statistics Database, OECD Economic Outlook Database*.

StatLink https://doi.org/10.1787/888933833445

Figure 1.4. Sub-national governments raise relatively little tax revenue

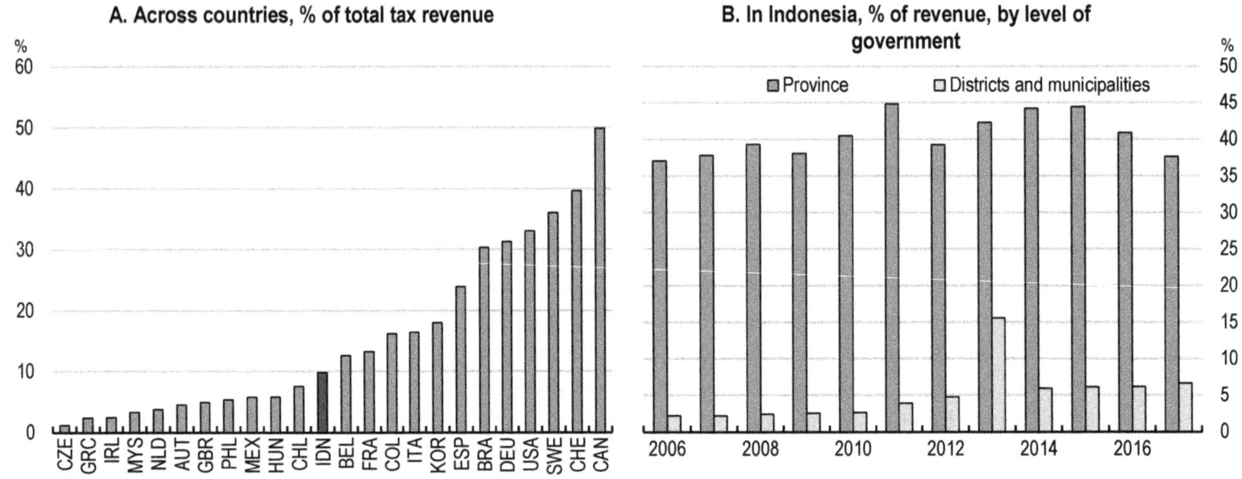

A. Across countries, % of total tax revenue

B. In Indonesia, % of revenue, by level of government

□ Province   □ Districts and municipalities

Note: Data in Panel A are for 2016 or latest available. Panel B shows tax revenues relative to total revenue at that level of government.
Source: OECD (2017), *Revenue Statistics in Asian Countries: Indonesia, Japan, Kazakhstan, Korea, Malaysia, the Philippines and Singapore;* OECD (2017), *Revenue Statistics: 1965-2016*, OECD et al. (2018), *Revenue Statistics in Latin America and the Caribbean 2018*; Statistics Indonesia.

StatLink ᔕᓕᔕᔪ https://doi.org/10.1787/888933833464

Administrative reform remains a priority

Reforms to tax administration are improving performance

The authority for administering the bulk of tax revenue lies with the Ministry of Finance's Directorate General of Taxes. The other key authorities are the Directorate General of Customs and Excise and sub-national levels of government. The government has made major efforts to increase registration and filing rates, including through better co-operation between parts of the government, new mobile tax units, e-registration, same-day registration service, e-filing options and amnesties on penalties for not previously registering. A high-profile tax amnesty from July 2016 to March 2017 saw IDR 4 884 trillion (USD 329 billion) of assets declared and resulted in 52 700 new taxpayers (Box 1.2). Reflecting these efforts, the number of registered taxpayers has been growing steadily (Figure 1.5, Panel A). Nonetheless, registration levels remain low by international standards (Table 1.2). Filing rates have risen, particularly for individuals with non-wage income (Panel B). The share of income tax returns filed electronically reached 82% in 2017 but still lags behind Brazil, Chile and Mexico where rates approach 100%.

Box 1.2. The 2016-17 tax amnesty

The aims of the amnesty were to raise revenue via a "clearance levy", to help reduce future tax evasion and to boost repatriation of assets for investment in Indonesia. Key elements were:

- A "clearance levy" was calculated as a rate applied to net asset values. Funds that were repatriated in the first phase were subject to a levy of just 2%. The rate increased twice during the programme (in October 2016 and January 2017). It

---

was lower for firms and self-employed individuals with gross turnover below IDR 4.8 billion (USD 323 000). It was higher if the assets were not repatriated.

- Assets that were repatriated must be kept in an approved vehicle for three years. Domestic assets may not be transferred out of Indonesia for three years. A breach would lead to income tax obligations of 30% on the declared assets.

- Participation conferred protection from investigation by other parts of the government, including from law enforcement agencies.

The amnesty collected IDR 135 trillion (USD 9 billion) in payments and saw IDR 4 884 trillion (USD 329 billion) of assets declared, although only 3% of that was repatriated (Table 1.1). Three-quarters of offshore assets were in Singapore. In terms of assets declared raised it was the world's most successful campaign (World Bank, 2017a). However, there were only 52 700 new taxpayers, which was below expectations. The bulk of assets declared and income raised was from individuals (87% of income). Large firms accounted for a further 13% of income raised.

Table 1.1. Value of the tax amnesty

	IDR trillion	% of GDP
"Clearance levy"	135	1.1
Total declared assets	4 884	38.4
Declared domestic assets	3 701	29.1
Repatriated assets	147	1.2
Declared foreign assets	1 037	8.2

Source: Directorate General of Taxes.

Figure 1.5. Registration and compliance have improved

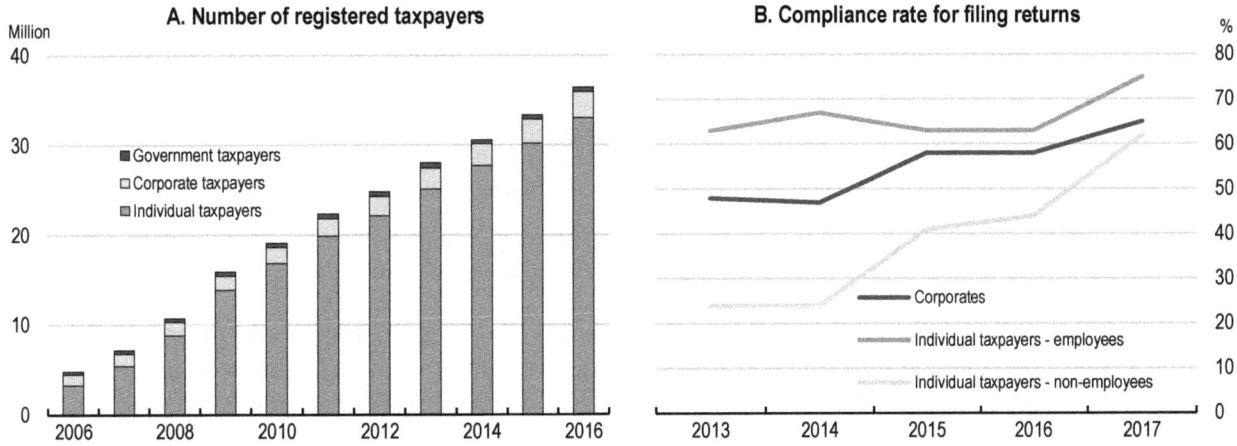

Note: Married couples typically pay tax as a household using the same taxpayer number. Compliance rates are calculated as the number of annual income tax returns filed in a fiscal year as percentage of those obliged to file a return at the beginning of that year. Unregistered taxpayers are not included. "Non-employees" are individuals with non-wage income, including professionals.
Source: Directorate General of Taxes.

StatLink ᵐˢˡ https://doi.org/10.1787/888933833483

Besides registration and filing rates, the tax administration can be assessed against other core functions including effectiveness of assessment, collection of overdue payments and dispute resolution (OECD, 2017a). Data are limited, but on available metrics Indonesia's performance is still mixed. In 2015 around 40% of personal and corporate income tax returns were filed late, which is similar to the rates in the average OECD emerging market economy (Table 1.2). Tax debt is low relative to revenue, and the rate of disputes is also comparatively low. Yet, the tax office wins a relatively small share of cases compared to other countries, suggesting that it may have inadequate legal resources or documentation (OECD, 2012). Darussalam (2017) argues that the nature of disputes indicates a lack of "co-operative compliance" and that dispute-resolution mechanisms like mediation are needed. Therefore, key reforms should include strengthening the tax administration, lowering compliance costs and increasing enforcement as discussed below. Investing in the tax administration could reap dividends: evidence from OECD countries highlights a positive relationship between expenditure on the tax administration and tax capacity and therefore revenue (Akgun, Bartolini and Cournède, 2017).

Table 1.2. Tax administration performance indicators

	Indonesia	Non-OECD average	OECD emerging market economies	OECD average
Registered personal income taxpayers (% of population aged 15+)	Between 17.8[1] and 35.7	56.1	73.6	87.6
On-time filing (%)				
- Personal income taxpayers	60.6	78.6	63.5	90.6
- Corporate income tax	57.6	71.9	59.8	84.5
On time payment – VAT (%)	86.0	90.4	..	93.3
Tax debt (% of revenue)	8.6	30.3	42.6	23.4
Disputes				
- Number of cases initiated per 1000 active taxpayers	0.7	4.4	1.8	12.4
- % of cases resolved in favour of tax office	32.5	61.6	58.3	69.3

Note: Data are for 2015 except for on-time payment, which is 2014 for Indonesia. The number of countries covered varies with response rates to the questionnaire, up to 54 countries. "OECD emerging market economies" is the average of Chile, Hungary, Mexico, Poland and Turkey; the average is not shown where there is only data for one country.
1. Calculated from data provided by the Directorate General of Taxes. Registered taxpayers are at end 2016. Note that married individuals typically pay tax at the household level; the lower bound is calculated by adjusting the number of taxpayers for the share that file tax jointly and the upper bound assumes that every taxpayer represents a two-taxpayer household.
Source: OECD (2017), *Tax Administration 2017: Comparative Information on OECD and Other Advanced and Emerging Economies*, OECD Publishing, Paris; Directorate General of Taxes; OECD calculations.

The current reform agenda rightly focuses on improving human resources and information systems. Spending on staff has risen to be comparable with other non-member countries by 2016 (Table 1.3). The administration has been expanding and now has around 40 000 staff, but in 2015 there were still almost 5 000 adults per staff member compared to 3 000 in the average non-OECD country with such data (Table 1.3). The relatively low number of active taxpayers mitigates the number of staff currently needed; as the tax base expands, exploiting economies of scale and greater use of technology may slow staffing needs. As well as hiring, the tax administration has been upskilling existing staff. Nonetheless, important employees such as auditors, analysts and IT professionals are still in short supply. New units, such as the Centre for Tax Analysis, can concentrate expertise. Further training will be crucial in strengthening the administration and enabling staff to adapt to new technologies and challenges. Building a reputation for staff integrity can help raise taxpayer morale, which is particularly important following high-profile cases of corruption. Recent steps to limit staff meeting taxpayers outside the tax administration reduce the risk of corruption; such reforms should continue so that taxpayers' confidence in the system increases.

Transformation has been hampered by the administration's lack of power to change its organisational structure and skill mix. All changes to its structure must be approved by the Ministry of Administrative and Bureaucratic Reform and it does not have the power to dismiss staff. One option is to establish the tax administration as an agency outside the Ministry, as is the case in many OECD countries, although the powers of such agencies vary across countries (OECD, 2017a). An alternative would be to temporarily give the tax administration more autonomy to make the transformation it needs, with appropriate oversight. Skills gaps can be filled through a combination of hiring, training and reallocation. Attention should be also be given to human resources at sub-national level, where constraints are even larger. The central tax administration has a help desk and provides training. Further initiatives could include secondments to the central tax administration and more sharing of best practices within provinces. Technology could deliver more training and also be used to upgrade processes.

The current modernisation programme aims to replace ageing IT infrastructure through a seven-year programme beginning in 2018. This is crucial, given the enormous amounts of data being generated from electronic reporting and third-party systems and the need to improve monitoring of the tax administration and taxpayers. The new "core tax administration" system is expected to capture all business processes including compliance system management, taxpayer account management, internal knowledge-management systems and managing new sensitive data, for example arising from exchange of information. Investment appears overdue: the recurrent IT budget is small compared to other countries, suggesting past under-investment (Table 1.3). (Although in 2015 capital expenditure from external suppliers increased 3.5-fold (OECD, 2017a)). The new system is estimated to cost around IDR 3.1 trillion (USD 209 million). Managing important risks, especially procurement of new IT systems and their implementation, will be critical for realising the potential benefits. The procurement process should be clear, transparent and adhere to good procedures. Training will need to be stepped up so that staff can adapt to these new technologies.

Table 1.3. Indicators of tax administrations' resources

	Indonesia	Non-OECD average	OECD emerging market economies	OECD average
Citizens (15 + years) per staff member	4 893	3 030	1 917	1 269
Active personal income taxpayers per staff member	446	562	1 065	635
Total budget as % GDP	0.08	0.12	0.14	0.19
Staff costs as % total recurrent budget	61.0	64.3	74.9	72.6
Training budget as % total recurrent budget	0.4	0.3	1.2	0.5
Recurrent IT budget as % total recurrent budget	3.3	11.0	3.8	13.4

Note: Data are for 2015 except for staff costs, which are 2016 for Indonesia to improve comparability. The number of countries covered varies with response rates to the questionnaire. "OECD emerging market economies" is the average of Chile, Hungary, Mexico, Poland and Turkey.
Source: OECD (2017), *Tax Administration 2017: Comparative Information on OECD and Other Advanced and Emerging Economies*, OECD Publishing, Paris; Directorate General of Taxes; OECD calculations.

Voluntary compliance and enforcement should be raised together

Compliance costs for businesses appear high relative to other countries, although progress has been made in recent years. For instance paying some taxes is still time-consuming (Figure 1.6). Payments are monthly, whereas many countries allow less frequent payments for small firms, for example (OECD, 2017a). High compliance costs can deter formalisation and, due their fixed nature, disproportionately burden small firms. Greater use, and ease, of online filing could reduce these costs. The refund process has been especially burdensome, which can particularly affect SMEs' cash flows. In general, refund requests trigger a compulsory audit, which can take up to 12 months. Until 2018, only relatively few "golden taxpayers" that were deemed low risk received refunds automatically. In 2018 reforms provided for certain low-risk taxpayers to receive VAT refunds within one month and income tax refunds within three months, with audits later. To be effective the group of eligible taxpayers will need to be sufficiently broad but with monitoring to guard against fraud. Technology should be used to expand risk-based auditing.

Figure 1.6. Complying with taxes takes firms longer than elsewhere

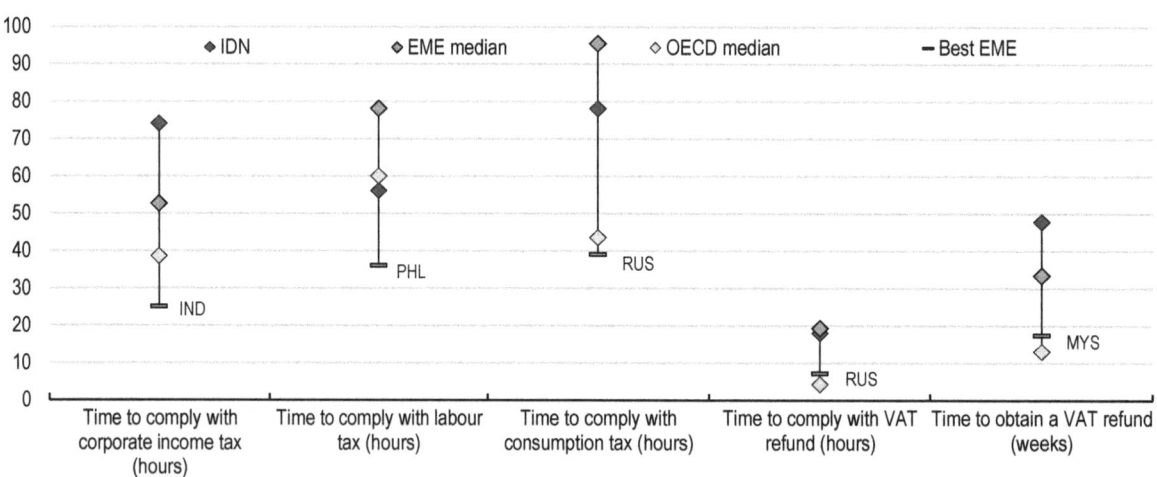

Note: Emerging market economies (EMEs) comprise Brazil, Chile, China, Colombia, India, Malaysia, Mexico, Philippines, Russia, and Turkey. The time required is based on a case study company.
Source: World Bank / PwC (2018), *Paying Taxes 2018*.

StatLink ᵃᵐˢᴾ https://doi.org/10.1787/888933833502

Indonesia uses withholding taxes extensively to shift the compliance burden from more risky taxpayers to designated taxpayers, with the aim of increasing overall compliance. Tax is withheld on wages, interest, royalties and dividends, as is common, as well as rental income and 62 types of business activities (for example, accounting, consulting, mining support, gardening and childcare services). Withholding taxes are also imposed on imports, which are credited against company income tax liabilities; in 2018 these were raised as part of the government's policies to reduce the current account deficit. In addition, construction activities are subject to final withholding tax at rates of 2-6%, depending on firm size and the type of activity. Lower-income countries often use withholding taxes to shift the burden of compliance to more trusted taxpayers, as do some OECD countries, for particular business activities, SMEs or self-employed taxpayers (OECD, 2017a; Joshi, Prichard and Heady, 2014; OECD, 2009).

Empirical evidence on the overall effectiveness of withholding taxes on business income is still patchy (Joshi, Prichard and Heady, 2014). In the near-term the priorities are to ensure that businesses are aware of their obligations, to minimise the associated compliance burden and to ensure that penalties for administrative mistakes are not disproportionate (Darussalam, 2018). The current pilot programme of e-withholding returns is being extended progressively and is a step in the right direction. Looking ahead, growing capabilities to monitor actual and potential taxpayers may reduce the need to cover so many business activities, as well as for differential treatment of income from construction-related activities. The costs and benefits of these business withholding taxes should be evaluated in light of other administrative reforms, and revisions made accordingly.

Complexity and uncertainty add to compliance costs and create opportunities for tax evasion. The tax regime is perceived as more contradictory and less consistently enforced than in most regional comparators but is perceived to have improved in recent years (Deloitte, 2017). Investors highlight uncertainty surrounding the tax environment as one of their concerns in Indonesia (IMF/OECD, 2017). Legislative ambiguity and overlaps create multiple interpretations and lead to different advice from tax administration staff. This uncertainty generates costs when firms seek advice and dispute interpretations. Frequent and hasty policy changes have added to uncertainty and caused implementation problems, which must be redressed. For example, the requirement to record an electronic identification number for all customers was initially announced with only three weeks for implementation, but an outcry led to its delay. Government plans to revise the income tax legislation to clarify key ambiguities are welcome. It should consult widely, ideally allowing public comments. A more stable environment could be established by focussing more tax changes in an annual window (e.g. following the budget) and standardising procedures for public consultation, as in South Africa.

Technology is easing compliance costs, for example through online filing and more payment options. Electronic invoice systems that report data automatically have been piloted since 2015 and will be rolled out nationwide in 2018. The tax administration uses multiple platforms, including social media, to increase the reach of its communication, and offers assistance via its call centre and live chat service. Planned changes to the tax administration's website are expected to make it more user-friendly. Clear and simple explanations of current obligations and online calculators, for example, would assist taxpayers in complying. However, alternatives to online processes will need to be retained while ICT infrastructure and internet connectivity are still developing. Greater use of technology can further reduce administrative burden, for instance online verification systems could validate data as they are submitted (OECD, 2017a). Systems for monitoring firms more closely can predict payment difficulties and facilitate early intervention. Using third-party data to pre-fill returns would lower the compliance burden. Risk-based auditing should continue to be expanded as it is an effective way of allocating limited resources.

Increasing registration and compliance of self-employed workers is an ongoing challenge, as in many emerging economies. Self-employed workers account for 40% of all employment, and around 70% appear to be informal. Reducing informality and under-reporting requires increasing the probability of detecting non-compliance as well as inducing voluntary compliance. The tax administration is raising the probability of detection of evasion by using third-party data, such as bank accounts and social media presence. Other countries have reported success in fighting under-reporting of income through e-invoicing and campaigns against cash payments in sectors such as construction (in Canada and New Zealand) (OECD, 2017b). Some have found that incentives for taxpayers to adopt e-invoicing paid for themselves (OECD, 2017b). Several European countries, Mexico, Uruguay and India limit the value of cash payments (OECD, 2017c; Sands et al., 2017). The Chilean government provides online accounting software that allows small businesses to record transactions and generate pre-filled tax returns. In Indonesia, a turnover tax for SMEs (discussed below) aims to encourage formalisation but it should be linked more closely to access to additional non-financial benefits.

Fighting tax evasion by wealthy individuals remains a priority, particularly to reinforce the success of the tax amnesty. Indonesia's participation in the Automatic Exchange of Information under the Common Reporting Standard contributed to the credibility of the amnesty and will provide the tax administration with significant amounts of data. As at late September 2018 86 countries had activated the Multilateral Competent Authority Agreement with Indonesia, including Singapore, which is particularly important, as almost three-quarters of offshore assets declared under the tax amnesty were there. The first Automatic Exchange of Information was in September 2018. In addition, in 2017 the tax administration gained access to domestic bank account information. The challenge is therefore to use these new tools effectively, as they will create huge demands on staff and IT systems. Setting up dedicated units within the tax administration in high-risk areas would concentrate valuable expertise.

Given the low rate of registration, enforcement efforts should be complemented by developing a stronger culture of voluntary compliance built on fairness and trust. The administration is shifting in this direction with the ending of the "gizjeling" practice (imprisoning taxpayers until they paid their taxes) and greater use of behavioural nudges like reminding people by SMS to pay their tax. Other penalties should be reviewed to ensure that they are appropriate and are not preventing formalisation. Fairness can be increased by making the tax legislation gender-neutral: it is written for a household headed by a man, which means that women must complete paperwork to change their taxpayer type and file returns as an individual. Women cannot claim the dependent allowance unless they prove that their husband has no income. Continuing to invest in service centres for taxpayers, including staff training, and enhancing taxpayer rights through a stronger ombudsman would help to create a culture of co-operative compliance (Darussalam, 2017).

Education and awareness campaigns are expanding. Tax literacy has been introduced into education curricula through programmes like "Pajak Bertutur". In 2016 eight tax offices began offering business development services to SMEs. From July 2018 all regional offices must offer such services, although they have discretion over the content. Services have included fairs bringing SMEs and large retailers together, as well as seminars on paying taxes and account keeping. Regional tax offices may also use private providers. SMEs are being targeted for participation based on the tax administration's databases although some offices use other methods, such as social media, to advertise these events. Monitoring and evaluating these programmes will enable the services to be better targeted over time. The range of services should also be expanded based on lessons learned across the country.

Income taxes are levied on narrow bases

At 5% of GDP, income tax revenues are low relative to other emerging-market and OECD economies (Figure 1.7, Panel A). Other emerging market economies and OECD countries also typically rely more heavily on social security contributions and payroll taxes. The prevalence of informal employment and micro-enterprises in Indonesia makes for a narrow tax base: labour force data suggest that just under half of all employees and 28% of self-employed were formally employed in 2017. By some estimates, 93% of firms are informal (Rothenberg et al., 2016). There has been some progress in raising personal income tax revenue, even abstracting from the tax amnesty, which likely reflects the rise in the number of taxpayers (Panel B). On the other hand, corporate income tax revenue has grown more slowly than GDP.

Figure 1.7. Income tax and social security collections are low

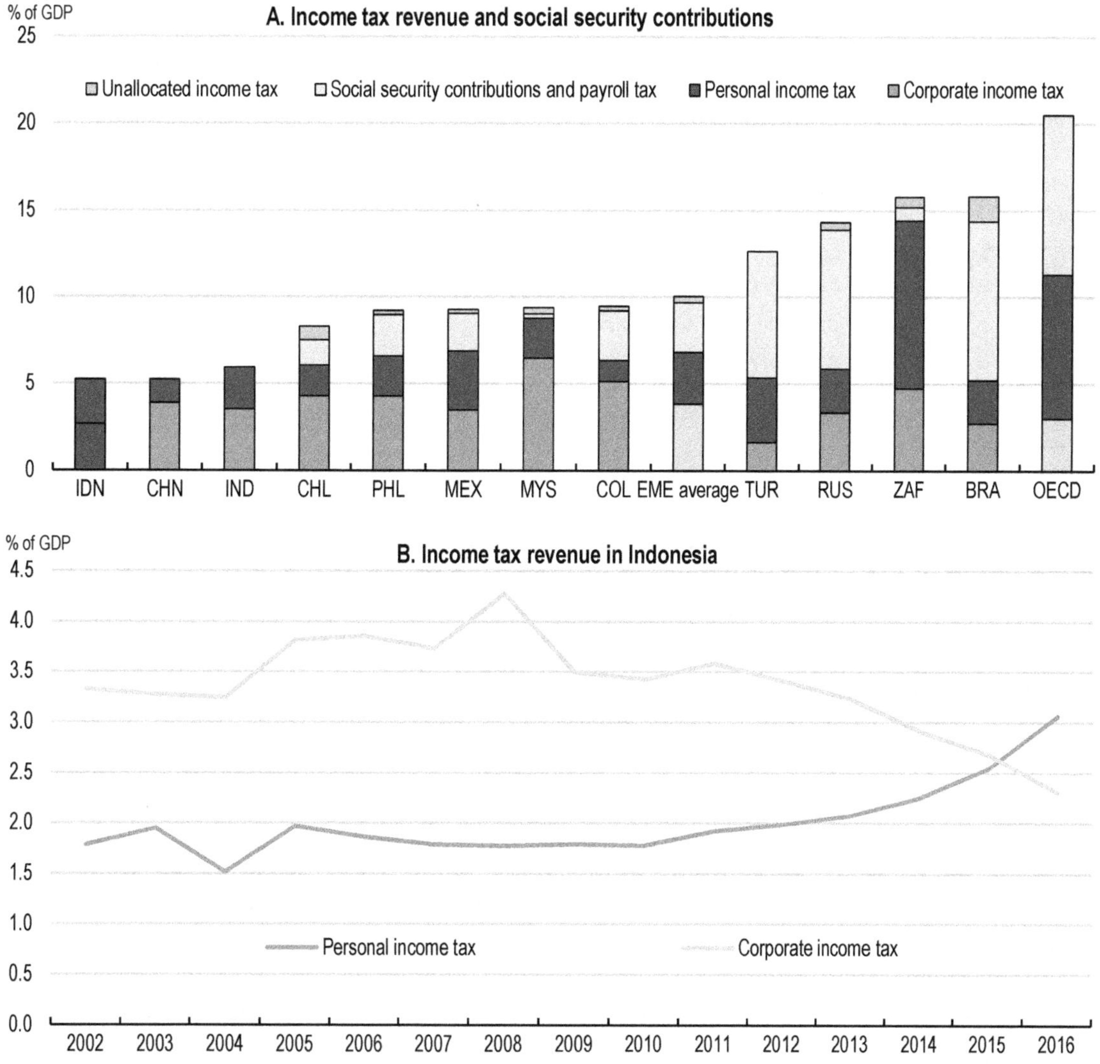

A. Income tax revenue and social security contributions

B. Income tax revenue in Indonesia

Note: "EME average" is the unweighted average of emerging-market economies shown. OECD is an unweighted average across OECD member countries. Indonesia's income tax data for 2016 includes revenue from the tax amnesty, of which individuals contributed the equivalent of 0.7% of GDP and companies 0.1% of GDP. Social security contributions are not included for Indonesia; those that would be classified as tax revenue are estimated to be equivalent to less than 0.5% of GDP in 2016.

Source: OECD, *Revenue Statistics Database*; CEIC; OECD calculations.

StatLink ⟶ https://doi.org/10.1787/888933833521

Relatively few individuals must pay personal income tax

Personal income taxes are charged on income at progressive marginal rates of 5%, 15%, 25% and 30%, typically at the household level. There is a standard tax allowance of IDR 54 million (USD 13 000 PPP-adjusted) and additional allowances for dependents (up to one spouse and three children). In 2015 and 2016 the tax allowances were increased sharply to stimulate consumption: the threshold for beginning to pay tax jumped from 1.2

times average employee earnings in 2014 to just over twice by 2016, (and almost three times for taxpayers with a dependent wife and three dependent children) (Figure 1.8, Panel A). This substantially reduced the number of personal income taxpayers as well as effective tax rates. The top tax rate is not payable until high multiples of income – around 20 times the average wage – although bracket creep has reduced this ratio over time (Panel B).

Figure 1.8. The threshold for paying tax increased but tax brackets have narrowed overall

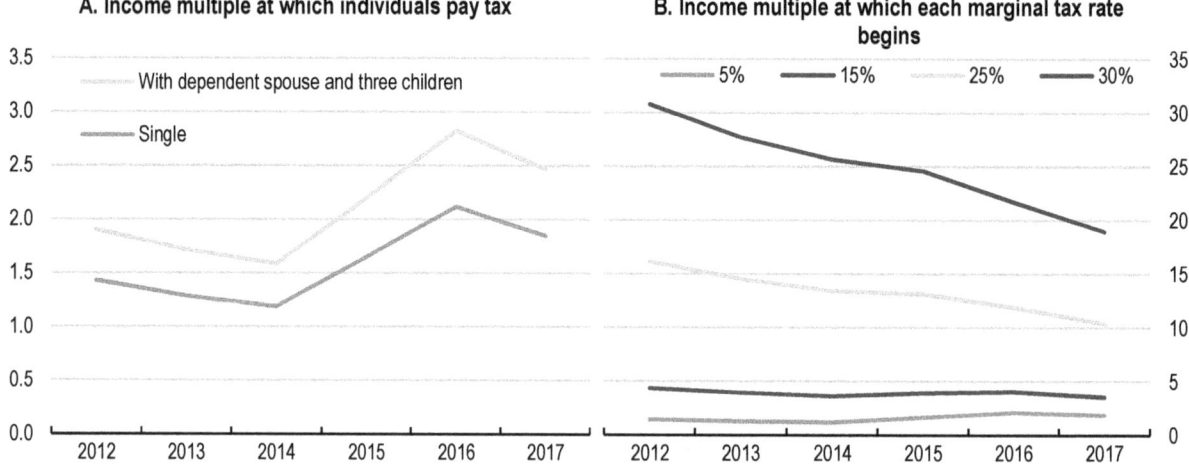

Note: There is a standard allowance of IDR 54 million and a further allowance of IDR 4.5 million for each dependent up to one spouse and three children. Panel B shows the rates for a single taxpayer. Data shown are based on the ILO harmonised measure of mean nominal monthly earnings of employees. The general trend over time also holds if average income is proxied by GDP per capita.
Source: ILO, *ILOSTAT Database*; OECD calculations.

StatLink ▒▒▒▒ https://doi.org/10.1787/888933833540

The social security system has been expanding, most recently in 2015 with a new pension plan. Employees must now pay 2% of their monthly gross salary towards health insurance and pension contributions and employers pay 6.54-8.04% of the salary (contributions for work-accident insurance vary across sectors). Health insurance and pension contributions are capped. Even after recent changes to increase social security contributions, the average (and marginal) tax wedge for average income earners is still low in international comparison, partly because workers with average earnings do not pay tax (Table 1.4). (Employees and employers also contribute a combined 5.7% of the salary to compulsory old age insurance but as this is a defined contribution scheme it is not included in the tax wedge.) The low tax wedge helps reduce the disincentive to work in the formal sector. The government's drive for universal health coverage with contributions from all but the poorest individuals will, in principle, contain the gap between taxes on informal and formal employment for low-income earners. However, in practice, registering all informal workers will be challenging (Dartanto, 2017).

Table 1.4. The average tax wedge is low

Income tax plus employee and employer contributions less cash benefits (% of labour costs, 2016)

	Family type						
	Single, no children			Married, 2 children			Married, no children
Wage level (% of average wage of each earner)	67	100	167	100-0	100-33	100-67	100-33
Brazil	32.5	32.5	36.3	32.5	30.4	32.5	32.3
China	32.4	32.9	35.2	32.9	34.8	32.7	34.8
India (if no social security contributions)	0.0	2.2	1.6	2.2	1.7	1.3	1.7
India (with social security contributions)	26.1	8.3	7.7	8.3	13.1	15.9	13.1
Indonesia	**7.8**	**7.8**	**7.8**	**7.8**	**7.8**	**7.8**	**7.8**
South Africa	11.4	15.2	20.7	15.2	12.1	13.7	12.1
OECD unweighted average	32.3	36.0	40.4	26.6	28.2	30.9	32.8

Note: Social security contributions are defined as a tax if they are compulsory unrequited payments to general government.
Source: OECD, *Taxing Wages Database.*

The distribution of income, together with the current personal income tax rate structure means that relatively few individuals must pay income tax. Only 20 million taxpayers were obliged to file a return in 2016. This is a small fraction of the adult population (even if some taxpayers represented two-income households rather than individuals). In 2012 over half of all personal income tax revenues were paid by less than 0.5% of households (Jellema, Wai-Poi and Afkar, 2017). Data for 2016 suggest the distribution remains highly skewed. Each taxable income bracket is reached at a much higher multiple of income than in Brazil, China or South Africa (Figure 1.9, Panel A). The relatively high thresholds for paying higher marginal rates of tax make the system less progressive than in many other countries, including emerging economies (Panel B). Moreover, the top statutory tax rate is relatively low compared to the OECD average and other emerging economies, although it is closer to other Asian countries' rates (Panel C). A more progressive tax structure with lower tax thresholds, for example, would be closer to that in other emerging economies and help address distributional concerns by increasing the effective tax rate of higher income earners.

Figure 1.9. Top personal income tax rates bite at high levels of income

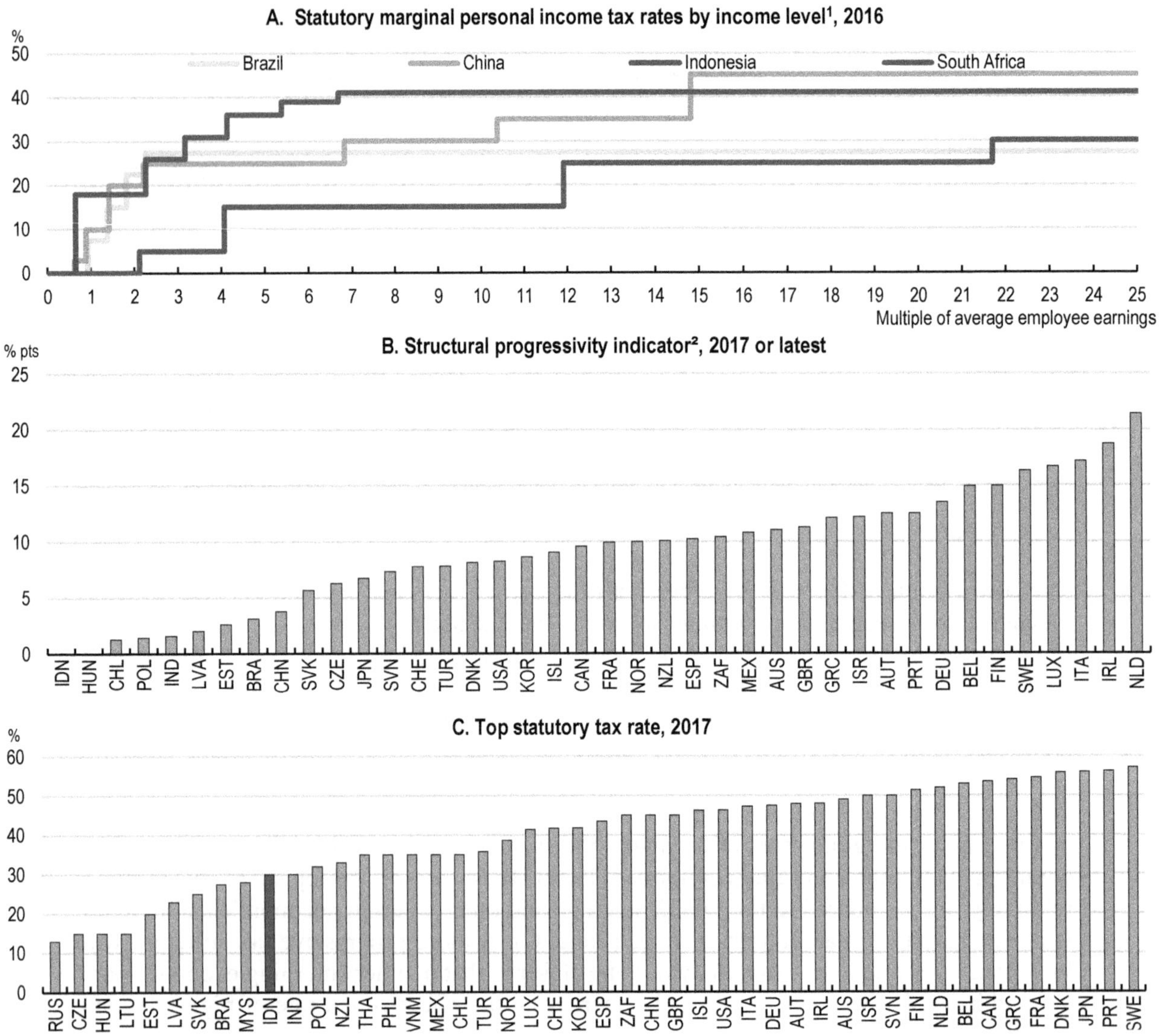

A. Statutory marginal personal income tax rates by income level[1], 2016

Legend: Brazil — China — Indonesia — South Africa

B. Structural progressivity indicator[2], 2017 or latest

C. Top statutory tax rate, 2017

1. Calculations are for a single earner. Rates shown are statutory rates. They take into account the basic tax allowance but do not include other tax allowances that reduce effective tax rates.
2. The structural progressivity indicator shown measures the percentage point change of the average effective tax rate for a single person with no children if their income increases from 67% to 167% of the average wage.
Source: OECD, *Taxing Wages Database, Tax Database*; ILO, *ILOSTAT Database*; EY (2016), *Worldwide Personal Tax and Immigration Guide 2016-17*; PwC, *Worldwide Tax Summaries Online*, OECD calculations.

StatLink 🔗 https://doi.org/10.1787/888933833103

Tax exemptions and deductions also narrow the tax base. Fringe benefits paid to workers and employer allowances (for transport, for example) are not included as taxable income, which benefits high-income earners relative to low-income earners (OECD, 2012). (These benefits are taxed at the company level as they are non-deductible expenses for employers.) Such benefits account for 2% of income among the top 5% of earners in the labour force survey compared to 0.8% among the top 15% (according to 2017 labour force survey data). Other allowances include a 5% tax allowance for employees' expenses (which is almost a basic tax allowance in practice) and for contributions to approved pension or saving funds. These are capped, which limits the fiscal cost of these allowances but they are still likely to be regressive across taxpayers. Estimates of forgone revenues would inform such assessments. These estimates should be published annually in future tax expenditure reports. Discussions are underway to recognise fringe benefits as personal taxable income and as expenses for corporate income tax. Incorporating non-monetary compensation in the tax base would broaden it and improve horizontal and vertical equity.

Options for raising more revenue include lowering the standard tax allowance, narrowing the brackets or increasing rates. Lowering the standard tax allowance would increase the number of taxpayers but may be difficult in practice, given that the allowance has recently been raised. It should therefore be held constant in nominal terms for several years: if the average wage grew by 10% per year, the allowance would return to the average wage after five years. Lowering the top threshold to be IDR 300 million (10 times average earnings in 2017), for example, could raise an additional 0.9% of total tax revenue, under simplifying assumptions including that there was no behavioural response. Lowering the second-highest threshold to be IDR 150 million (5 times average earnings) could raise a little more (2.7%). Increasing marginal tax rates can be ineffective in the presence of a large informal sector (Besley and Persson, 2014). High-income earners can more easily engage in tax planning than those with lower incomes. In both cases, the elasticity of tax revenue may be low (*ibid*). Simulations of similar reform combinations also highlighted the potential drag on economic growth from raising rates (Nugroho and Tenrini, 2014). The administration would need to monitor the effects of such changes to ensure they do not increase informality or avoidance.

Investment income is currently taxed at different rates depending on its source and to whom it is paid. Resident individuals typically face a final withholding tax, at rates of 10% (on dividends and rental income from land and buildings), 15% (on interest income from bonds) and 20% (on interest from bank accounts). Foreign-sourced capital income is taxed as ordinary income. Non-residents are subject to higher rates of taxation unless their country of residence has a tax treaty with Indonesia. Individuals' capital gains are taxed as ordinary income, except the sale of Indonesian real estate (taxed at 2.5% of the property's value) and listed shares (0.1% of the value). Such large differences in tax rates distort saving decisions and open up tax planning opportunities. For instance, combined marginal tax rates for high-income earners range from 10% for rental income to 32.5% on dividend income (including the 25% corporate income tax rate). While effective tax rates will depend on holding periods, in general this differential creates incentives to invest in real estate, diverting funds from Indonesia's already thin capital markets. The tax rates should be reviewed and adjusted to minimise such distortions.

Corporate income taxation can be broader and more growth-friendly

Slower economic growth, lower commodity prices and policy decisions have weighed on corporate income tax revenues. Between 2008 and 2010 the standard statutory rate was lowered in two steps from 30% to 25%, which is around G20 and OECD averages. A raft of tax incentives were introduced and expanded, including an import duty facility (2009), tax allowances for specific investment (2011 and 2016) and tax holidays (2011, 2015 and 2018). The number of special economic zones is increasing. In April 2018 eligibility for tax holidays was broadened and the process simplified to try to attract more investment. New incentives are planned, including for smaller investments that do not qualify for tax holidays, R&D investment and provision of vocational education and training.

There is now a long list of tax incentives aimed at attracting investment, especially to particular locations (special economic zones and free trade zones) and sectors (Table 1.5). Indeed, even before the latest changes Indonesia's tax incentives were relatively generous for certain investments (OECD, 2018a). Under specific assumptions, tax incentives would reduce the effective average tax rate that a manufacturing firm could face by 13 percentage points (Figure 1.10). The Investment Coordinating Board is promoting these incentives to investors together with regulatory reforms and faster licensing processes.

Table 1.5. Overview of tax incentives

Type of incentive	Description
Tax allowance incentive	Targets new investment or expanding a current business. Eligible investments: 71 categories of business sectors and 74 other categories of industries in certain locations may qualify for the tax incentives. Industries include subsectors of agriculture, power generation, oil & gas and manufacturing. Instruments: • Accelerated depreciation and amortisation • Extended period of 10 years for the carry-forward of a tax loss (normally 5 years). • Reduced tax rate of 10% for dividends paid to non-residents (normally 20%). • Investment allowance: reduction of net income by 30% of the amount invested in land and buildings, and plant and equipment. Claimed over six years at 5% per year. Other requirements include: investment value or export orientation, labour intensity, local content and project location.
Tax holiday	Targets new taxpayers in "pioneer industries", defined as having a wide range of connections to other parts of the economy, providing additional value and high externalities, introducing new technologies, and having strategic value for the national economy. 17 industries are specified but a taxpayer may still qualify if approved by the Ministry of Finance, other relevant Ministries and the Investment Co-ordinating Board (BKPM). Industries include: upstream metal; refinery; petrochemicals; chemical industry; types of manufacturing; economic infrastructure. 100% corporate income tax holiday for 5-20 years depending on the size of the investment, with a minimum investment of minimum capital investment of IDR 500 billion (USD 34 million).
Special economic zones and other special locations	Special economic zones allow for incentives such as additional corporate income tax deductions for up to 25 years, VAT exemptions on imports of raw materials and duty-free importation. Other zones also benefit from exemptions on trade taxes and VAT and tax holidays in some cases.
Other incentives	A reduction of the withholding rate on dividends paid to non-residents to 10%. Reduced CIT rate of 20% for companies that are publicly listed (at least 40% traded). A reduced CIT rate of 12.5% for qualifying SMEs on the first IDR 4.8 billion of income. Income earned by venture capital companies in the form of profit sharing from investments in Indonesia is permanently exempt from tax (under some conditions).

Source: OECD (2018), *OECD Investment Policy Reviews: Southeast Asia*; EY (2018), *Worldwide Corporate Tax Guide*; Ministry of Finance.

International experience cautions against tax holidays and income tax exemptions, particularly for specific sectors (IMF et al., 2015; IADB, 2013; IMF, 2011). Sector- and location-specific tax incentives, particularly tax holidays, can be costly in fiscal and economic terms by eroding the revenue base, creating tax-planning opportunities, distorting competition and creating the potential for policy capture (OECD, 2018a; OECD, 2012). Other sectors and locations face a competitive disadvantage. Moreover, tax holidays are inefficient, as they do not address the non-tax related factors that are often more important determinants of investment decisions. For instance, executives cite corruption and inefficient government bureaucracy as the most problematic factors for business in Indonesia, well ahead of tax rates (7th) or tax regulations (9th) (World Economic Forum, 2017). A lack of infrastructure has also hampered investment by adding to transport costs, for example. The current incentives also impose a heavy administrative burden, even after the recent changes, for instance due to the need to monitor attached conditions.

Figure 1.10. Incentives substantially reduce corporate income tax bases

Effective average tax rates (EATRs) with and without incentives

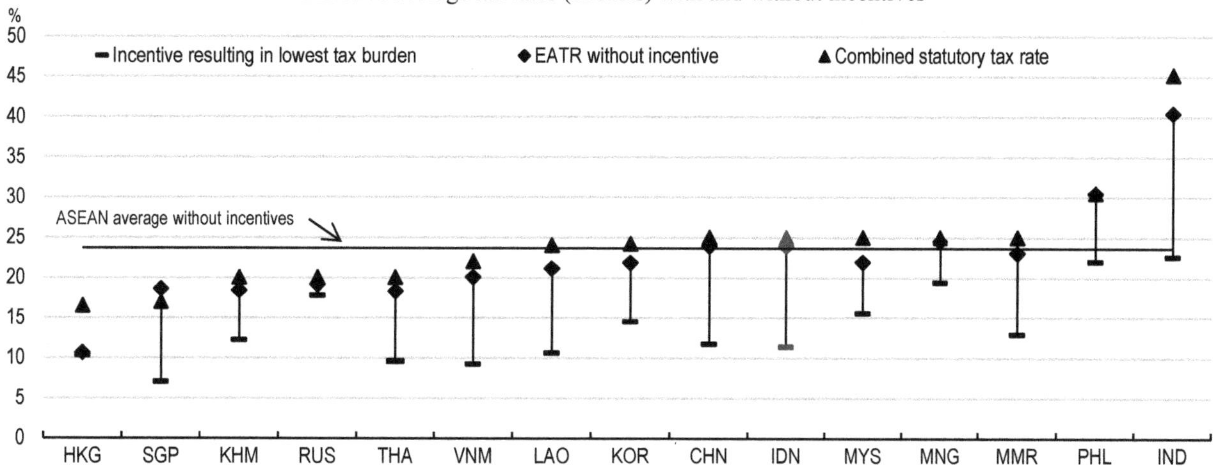

Note: The effective average tax rate is based on a manufacturing firm with assets in the form of buildings, intangible assets, machinery, financial assets and inventory (20% each). Finance is from retained earnings (55%), new equity (10%) and debt (35%). The real interest rate is 5%, pre-tax real rate of return is 20% and the inflation rate is 2%.
Source: V. Wiedemann and K. Finke (2015), "Taxing investments in the Asia-Pacific region: the importance of cross-border taxation and tax incentives", *ZEW Discussion Papers*, No. 15-014.

StatLink ⋙ https://doi.org/10.1787/888933833559

Rethinking tax incentives could broaden the tax base and be more effective in encouraging investment. The publication in late September 2018 of detailed tax expenditure estimates for 2016-17 increases transparency and is a welcome first step in evaluating the incentives. The tax expenditure report should be published annually, as planned. Because many countries in the region offer tax holidays, Indonesia could lead a co-ordinated approach within ASEAN. It would be preferable to shift away from tax holidays to cost-based incentives (tax deductions or credits) linked to investment in capital or skills (OECD, 2018a; IMF et al., 2015). Cost-based incentives could include the planned R&D tax credit, or allowances or credits for providing workplace training or for incorporating SMEs in supply chains, as in Malaysia (OECD, 2018a). Such incentives would better target new investment by more effectively lowering the cost of capital, even when profitability is low (IMF et al., 2015). They would still require ensuring sufficient administrative capacity to oversee them.

All incentives should be monitored carefully to detect abuse and subject to a sunset clause to ensure regular reviews. Investor concerns related to the regulatory environment would be better addressed directly rather than through the tax system. The special economic zones should focus on promoting a more business-friendly regulatory and legal environment, as in the new tourism economic zones, or piloting less stringent employment regulations, as previously recommended (OECD, 2016a).

A final turnover tax was introduced in 2013 for firms with turnover up to IDR 4.8 billion (USD 323 000) to encourage formalisation and increase voluntary compliance. By 2017 the regime had attracted 1.5 million registrants, of which 205 000 were incorporated businesses and 1.3 million were individuals. While this growth is impressive, the sheer number of SMEs in Indonesia means that increasing registration remains a challenge (Table 1.6). The rate was initially 1% but was halved in July 2018 to further encourage formalisation. This will, however, generate windfall gains for firms that were already registered. In addition to awareness and willingness amongst businesses, take-up is hindered by the large standard tax allowance in the personal income tax scheme which is an alternative for unincorporated micro enterprises and that many professions are excluded from the scheme. From July 2018 access to the turnover tax is limited to three years for incorporated firms and to up to seven years for individuals. Larger SMEs with turnover below IDR 50 billion (USD 3.4 million) pay half the statutory corporate income tax rate – 12.5% – on income up to IDR 4.8 billion; this smooths the transition to the standard regime somewhat.

Table 1.6. Micro enterprises dominate the business landscape

	Cut-off values for each category (IDR)		By number		By employment	
	Net assets (excluding premises)	Annual revenue	Thousand	% of total	Thousand	% of total
Micro enterprises	50 million	300 million	23 864	89.3	41 032	58.4
Small enterprises	500 million	2.5 billion	2 399	9.0	12 609	17.9
Medium enterprises	10 billion	50 billion	412	1.5	8 132	11.6
Large enterprises			35	0.1	8 547	12.2
Total			26 711		70 320	

Note: Data are for establishments in 2016 and exclude the agriculture, forestry and fisheries sector, government administration, defence and social security sector, and household activities as employers or own production sector. Unregistered businesses are included.
Source: Statistics Indonesia, *Economic Census 2016*.

A presumptive turnover tax has the advantage of simplifying taxation for start-ups and for small firms that have low growth prospects. But it has two drawbacks: (i) that the effective tax rate is higher for low-profit firms than their more profitable counterparts; and (ii) that any size-related incentive can reduce incentives to grow, reducing productivity (Benedek et al., 2017). In Indonesia's case, these effects are mitigated by the fact that firms can choose whether to opt into this scheme or the regular system and that there is a time limit on the scheme. Nonetheless, the threshold is high compared to those in other countries with turnover taxes, which adds to the fiscal cost of the scheme (Box 1.3). The threshold should be lowered so that the scheme better targets very small firms, which would also contain its cost. Estimated costs of the scheme should be included in forthcoming tax expenditure reports. The time limit will disadvantage firms that do not have the capacity to comply with the standard tax system. Micro enterprises could be allowed to remain on the simplified scheme. Firm behaviour should be monitored, particularly to ensure that firms are not being "reborn" to avoid joining the regular corporate income tax regime or bunching just below the turnover threshold.

The trade-off for registration should be improved by offering more benefits linked to registration for the turnover tax. Such benefits include further simplifying processes (for example allowing quarterly filing of tax and social security contributions) and clearly linking registration to access to additional services such as account-keeping applications and business development programmes. In Brazil, Mexico and Colombia such non-tax benefits appear to have helped increase formalisation. A more lenient approach to honest mistakes may also lower barriers to formalisation. The cross-country evidence suggests that measures to broaden the tax base to small firms are unlikely to generate substantial short-term revenue, they can form part of a longer-term strategy to encourage firms to grow

(Joshi, Prichard and Heady, 2014). To further smooth firms' transition to the standard regime, all small firms could be allowed to make less frequent payments.

Box 1.3. Examples of simplified tax schemes from other countries

Many OECD and non-OECD countries offer simplified tax regimes to lower the burden on firms that may otherwise operate informally. Two common approaches are a lump-sum tax, which typically targets the smallest firms, or a turnover tax. The appropriate thresholds must then be determined based on the targeted group of firms. Some examples of these are:

Brazil has three presumptive tax schemes, targeted at micro, small and medium-sized businesses. A lump-sum tax is available for individuals with up to one employee and revenue below BRL 60 000 (USD 14 000). This replaces other taxes and contributions and offers other benefits including social security. At the other end, a turnover-based scheme with rates varying by sector (an indicator of profit margins) is available for firms with turnover up to BRL 78 million (USD 19 million).

Hungary has a lump-sum scheme for very small self-employed taxpayers with revenue up to HUF 8 million (USD 29 000). This replaces income taxes and social security contributions. Firms with turnover below HUF 30 million (USD 107 000) can calculate taxable income as 37% of turnover. This replaces value-added tax and income taxes. Firms with up to 25 employees and both turnover and assets below 500 million (USD 1.8 million) may pay a reduced tax rate of 13% of the tax base, which is based on cash-flow profit and increased by staff costs.

Italy has a turnover tax for businesses with revenue thresholds varying by sector, from EUR 15 000 (for professionals) to EUR 40 000 (for trade and hospitality) (USD 17 000 to 46 000). This replaces all other taxes for businesses.

Source: A. Thomas et al. (2017), "Taxation and investment in India", *OECD Economics Department Working Papers,* No. 1397, OECD Publishing, Paris; OECD (2015), *Taxation of SMEs in OECD and G20 Countries*, OECD Publishing, Paris.

In Indonesia, as in many countries, the growing digital economy is challenging the effectiveness of the existing income tax system to deal with new business models. This may raise equity issues across firms if income from such models and from more conventional models are not taxed similarly. It may also lead to misalignments between the location in which profits are taxed and where value is created because of the difficulties in determining where and how much value is being created. Countries are working toward a consensus-based solution within the OECD's Inclusive Framework on Base Erosion and Profit Shifting (BEPS). Indonesia and some other countries are considering moving ahead with unilateral non-income tax measures in the interim (OECD, 2018b). However, there is no consensus in the Inclusive Framework on the need or merit of taking such action.

The Inclusive Framework on BEPS Interim Report on tax challenges arising from digitalisation includes guidance on design principles that need to be taken into account by countries considering taking immediate unilateral measures, such as Indonesia's planned tax on some e-services. These principles include that the measure should be temporary and targeted and should minimise over-taxation, compliance burdens and the effect on start-ups (OECD, 2018b). To ensure fair treatment of firms (and also employees) that earn income through online platforms, the authorities could follow the examples of Estonia, Finland,

Mexico and Ecuador, where governments have worked with platforms to obtain access to their data (*ibid.*).

More generally some international tax challenges, including base erosion and profit shifting, are of particular concern in emerging economies, where corporate income tax is a more important revenue source (Thomas et al., 2017). Indonesia has committed to implementing the minimum standards of the Inclusive Framework on BEPS. This is a key step in the fight against cross-border tax planning and will help to level the playing field between domestic and multinational firms (OECD, 2018b). Incorporating more measures from the Inclusive Framework on BEPS could yield substantial benefits (IMF, 2017). But more broadly, the complicated and intricate nature of cross-border taxation means that building up core teams of highly skilled staff is crucial, both in tax policy-making and administration. A transfer pricing taskforce was established to work on policy, but a unit could be established in the tax administration. The Tax Reform Team could conduct a study of international taxation. Given the complexity of the topic, an OECD study may be helpful.

Taxes on goods and services have further potential

Taxes on goods and services are the largest source of revenue – raising almost 5% of GDP in 2016 – but their GDP share is only half that of other emerging-market and OECD countries (Figure 1.11). This is partly because value-added tax, the most important, raises a small amount of revenue relative to most other countries. Excise taxes are the next largest type. As in many emerging economies, trade taxes are not negligible; Indonesia levies import tariffs as well as export taxes on some unprocessed commodities. There is also a luxury goods sales tax of 10-125% depending on the product, but it raises little revenue (0.2% of GDP). Revenues from local government taxes on goods and services totalled around 0.5% of GDP in 2016, primarily due to motor fuel and cigarette tax at the provincial level and district and municipal taxes on restaurant and hotel sales and on electricity consumption ("street-lighting tax").

Figure 1.11. Goods and services tax revenues are low and rely on value-added tax

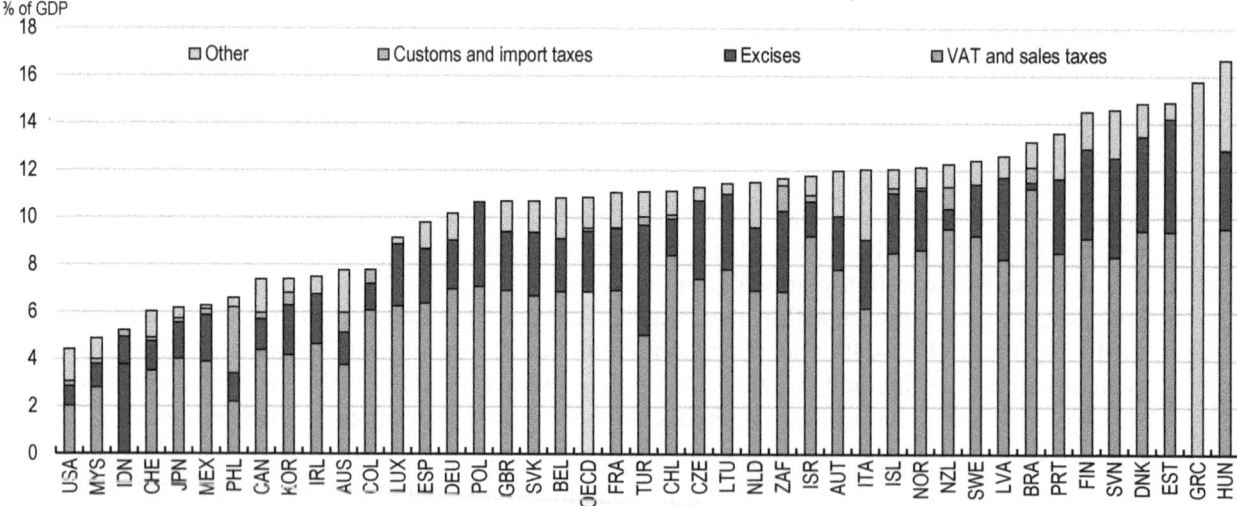

Note: Data are for 2016 or latest available year. The VAT for Indonesia includes the luxury goods sales tax, but this is just 3% of the VAT amount shown. Other taxes include taxes on exports, investment goods, specific services and the use of goods.
Source: OECD, *Revenue Statistics Database, OECD Economic Outlook Database*; Ministry of Finance; OECD calculations.

StatLink https://doi.org/10.1787/888933833578

A more efficient value-added tax would raise more revenue

Indonesia's VAT has only two rates: (i) 10% applied to domestic supplies of goods and services and imports of goods and certain services, and (ii) 0% applied to exports of goods and certain services. By comparison, the OECD average standard rate is 19%, but countries with high rates typically have reduced rates on some goods and services, which aim to increase equity but in fact create distortions. A zero rating on exports is in line with the destination-based principle of VAT (although in other countries a wider range of services have a zero rating than is the case in Indonesia).

Despite having a single standard rate, the design of the VAT is relatively complicated. There are numerous exemptions (that remove the right to deduct input tax), which limit its efficiency and add to its compliance costs. Exemptions include:

- "basic necessities" (rice and some other grains, corn, table salt, soybean, meat, eggs, milk, fruit, vegetables, sago, tubers, sugar and spices);
- financial and insurance services (fundraising, mortgages, insurance, money orders);
- social-type services (education services, medical services, orphanages, funerals, religious services, public transport, public services, postal services);
- "strategic goods" (plant machinery and equipment, livestock, poultry, fish feed, seeds, clean piped water, low-wattage electricity);
- services for which there are local government sales taxes (entertainment, restaurants, hotels, parking);
- goods and services delivered inside free-trade areas;
- other goods and services such as: money and valuable documents; coal, oil and other raw mining or drilling products; catering services; and services supplied to local shipping companies.

While many countries exempt financial and insurance services and meritorious services like education and health care from VAT, the application of exemptions in Indonesia is particularly broad. Not only do exemptions narrow the tax base but they also weaken the self-enforcement mechanism of the VAT, because customers of VAT-exempt suppliers of goods or services cannot claim back VAT paid on their inputs, which reduces their incentive to demand compliance from their suppliers. Exemptions on intermediate inputs generate distortions, because non-deducted tax is passed on at each step of the supply chain ("cascading") (OECD, 2016b). In terms of revenues, this leads to overpayment of VAT, which may slightly offset the losses from the exemptions on final consumption (by 0.1% according to IMF estimates) (IMF, 2017). But because exemptions also indirectly reduce revenue by weakening compliance, the net revenue effect of reducing exemptions could be positive overall.

One way of assessing the VAT is to compare revenue collected to potential revenue. By this measure – the VAT Revenue Ratio – Indonesia's performance was above the median of OECD and other Asian economies in 2014, although it has fallen since (Figure 1.12). This measure is an approximation; overpayment due to exemptions on intermediate consumption and difficulties in obtaining refunds discussed above inflate the revenue ratio. With more detailed data on consumption and tax expenditures this recent decline could be apportioned to: (i) reduced compliance; (ii) policy changes; and (iii) changes in consumption patterns; or (iv) changes in VAT refund policy on exported goods and services.

One factor behind the decline is the eight-fold increase in the turnover threshold for VAT registration and collection in 2014 to IDR 4.8 billion, which considerably reduced the number of firms covered by the VAT (IMF, 2018). The expansion of exemptions to include "strategic goods" has also likely played a role. So has the decline in the international oil price: the VAT revenue ratio is strongly correlated with the US dollar oil price, which is consistent with the link between oil prices and import VAT highlighted by World Bank (2017b) but also implying that an improvement is likely in 2018. National accounts data suggest that shifts in consumption towards goods taxed at lower rates do not explain the decrease.

Figure 1.12. The performance of the VAT is reasonable but has deteriorated

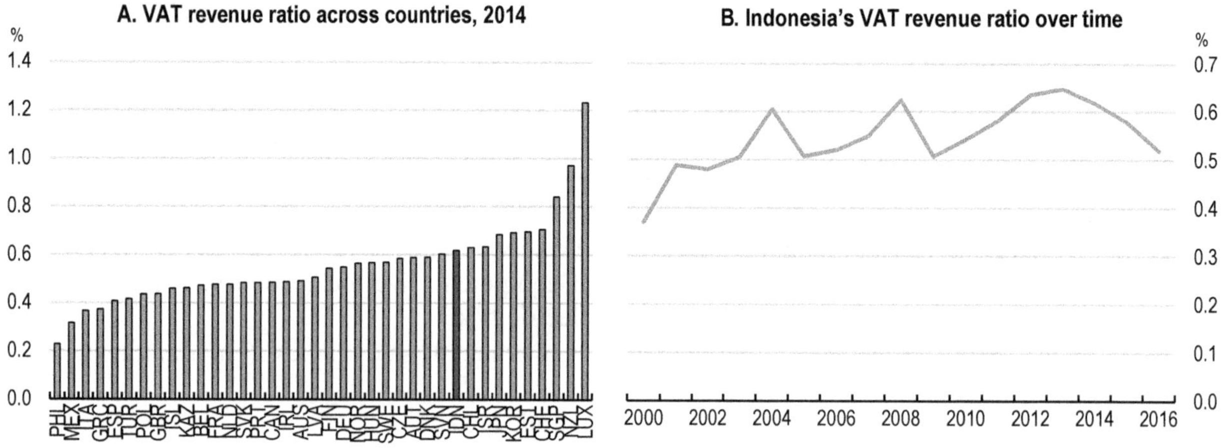

Note: The VAT revenue ratio is calculated as the ratio of VAT revenues collected to the potential tax base (total consumption less VAT revenues multiplied by the standard VAT rate).
Source: OECD (2016), *Consumption Tax Trends*; OECD (2017), *Revenue Statistics in Asian Countries: Trends in Indonesia, Japan, Kazakhstan, Korea, Malaysia, the Philippines and Singapore*; OECD, *OECD Economic Outlook Database*; Directorate General of Taxes (2017), *Laporan Tahunan 2016* [Annual Report 2016]; OECD calculations.

StatLink https://doi.org/10.1787/888933833597

The near-term priority is to broaden the VAT base by removing exemptions and lowering the threshold for VAT registration. Such changes would harness the efficiency of the VAT and raise more revenue without increasing the rate. The VAT exemptions for strategic goods and other intermediate inputs are not an effective or efficient way of raising investment. However, the exemptions on basic food necessities appear reasonably well targeted. Expenditure data (from Susenas) show that poorer households spend a larger share of their budgets on items such as cereals and tubers than the better-off (Figure 1.13). However, affluent households spend much more on meat, suggesting that this particular tax exemption is regressive. Overall, the expenditure pattern for "basic necessities" is consistent with research that finds that Indonesia's VAT has a broadly neutral distributional effect (Jellema, Wai-Poi and Afkar, 2017). Imposing a reduced VAT rate, or even a 0% rate, on necessities would be a "second best" way of supporting low-income households until coverage of social protection systems is more complete (OECD/KIPF, 2014). It would also create incentives for VAT compliance, because input tax credits could be claimed. The definition of basic necessities could be narrowed (for example, excluding meat), but this may be difficult in practice.

Making restaurant, hotel, entertainment and parking expenditure subject to VAT rather than sales tax would improve efficiency and may increase overall revenue through better compliance, even though VAT on inputs could be deducted. Over 90% of local governments now impose hotel and restaurant tax, but the proceeds are modest compared to consumer spending, suggesting that compliance is low. In 2016 revenues were the equivalent of 1.2% of consumer spending on hotels and restaurants (based on national accounts data), which was barely changed from 2010 (1.1%). Replacing these taxes with VAT would strengthen compliance by creating an incentive for hotels and restaurants to pay tax. It could therefore increase overall revenues. Transfers to local governments could be increased to compensate for lost revenue from the removal of sales taxes. Local governments could also be allowed to supplement their revenue with a small occupancy (accommodation) tax, as proposed in Chapter 2 to incentivise them to encourage tourism. Compliance costs associated with switching to VAT (and e-invoicing) would be mitigated by the VAT registration threshold, but a transition period could also be allowed.

Figure 1.13. VAT exemptions for food generally benefit poorer households

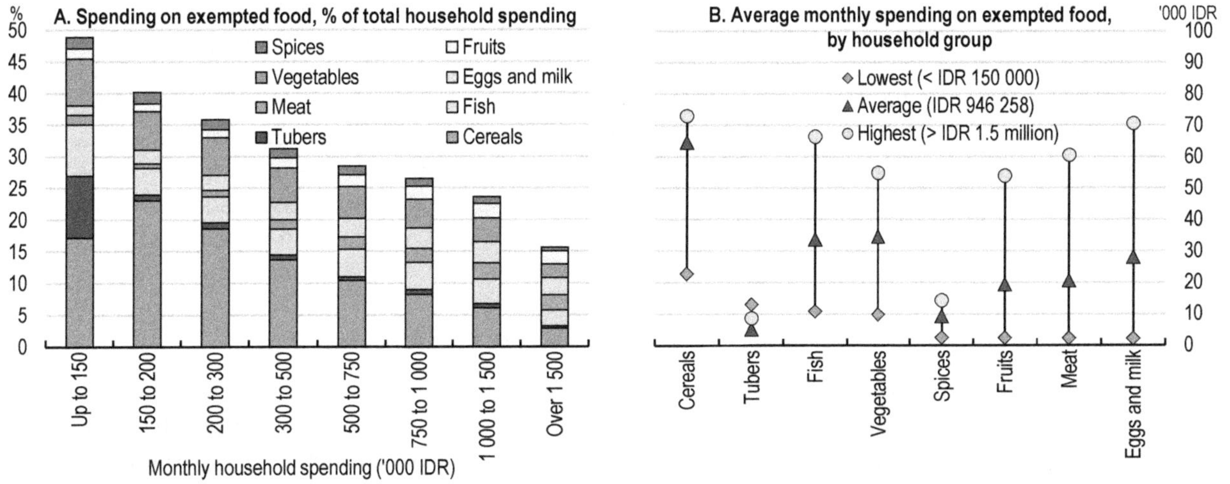

Note: Data are for 2016. Salt and soybeans are also exempt from VAT but are not shown here. In Panel B food items are ordered by the spending of the poorest households.
Source: Statistics Indonesia.

StatLink https://doi.org/10.1787/888933833122

As elsewhere, there are concerns that digitalisation and the growth of international e-commerce are eroding the VAT base. Over the last decade e-commerce transactions are estimated to have grown by 17% annually (The Jakarta Post, 2018). While they are only 1.3% of household consumption, further rapid growth is expected (*ibid*). Indonesia currently uses a reverse-charge mechanism, in line with the OECD's *International VAT/GST Guidelines*, for business-to-business transactions in services and intangibles. However, business-to-consumer transactions have proved more difficult to capture. The OECD's *Guidelines* point to ways of taxing such transactions. Such measures are usually supported by simplified supplier registration. These measures have boosted VAT revenues where they have been implemented: for instance, South Africa collected ZAR 585 billion USD 39 million) through these measures (OECD, 2018b). The 2015 BEPS Action 1 Report outlines options to facilitate collection of VAT on the importation of low-value goods via online sales (OECD, 2015b). In addition to levelling the playing field with other retailers, the revenue gains could be sizeable.

Lowering the threshold for VAT registration would strengthen the self-reinforcing nature of the VAT. The turnover threshold of IDR 4.8 billion is around USD 323 000 at market exchange rates, or USD 1.1 million at 2017 purchasing power-adjusted exchange rates. This threshold is well above those applied in OECD countries (which range from zero in Chile and Mexico to USD 119 000 in the United Kingdom). It is also well above the USD 100 000 that is typically prescribed to leave firms who are unable to keep adequate accounts outside the VAT system (IMF, 2011). Broadening the VAT base by lowering the threshold could also reduce the risk of "bad" VAT chains forming, whereby firms have incentives to buy inputs from other vendors outside of the system (de Paula and Scheinkman, 2007). Evidence from Chile shows that the self-enforcing mechanism of VAT is important up the VAT chain (Pomeranz, 2015). Small businesses in upstream industries (e.g. manufacturing and wholesale trade) in the Indian state of Karnataka were found to be willing to bear an administrative cost of 1% of turnover to be part of the VAT regime rather than the simplified turnover tax regime (Rios and Seetharam, 2017).

A combination of changes that lifted the efficiency of the VAT by 13 percentage points (equivalent to raising the VAT Revenue Ratio to its 2013 level) would have increased VAT collection in 2016 by IDR 100 trillion, or 0.8% of GDP. Some estimates of revenue forgone due to exemptions and zero-rated goods and services have recently been published. They should continue to be improved and expanded to assist policymakers in evaluating VAT performance in coming years. After the design of the tax regime is made more efficient, further revenue could be raised by increasing the VAT rate. Assuming the same performance as in 2016, a 1 percentage point increase would have raised an additional IDR 41 trillion – 0.3% of 2016 GDP. The effect of the VAT increase on poor households could be mitigated using existing cash or non-cash transfers.

Higher excise taxes can raise revenue and improve health outcomes

As in most OECD countries Indonesia is increasingly using excise taxes to influence consumer behaviour to achieve health outcomes as well as raise revenue. Almost all excise collected is from tobacco tax (1.2% of GDP in 2016). Local governments may also impose tobacco tax, although the rate is capped; such revenues amount to around 0.1% of GDP. Revenue from alcohol excise tax is comparatively low, at 0.04% of GDP, reflecting low consumption (OECD, 2017d). Both alcohol and tobacco are also subject to import duties. Empirical research based on OECD countries suggests that there is no growth penalty of excise tax (Akgun, Cournède and Fournier, 2017). This may result from the relatively inelastic tax base, which makes the tax efficient. The distributional impact depends on consumption patterns but is mitigated by the distribution of health costs, which are often higher for poorer individuals as well.

There is a strong case to increase the taxation of tobacco. Indonesia has one of the highest rates of smoking and tobacco use – three-quarters of men smoke, though few women do – and is one of the few countries where rates of smoking have increased in the past decade (Figure 1.14, Panel A) (OECD, 2017d). Moreover, taxation has proved to be a cost-effective means of reducing smoking (WHO, 2017). Indonesia's tax rates are still below the World Health Organisation's recommended level of 70% of the retail price and other countries' rates (Panel B). The number of levels in the excise structure was reduced from 12 to 10, but it should be simplified further, as planned, to limit substitution across products and tax avoidance more generally. Tobacco tax appears less regressive than may be expected: spending on tobacco and betel accounted for a lower share of the poorest households' budgets (5% for those spending less than USD 48 PPP-adjusted monthly), than for households with incomes of USD 119-239 PPP-adjusted (9%). Tobacco excise increased by 10% on 1 January 2018, but the rate could be raised further. Providing a predictable path for excise would help farmers to adjust.

The government is considering implementing a sugar tax, which is an increasingly common tool to fight obesity in OECD and emerging economies, including Hungary and Mexico (OECD, 2017e; OECD, 2018c). Indonesia's obesity rates are still comparatively low (at 5% for men) (OECD, 2017d). But the incidence of being overweight or obese has almost doubled over two decades to one-quarter in 2014 (Aizawa and Helble, 2016). The incidence of diabetes and other non-communicable diseases linked to lifestyle are rising (Fountaine et al., 2016). Stronger preventative action is needed to contain future human, economic and fiscal costs. Policy tools include regulatory measures, education, voluntary initiatives with agreed targets and taxes that increase the price of these goods (Sassi, 2016).

A simple tax on sugar-sweetened beverages could reduce consumption of taxed products and, if the tax is sufficiently high, can have positive health outcomes (Thavorncharoensap, 2017). Studies from Mexico's tax on sweetened beverages shows a correlation with lower consumption when healthier untaxed alternatives were available (OECD, 2018c). Lower socio-economic groups would likely experience greater health improvements (Sassi et al., 2014). The soft drink market (excluding consumption at restaurants and hotels) was estimated at 0.8% of GDP in 2015, implying that a 20% tax would raise around 0.2% of GDP in revenues (but less to the extent that consumption falls or producers reduce the sugar content of their drinks).

Figure 1.14. Tobacco use is high, and taxes are relatively low

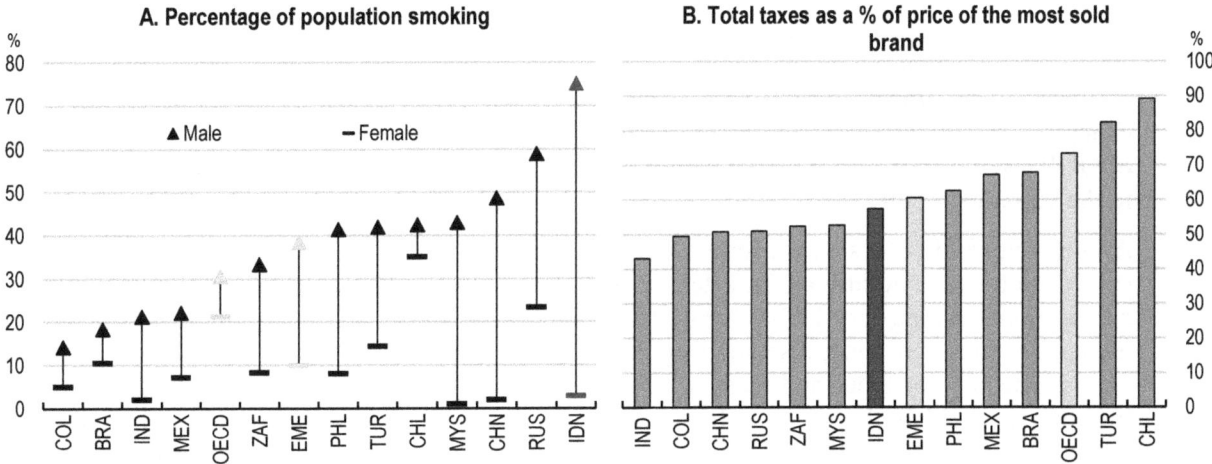

Note: "EME" is an unweighted average of the emerging market economies shown. Data in Panel A are for 2015 and in Panel B for 2016.
Source: World Health Organisation (2017), *WHO Report on the Global Tobacco Epidemic 2017*, Appendix IX and X.

StatLink ᵐˢ᷉ https://doi.org/10.1787/888933833141

Well-designed environmental tax reform could work toward several goals

Environmentally related tax revenue is relatively low in Indonesia. OECD estimates suggest that it is equivalent to less than 1% of GDP, compared to an average of 2.3% across OECD and non-OECD economies. Revenue is mostly from sub-national government taxes on motor vehicles (around 0.5% of GDP), in contrast to most countries where taxes on transport fuels are the largest source. As Indonesia's economy grows, environmental pressures will intensify. By increasing the price of pollution or of other negative environmental externalities, taxes and charges can reduce their production in a cost-effective way by creating incentives for behavioural change, as well as raising revenues (OECD, 2017f).

Air pollution is already an environmental and health challenge, with three-quarters of Indonesia's population exposed to pollution levels above World Health Organisation guidelines ($PM_{2.5}$ concentrations). Exposure to particulate matter and ozone is projected to cause around 115 000 premature Indonesian deaths annually by 2060 (OECD, 2016c). According to OECD estimates accounting for direct and indirect effects, air pollution could lower annual GDP by 0.8% in 2060 (*ibid*). Likewise water pollution and waste are growing (OECD, 2016d; OECD, 2014). To address the threat of climate change the government has committed to lowering greenhouse gas emissions by 29% by 2030 compared to "business as usual", which will require bold measures. There is scope to use existing taxes more effectively to address these challenges, as well as to introduce new taxes and charges.

Motor vehicle taxes are paid at the time of purchase as well as annually. They include luxury goods sales tax, transfer fees and annual registration fees (Table 1.7). The government has started incorporating environmental objectives into the design of these taxes. In 2013 it lowered the rate of luxury goods sales tax for "low-cost green cars" (with small engines and minimum fuel efficiency) that meet local-content requirements. But focusing on fuel efficiency (or CO_2 emissions) can favour diesel cars, which often emit more air pollutants. Moreover, higher rates on imported vehicles (including hybrids and electric vehicles), along with import tariffs, mean that environmental and industry protection objectives are working at cross purposes. The Ministry of Finance and the World Bank estimate that aligning motor vehicle taxes better with negative environmental externalities by converting the luxury goods sales tax on vehicles to a specific tax and changing the rates according to environmental impacts could raise the equivalent of 0.6% of GDP (World Bank, 2018). This would also reduce opportunities for tax avoidance (due to the current structure).

Annual registration fees vary with the assessed value of the car. In Jakarta there is a 0.5% surcharge for each additional car after an individual's first car to deter car ownership and an additional charge for SUVs. Using the car's assessed value as the tax base means that the tax declines over time, discouraging fleet renewal. Converting the tax to a flat tax that varies based on car types and their emissions would provide a more effective signal. For instance, it could be based on cylinder volume (which would exempt electric cars and provide a reduction for hybrids). Higher fees could be charged for additional cars, as in Jakarta.

Tax rates on energy and associated CO_2 emissions, and associated revenues, are among the lowest across OECD and G20 countries (OECD, 2018d). There is no fuel excise tax at the national level and only a low tax at the provincial level, which is charged on fuel for road transport and capped to maintain competitiveness. There is also a small sub-national electricity tax ("street lighting tax") with a capped rate. Indonesia has made important progress in reducing energy subsidies, which is a first step towards better pricing of the externalities associated with its use, including carbon emissions. But subsidies for production and consumption, price caps and tax exemptions still serve to lower the relative price of energy. Because of the close link between the carbon content of fuels and the associated CO_2 emissions, higher fuel taxes would be an efficient tool to reduce these emissions. In the near term the cap for regional governments could be raised. Coverage could eventually be extended to off-road fuel usage, taking into account effect on poorer households. Congestion charges or distance-based driving charges are efficient tools for addressing other driving-related externalities like congestion, air pollution and road damage (van Dender, forthcoming).

Table 1.7. Key environmentally related taxes

Tax	Tax base	Level of government with the taxing power	Revenue sharing across government (central/regional/local)	Maximum tax rate allowed	2016 revenue as % of GDP
Vehicles					
Motor vehicle taxes (annual registration fee, transfers)	Vehicle value	Province	0 / 70 / 30	5% for annual registration fee, 10% for transfers	0.52
Luxury goods sales tax	Vehicle value	Central	n.a.	200%	0.01
Energy use					
Motor vehicle fuel tax	Fuel consumption excluding VAT	Province	0 / 30 / 70	5%, 7% in some regions	0.13
Street lighting tax	Electricity consumption, excluding VAT	Local		1.5% for self-produced, 3% for industry, 10% for households	0.08
Other					
Surface and ground water extraction taxes	Water consumption	Province	0 / 30 / 70	10% and 20%	0.01
Parking tax	Parking fees	Local		30%	0.01
Swallows nest tax		Local			0.00

Note: Import tariffs on motor vehicles are not included.
Source: A. Nasution (2016), "Government decentralization program in Indonesia", *ADBI Working Paper Series*, No. 601; L. Hakim, (2016), Pajak *Daerah - Pajak Penerangan Jalan (Regional Tax and Regional Levies: Local Taxes - Street Lighting Tax)*, http://padjakdaerah.blogspot.com/2016/04/pajak-penerangan-pajak.html; Ministry of Finance; OECD calculations.

As proposed in the 2012 OECD *Economic Survey*, a carbon tax could be introduced to ensure prices better reflect climate-change-related externalities and help put Indonesia on a low-carbon growth path. Although the government began considering a carbon tax in 2009, there has been little progress since. Meanwhile, numerous emerging market economies have introduced a carbon prices, including Mexico, Chile and Colombia and others, such as South Africa and Thailand, plan to. Introducing a carbon tax at a modest level initially, scaling up over time, could help overcome resistance to the tax and allow firms to adjust. To be effective and efficient, the tax should ideally apply a uniform marginal rate across all sources of emissions, particularly within the same sector. Competitiveness concerns are mitigated by the growing threat of border taxes and the rising number of countries levying carbon taxes. Acting sooner, while the economy is less carbon-intensive, would help reduce the carbon intensity of Indonesia's growth at lower cost. Recent OECD research suggests that income-related transfers are the most efficient tool to address energy affordability concerns (Flues and van Dender, 2017). Accordingly, a combination of current social assistance programmes and income tax credits could be used.

There is scope to broaden taxation of other environmental "bads" to simultaneously reduce harmful behaviour and raise revenue. Because many environmental externalities are local (e.g. water pollution), these could be sub-national taxes. Poorer local populations would likely benefit disproportionately from lower pollution. Environmentally related taxes could include taxes on plastic bags, chemicals (especially pesticides) and waste, such as tyres, in line with the polluter-pays principle. Indeed, the 2018 national budget proposed a plastic bag tax, which could raise around IDR 1.9 trillion; although this is equivalent to only 0.01% of GDP it could mitigate the growing problem of plastic marine pollution, which has propelled Indonesia to be the world's second-largest marine polluter (Jambeck et al., 2015). Such reforms should be reinforced by regulatory measures and complemented with increased enforcement (OECD, 2005). Enforcement of existing taxes should be stepped up. The Jakarta government is increasing enforcement of water abstraction fees, which will also bring lessons for other governments. Fees for wastewater could also be charged but would need to be well regulated. The relationship between taxation, regulation and enforcement underscores the importance of involving environmental authorities in planning the expansion of environmentally related taxes.

Property tax is currently low

Property taxes raise around 3.5% of tax revenue (0.4% of GDP), well below other countries' shares (Figure 1.15). Recurrent taxes on immovable property account for around three-quarters of property tax revenue, but, unlike many other countries, they come mostly from taxes on plantations, mining and forestry properties, and are collected by the central government. Following devolution of responsibilities over 2009-13, local governments levy recurrent taxes on urban and rural land and buildings and transfer taxes on motor vehicles and real estate. These taxes each raise revenue equivalent to 0.1% of GDP, or around one quarter of total district and municipality tax revenues.

The low level of revenues from property taxation suggests that there is considerable unexploited potential to increase revenues, particularly given the empirical evidence that some types of property tax are less harmful for growth than taxes on incomes or consumption (Akgun, Cournède and Fournier, 2017; Blöchliger, 2015; Acosta-Ormaechea and Yoo, 2012). In particular, recurrent taxes on immovable property are considered least distortionary, whereas transaction taxes deter households from moving to another location for work, for example, or individuals or firms from reallocating assets to their most valuable use (Arnold et al., 2011). Property taxes can also help address high levels of wealth inequality: the wealthiest 1% of Indonesian households are estimated to hold 45% of total wealth (Credit Suisse, 2017).

Figure 1.15. Revenue from property tax is low in Indonesia

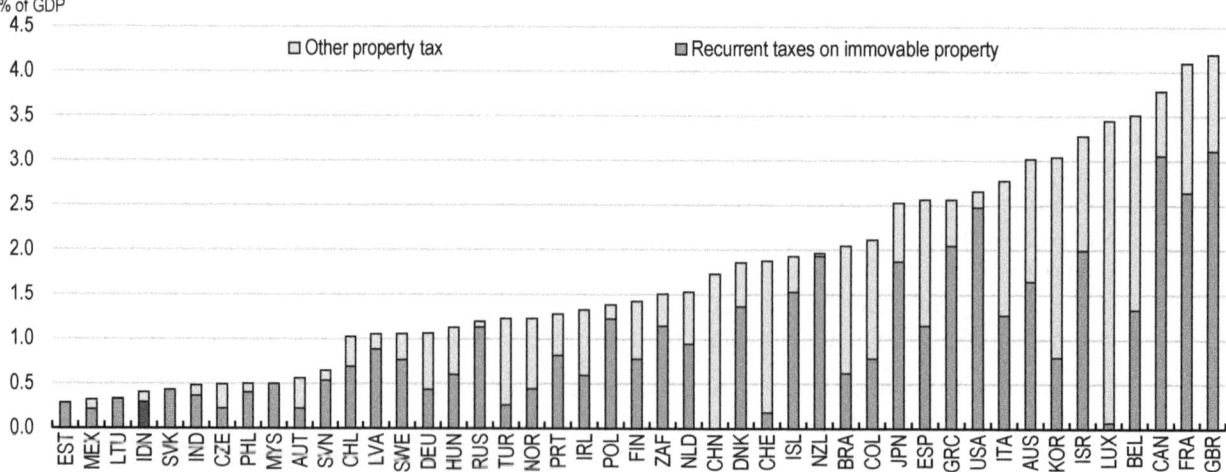

Note: Data are for 2016 or latest. Data for Indonesia are from national sources. OECD is an unweighted average of OECD member countries. Data for China, India and Russia are for 2009, 2009-10 and 2010, respectively and taken from Prakash (2013).
Source: OECD, *Revenue Statistics Database*; Ministry of Finance; P. Prakash (2013), "Property taxes across G20 countries: can India get it right?", *Oxfam India Working Papers Series*, XV, January; OECD calculations.

StatLink 🔗 http://dx.doi.org/10.1787/888933833160

Recurrent taxes on immovable property are underused

For recurrent taxes levied on land and buildings which are the responsibility of sub-national governments, the tax is typically levied at low and progressive rates. But their application appears heterogeneous. National legislation sets a minimum exemption of IDR 10 million (USD 673) and a maximum rate of 0.3% on the taxable value. This cap limits the revenue that can be raised in some areas. But local property taxes have also been found to be far below their revenue-maximising level given current legislation (von Haldenwang et al., 2015). There are strong arguments for raising more revenue from recurrent tax on immovable property by increasing the cap on tax rates: it can in principle raise additional revenues for local governments in an economically efficient way, and increase local government accountability; moreover, evasion is difficult. Allowing a higher rate would also mitigate the incentive for governments to inflate property values to raise additional revenues. With 88% of Indonesians' wealth held in real, rather than financial, assets according to Credit Suisse (2017), greater use of this tax would also be progressive.

Updating property registers and establishing systems for fair and predictable valuations would lay the foundation for higher rates but to do this, local governments still need more support. Because there is no national cadastre, the property tax registers are at the local level. But when taxing powers were decentralised and the register transferred to local governments, the valuations and taxpayer information in the register were out of date (von Haldenwang et al., 2015). This means that even though regulations prescribe that valuations be undertaken every three years with a mass valuation method, there are likely to be many errors in the records. Moreover, in rural areas where property rights are less clear, raising taxes may be difficult. Smaller districts also appear more likely to struggle to manage arrears than larger districts (von Haldenwang et al., 2015). This can make the administrative costs of the tax outweigh the benefits and may explain why some governments appear unwilling to raise taxes (*ibid.*).

The central government already provides support to local governments and shares information from geographic information systems with them. Nonetheless, given the potential importance of the tax for local governments, the central or provincial governments should ramp up assistance so that it can be implemented well and rates can be raised. In particular local government staff need more training in using and updating their IT systems, updating business processes and improving client relations. Provincial governments could facilitate sharing of good practices and troubleshooting across local authorities. Local governments could be encouraged to use property taxes by offering matching grants and ensuring that the transfer formula does not penalise jurisdictions that enhance their revenue-raising capacity, as recommended in the previous *Survey* (OECD, 2016a).

Ensuring the tax is fair and linking it to better local services can improve its acceptance (Blöchliger, 2015). Appropriate exemptions or allowances can ensure that poor households are excluded from the tax. Many local governments appear do not appear to apply thresholds above the IDR 10 million minimum (von Haldenwang et al., 2015). It is possible to apply for tax relief due to individual circumstances, but the most vulnerable households, such as welfare recipients, could be explicitly exempted. Low-income older households could be allowed to defer their debt so that it is only payable when the property is sold (Blöchliger, 2015). In the South African City of Johannesburg there are rebates for pensioners, those below the poverty line and those temporarily without income (OECD, 2015c).

Transaction taxes are a significant local government tax

Transaction taxes on real estate and motor vehicle transfers raise one-quarter of district and municipal governments' tax revenues. A maximum rate of 5% may be charged on land and building transfers, payable by the purchaser, although some local governments, such as the city of Jakarta, have lowered this to stimulate development. There is also a central-government transaction tax of 0.1% of the value of listed shares when sold. Transaction taxes are common in emerging-market economies because they are easy to administer and perceived to affect wealthy households more than the poor. But because transaction taxes deter people from moving to take advantage of better opportunities and the reallocation of assets to more valuable uses, they should be phased out as other revenues increase.

Although there are taxes on asset transactions, there is no inheritance or gift tax. Since 2016 some local governments, including Jakarta's, ruled that transfers of land and buildings through inheritance to direct relatives are no longer subject to the 5% local government transfer tax. This benefit should be reconsidered as it disproportionately benefits wealthy households.

Better management of natural resources could raise related revenues

Indonesia's large and diverse natural resource wealth is a source of tax and non-tax revenue, as well as growth, employment and environmental services. In 2015 Indonesia produced 6% of the world's coal output, 2% of its gas and 1% of its oil (International Energy Agency, 2017). It is also the world's second-largest producer of fish, crustaceans and aquatic plants (OECD, 2017h). With 48% of its land forested – representing 2% of the world's forests – Indonesia is major timber producer as well as an important carbon sink. It is also the top producer of crude palm oil and has the largest geothermal energy potential. Mining, oil and gas contribute 7% of gross value-added. The government raises revenues by developing the resources itself or selling rights to do so. Under the Constitution, resources are under the power of the state; for decades the central government controlled access and retained the revenue that assets generated, but since the decentralisation of the early 2000s sub-national governments have received a larger share and received revenue-raising powers for some resources (Nasution, 2016).

Government revenues from natural resources had been sizeable before they collapsed over the past decade (Figure 16, Panel A). Most revenue is raised from crude oil via production-sharing contracts, which is common in the petroleum sector, but income tax is also significant (Panel B). A combination of the sharp oil price fall during 2014 and 2015 and an unattractive fiscal regime has weighed on activity and revenue (OECD, 2015d). Likewise, revenues from the gas industry have fallen dramatically. Mining is the next-largest source of revenue, with royalties usually being used as an alternative to production-sharing contracts. There are also a number of state-owned mining companies. Other revenue instruments include: the reforestation fund; levies on resource extraction; permits and concessions (in forestry); and levies and cost recovery (for fisheries). There are also export taxes on some raw materials. Each sector pays income taxes and recurrent property taxes calculated using the value of the land as well as production. Some of the revenues, such as from property tax on land and structures related to oil and gas, mining, forestry and plantations, are shared with local governments, while mining royalties for non-metallic and rock minerals are levied by local governments directly.

Figure 1.16. Revenues from natural resources

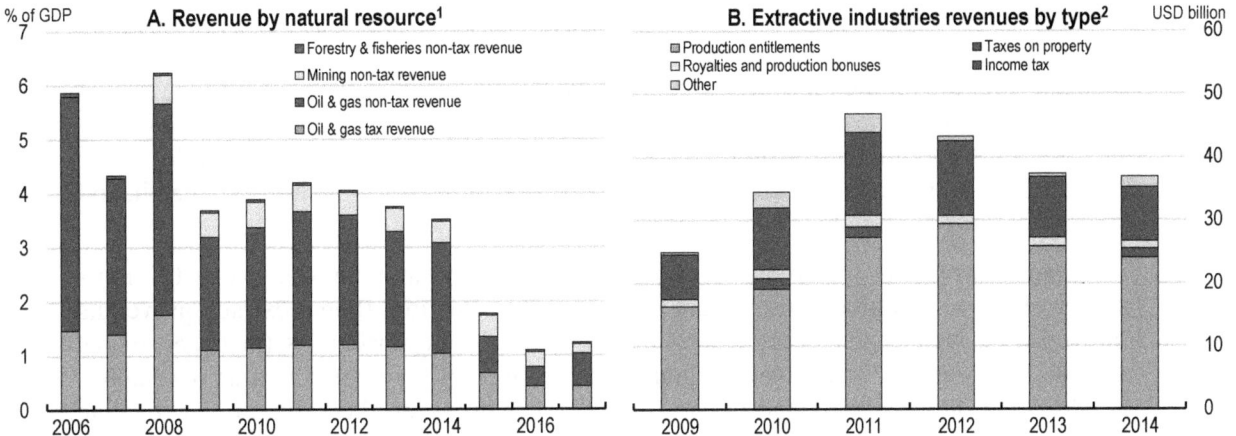

1. Tax revenues shown comprise income tax and property tax.
2. Data are the aggregates of reconciled company data published by the Extractive Industries Transparency Initiative.
Source: CEIC; Ministry of Finance; Directorate General of Taxes, Annual Reports; Extractive Industries Transparency Initiative; OECD calculations.

StatLink 🖳 https://doi.org/10.1787/888933833616

The fiscal regimes for oil and gas and mining have been overhauled in recent years. In oil and gas the government has switched from a cost-recovery method to a new "gross-split" scheme whereby production is split with the government based on a pre-determined percentage. The aim is to boost exploration in the oil sector, which has been depressed by uncertainty and the previous unattractive fiscal regime (OECD, 2015d; OECD, 2012). The gross-split system aims to provide more certainty for investors and removes the incentive for producers to inflate costs (as under a cost-recovery method). Nonetheless, the regime still involves challenges, particularly setting the split at a sufficiently attractive level. After the first bidding round for exploration tracts in 2017 saw no investor interest, the government responded with more favourable terms that led to a more successful later round. Another round is underway and will be an added test of the new regime.

A new fiscal regime for mining became effective in 2014, replacing the "Contract of Work" system, which was a contract between the government and a foreign mining company setting out the latter's rights (including the automatic right to exploit a deposit following its discovery) and obligations (OECD, 2015d). The new mining business licences (*Izin Usaha Pertambangan*, or IUPs) impose obligations to add value to raw materials through onshore processing as well as partial divestment. Exports of raw materials were initially restricted, but this was scaled back. Royalty rates are 2-7% of revenue depending on the mineral but may be changed by the government. The regime and subsequent amendments have generated considerable uncertainty, hurt exports and further reduced incentives to undertake exploration activity (Sullivan, 2017).

Economic theory points to the benefits of taxing economic rents rather than output (either value or volume) as a way of ensuring that the country benefits from windfall gains when commodity prices rise while maintaining incentives to invest. However, the design and implementation of a profit-based tax on resource rents often proves difficult in practice. Instead, countries often opt for royalty (output-based) regimes or state participation. Previous *Surveys* have recommended shifting towards greater taxation of resource rents

(OECD, 2015d, 2012). In the near term, however, there is little government appetite to change the fiscal regimes for extractive industries. But the government should work with mining firms to reduce uncertainty and some of the new costs. The Corruption Eradication Commission (KPK) (2015) argues that forest royalty rates are too low to capture economic rents and "provide implicit incentives for unsustainable forest management". These should be raised. The government plans to improve fisheries management through quotas, capacity rules and multi-stakeholder institutions managing 11 maritime areas. Giving well-defined rights to the resource creates incentives to reduce costs, rather than maximise the catch, and is therefore more sustainable (OECD, 2017h).

Governance problems including insufficient enforcement and unclear property rights hamper effective resource management and revenue collection. Illegal extraction weighs on revenues as well as generating environmental costs. For instance, KPK (2015) estimates that forestry revenues were only one-quarter to one-third of their correct value over 2003-14. Moreover, land clearing and higher timber prices drove up the value of lost revenue due to unreported timber production to USD 5-7 billion in 2013 (at current exchange rates) (*ibid*). Illegal fishing has depleted fish stocks (OECD, 2014). Likewise, illegal mining generates environmental costs through poorer environmental management and failure to rehabilitate the land afterwards (OECD, 2015d). The government has stepped up its fight against illegal (and unregulated and unreported) fishing and timber production since 2014. It has banned transhipment at sea, required all large boats (over 30 gross tonnes) to use vessel-monitoring systems, initiated a controversial campaign of sinking illegal (foreign) boats, and, in 2015, doubled the budget of the Ministry of Marine Affairs and Fisheries (OECD, 2017h). The crackdown has reportedly added to revenues. Technology should be used more in monitoring, law enforcement and inter-agency co-operation.

Property rights for resources are still not clearly allocated. Only 35% of the country is covered by the cadastre and the geospatial data are not co-ordinated (Design, 2017). For example, 89% of Indonesia's forests were under no regulation or permit in 2015 (OECD, 2015d). Conflicting maps are a common cause of land disputes, including when different government agencies grant competing rights in overlapping jurisdictions (MacDonald, 2017). The government's "One Map" initiative aims to create a single map for all of Indonesia's forests to clarify landholdings. Base maps to which thematic maps will be overlaid are now freely available online, but consolidation of overlapping property rights and therefore achieving a definitive map of property rights has been slow. Co-operation across institutions should be stepped up to meet the 2019 target completion date.

Stronger law enforcement and clearer property rights are also needed to fight corruption. Indonesia's participation in the Extractive Industries Transparency Initiative (EITI) is driving governance improvements in that sector; in March 2018 the government announced that beneficial ownership of mines must be revealed. Nonetheless, there is some way to go: according to the EITI one-quarter of mining-sector contracts do not include taxpayer identification numbers. Ambiguity in the national legislation together with the decentralised property registers also widens the scope for corruption in allocating property rights (Design, 2017). Allocating property rights appropriately and enforcing them are pre-conditions for maximising revenues from natural resources. It would also pave the way for more efficient fiscal regimes in the future.

Recommendations to raise revenues

(Key recommendations are shown in bold)

Tax administration and legislation

- **Increase investment in tax administration, particularly staff, electronic services and databases.**
- Establish standard procedures for public consultations on tax legislation before implementation.
- **Make greater use of information technology to strengthen monitoring and facilitate tax compliance.** Increase use of risk-based assessment for conducting audits of all taxes.
- **Continue to expand and improve tax expenditure estimates and publish them annually, as planned.**
- Build tax capacity at sub-national government level through training and sharing of best practices.

Income taxes

- **Freeze the basic tax allowance for individuals to broaden the tax base. Gradually lower thresholds for paying the top two rates of personal income tax.**
- **Include fringe benefits and employer allowances in taxable income.** Reduce differences in the tax treatment of personal savings across sources.
- Shift from tax holidays towards cost-based tax incentives. Impose sunset clauses on all new tax incentives to ensure regular reviews.
- **Tighten eligibility for the turnover tax to very small firms and link registration to access to additional non-financial benefits.**

Goods and services taxes

- **Broaden the VAT base by removing most exemptions, especially for intermediate goods, replacing local sales tax with VAT, and lowering the threshold for compulsory registration. Compensate sub-national governments for lost sales tax revenue.** Over the medium term, raise the VAT rate.
- **Increase and harmonise tobacco excise across products.**
- Link the level of motor vehicle taxes to their carbon emissions. Continue to phase out energy subsidies, then increase taxation of energy. Introduce a simple carbon tax at a low rate.

Property taxes

- **Increase training and assistance for sub-national governments to improve the quality of property tax databases, valuation methods and tax administration. Raise the cap on property tax rates.**

Non-tax revenues

- Finalise the One Map Initiative, and step up the fight against illegal resource extraction at all levels of government.

Bibliography

Acosta-Ormaechea, S. and J. Yoo (2012), "Tax composition and growth: A broad cross-country perspective", *IMF Working Papers*, No. 12/257, International Monetary Fund, Washington, DC.

Aizawa, T. and M. Helble (2016), "Socioeconomic inequity in excessive weight in Indonesia", *ADBI Working Paper Series*, No. 572, Asian Development Bank Institute, Tokyo.

Akgun, O., D. Bartolini and B. Cournède (2017), "The capacity of governments to raise taxes", *OECD Economics Department Working Papers*, No. 1407, OECD Publishing, Paris, http://dx.doi.org/10.1787/6bee2df9-en.

Akgun, O., B. Cournède and J. Fournier (2017), "The effects of the tax mix on inequality and growth", *OECD Economics Department Working Papers*, No. 1447, OECD Publishing, Paris, http://dx.doi.org/10.1787/c57eaa14-en.

Arnold, J. et al. (2011), "Tax policy for economic recovery and growth", *The Economic Journal*, Vol. 121/550, pp. F59-F80, http://dx.doi.org/10.1111/j.1468-0297.2010.02415.x.

Benedek, D. et al. (2017), "The right kind of help? Tax incentives for staying small", *IMF Working Papers*, No. 17/139, International Monetary Fund, Washington DC.

Besley, T. and T. Persson (2014), "Why do developing countries tax so little?", *Journal of Economic Perspectives*, Vol. 28/4, pp. 99-120.

Blöchliger, H. (2015), "Reforming the tax on immovable property: taxing care of the unloved", *OECD Economics Department Working Papers*, No. 1205, OECD Publishing, Paris, https://doi.org/10.1787/5js30tw0n7kg-en.

Corruption Eradication Commission (KPK) (2015), *Preventing State Losses in Indonesia's Forestry Sector Preventing State Losses in Indonesia's Forestry Sector: An Analysis of Non-tax Forest Revenue Collection and Timber Production Administration*, Komisi Pemberantasan Korupsi, Jakarta.

Credit Suisse (2017), *Credit Suisse Global Wealth Databook 2017*, Credit Suisse Research Institute.

Dartanto, T. (2017), *Universal Health Coverage in Indonesia: Informality, Fiscal Risks and Fiscal Space for Financing UHC*, Presentation at IMF-JICA Conference on "Regional Development: Fiscal Risks, Fiscal Space and the Sustainable Development Goals".

Darussalam (2018), *Menyoal Perluasan Withholding Tax Atas Penghasilan Usaha* [Questioning expansion withholding tax on business income], https://news.ddtc.co.id/menyoal-perluasan-withholding-tax-atas-penghasilan-usaha-13008 (accessed on 06 July 2018).

Darussalam (2017), *Arah Reformasi Pajak: Meningkatkan Penerimaan, Mengurangi Sengketa* [The direction of tax reform: increasing revenue, reducing disputes] in INDEF (ed.), *Menuju Ketangguhan Ekonomi: Sumbang Saran 100 Ekonom Indonesia*, Penerbit Buku Kompas.

de Paula, Á. and J. Scheinkman (2007), "The informal sector", *NBER Working Papers*, No. 13486, National Bureau of Economic Research, Cambridge, MA.

Deloitte (2017), *Shifting Sands: Risk and Reform in Uncertain times - 2017 Asia Pacific Tax Complexity Survey*.

Design, L. (2017), *Combatting Corruption in Mining Approvals: Assessing the Risks in 18 Resource-rich Countries*, Transparency International.

Égert, B., P. Gal and I. Wanner (2017), "Structural policy indicators database for economic research (SPIDER)", *OECD Economics Department Working Papers*, No. 1429, OECD Publishing, Paris, http://dx.doi.org/10.1787/39d69dff-en.

Fenochietto, R. and C. Pessino (2013), "Understanding countries' tax effort", *IMF Working Papers*, No. 13/244, International Monetary Fund, Washington DC.

Flues, F. and K. van Dender (2017), "The impact of energy taxes on the affordability of domestic energy", *OECD Taxation Working Papers*, No. 30, OECD Publishing, Paris, http://dx.doi.org/10.1787/08705547-en.

Fountaine, T. et al. (2016), *Tackling Indonesia's Diabetes Challenge: Eight Approaches from Around the World*, McKinsey & Company and Center for Healthcare Research and Innovation.

Gaspar, V., L. Jaramillo and P. Wingender (2016a), "Tax capacity and growth: Is there a tipping point?", *IMF Working Papers*, No. 2016/234, International Monetary Fund, Washington DC.

Gaspar, V., L. Jaramillo and P. Wingender (2016b), "Political institutions, state building, and tax capacity: crossing the tipping point", *IMF Working Papers*, No. 2016/233, International Monetary Fund, Washington DC.

IADB (2013), *More than Revenue: Taxation as a Development Tool*, Palgrave Macmillan US, New York.

IMF (2018), "Indonesia: Selected issues", *IMF Country Report*, No. 18/33, International Monetary Fund, Washington DC.

IMF (2017), "Indonesia: Selected issues", *IMF Country Report*, No. 17/48, International Monetary Fund, Washington DC.

IMF (2011), "Revenue mobilization in developing countries", *IMF Policy Papers*, International Monetary Fund, Washington, DC.

IMF et al. (2015), *Options for Low Income Countries' Effective and Efficient Use of Tax Incentives for Investment: A Report to the G-20 Development Working Group by the IMF, OECD, UN and World Bank*, www.oecd.org/tax/tax-global/options-for-low-income-countries-effective-and-efficient-use-of-tax-incentives-for-investment.pdf.

IMF/OECD (2017), *Tax Certainty: IMF/OECD Report for the G20 Finance Ministers*, IMF and OECD, www.oecd.org/tax/tax-policy/tax-certainty-report-oecd-imf-report-g20-finance-ministers-march-2017.pdf.

International Energy Agency (2017), *World Energy Balances 2017*, International Energy Agency, Paris.

Jambeck, J. et al. (2015), "Plastic waste inputs from land into the ocean", *Science*, Vol. 347/6223, pp. 768-71.

Jellema, J., M. Wai-Poi and R. Afkar (2017), "The distributional impact of fiscal policy in Indonesia", *Commitment to Equity (CEQ) Working Paper Series*, No. 40, Tulane University, New Orleans.

Joshi, A., W. Prichard and C. Heady (2014), "Taxing the informal economy: The current state of knowledge and agendas for future research", *The Journal of Development Studies*, Vol. 50/10, pp. 1325-1347.

MacDonald, L. (2017), *Can "One Map" Solve Indonesia's Land Tenure Woes?*, World Resources Institute, www.wri.org/blog/2017/06/can-one-map-solve-indonesias-land-tenure-woes.

Nasution, A. (2016), "Government decentralization program in Indonesia", *ADBI Working Paper Series*, No. 601, Asian Development Bank Institute, Tokyo.

National Legal Development Board (2013), *Analisis dan Evaluasi Tentang Pajak dan Redistribusi Daerah* [Analysis and evaluation of Tax and Regional Transfers], Ministry of Law and Human Rights, Jakarta, www.bphn.go.id/data/documents/ae_retribusi.pdf.

Nugroho, A. and R. Tenrini (2014), "The design of income tax system responding to the middle class growth, and its effects on income distribution", Paper presented at the International Conference on Economic Modeling, 16-18 July.

OECD (2018a), *OECD Investment Policy Reviews: Southeast Asia*, OECD Publishing, Paris, www.oecd.org/daf/inv/investment-policy/Southeast-Asia-Investment-Policy-Review-2018.pdf.

OECD (2018b), *Tax Challenges Arising from Digitalisation - Interim Report: Inclusive Framework on BEPS*, OECD/G20 Base Erosion and Profit Shifting Project, OECD Publishing, Paris, http://dx.doi.org/10.1787/9789264293083-en.

OECD (2018c), *OECD Economic Surveys: Czech Republic 2018*, OECD Publishing, Paris, http://dx.doi.org/10.1787/eco_surveys-cze-2018-en.

OECD (2018d), *Taxing Energy Use 2018: Companion to the Taxing Energy Use Database*, OECD Publishing, Paris, http://dx.doi.org/10.1787/9789264289635-en.

OECD (2017a), *Tax Administration 2017: Comparative Information on OECD and Other Advanced and Emerging Economies*, OECD Publishing, Paris, http://dx.doi.org/10.1787/tax_admin-2017-en.

OECD (2017b), *Technology Tools to Tackle Tax Evasion and Tax Fraud*, www.oecd.org/tax/crime/technology-tools-to-tackle-tax-evasion-and-tax-fraud.pdf.

OECD (2017c), *Shining Light on the Shadow Economy: Opportunities and Threats*, www.oecd.org/tax/crime/shining-light-on-the-shadow-economy-opportunities-and-threats.pdf.

OECD (2017d), *Health at a Glance 2017: OECD Indicators*, OECD Publishing, Paris, https://doi.org/10.1787/health_glance-2017-en.

OECD (2017e), *Tax Policy Reforms 2017: OECD and Selected Partner Economies*, OECD Publishing, Paris, http://dx.doi.org/10.1787/9789264279919-en.

OECD (2017f), *Environmental Fiscal Reform: Progress, Prospects and Pitfalls*, OECD Publishing, Paris, www.oecd.org/tax/tax-policy/environmental-fiscal-reform-G7-environment-ministerial-meeting-june-2017.pdf.

OECD (2017g), *OECD Economic Surveys: India 2017*, OECD Publishing, Paris, http://dx.doi.org/10.1787/eco_surveys-ind-2017-en.

OECD (2017h), *OECD Review of Fisheries: Policies and Summary Statistics 2017*, OECD Publishing, Paris, http://dx.doi.org/10.1787/rev_fish_stat_en-2017-en.

OECD (2016a), *OECD Economic Surveys: Indonesia 2016*, OECD Publishing, Paris, http://dx.doi.org/10.1787/eco_surveys-idn-2016-en.

OECD (2016b), *Consumption Tax Trends 2016: VAT/GST and Excise Rates, Trends and Policy Issues*, OECD Publishing, Paris, http://dx.doi.org/10.1787/ctt-2016-en.

OECD (2016c), *The Economic Consequences of Outdoor Air Pollution*, OECD Publishing, Paris, http://dx.doi.org/10.1787/9789264257474-en.

OECD (2016d), *Green Growth in Bandung, Indonesia*, OECD Publishing, Paris, http://dx.doi.org/10.1787/9789264264113-en.

OECD (2015a), "Making tax policy more efficient, fair and green", in *OECD Economic Surveys: Colombia 2015*, OECD Publishing, Paris, http://dx.doi.org/10.1787/eco_surveys-col-2015-5-en.

OECD (2015b), *Developing a Multilateral Instrument to Modify Bilateral Tax Treaties, Action 15 - 2015 Final Report*, OECD/G20 Base Erosion and Profit Shifting Project, OECD Publishing, Paris, http://dx.doi.org/10.1787/9789264241688-en.

OECD (2015c), *OECD Economic Surveys: South Africa 2015*, OECD Publishing, Paris, http://dx.doi.org/10.1787/eco_surveys-zaf-2015-en.

OECD (2015d), "Making the most of natural resources", in *OECD Economic Surveys: Indonesia 2015*, OECD Publishing, Paris, http://dx.doi.org/10.1787/eco_surveys-idn-2015-6-en.

OECD (2014), *Towards Green Growth in Southeast Asia*, OECD Publishing, Paris, http://dx.doi.org/10.1787/9789264224100-en.

OECD (2012), "Improving the tax system", in *OECD Economic Surveys: Indonesia 2012*, OECD Publishing, Paris, http://dx.doi.org/10.1787/eco_surveys-idn-2012-5-en.

OECD (2009), "Withholding & information reporting regimes for small/medium-sized businesses and self-employed taxpayers", Forum on Tax Administration Compliance Sub-Group Information Note, OECD Publishing, Paris, www.oecd.org/tax/administration/48449751.pdf.

OECD (2005), *Environmental Fiscal Reform for Poverty Reduction*, DAC Guidelines and Reference Series, OECD Publishing, Paris, http://dx.doi.org/10.1787/9789264008700-en.

OECD/KIPF (2014), "The distributional effects of consumption taxes in OECD countries", *OECD Tax Policy Studies*, No. 22, OECD Publishing, Paris, http://dx.doi.org/10.1787/9789264224520-en.

Pomeranz, D. (2015), "No taxation without information: deterrence and self-enforcement in the value added tax", *American Economic Review*, Vol. 105/8, pp. 2539-69.

Rios, J. and I. Seetharam (2017), "Propagating formality via value added tax networks: evidence from India", https://web.stanford.edu/~ishuwar/ValueAddedPremium.pdf.

Rothenberg, A. et al. (2016), "Rethinking Indonesia's informal sector", *World Development*, Vol. 80, pp. 96-113.

Sands, P. et al. (2017), "Limiting the use of cash for big purchases: Assessing the case for uniform cash thresholds", *RUSI Occasional Paper*, No. 80, Royal United Services Institute / Harvard Kennedy School.

Sassi, F. (2016), "Taxing sugar", *BMJ (Clinical research ed.)*, Vol. 352, p. h6904.

Sassi, F. et al. (2014), "Taxation and economic incentives on health-related commodities: Alcohol, tobacco and food", *HEC Paris Research Paper*, No. LAW 2014-1038, Cambridge University Press.

Sullivan, B. (2017), "Conversion of Contracts of Work - confusion heaped upon uncertainty", *Coal Asia Magazine*, May-June.

Thavorncharoensap, M. (2017), "Effectiveness of obesity prevention and control", *ADBI Working Papers*, No. 654, Asian Development Bank Institute, Tokyo.

The Jakarta Post (2018), *E-commerce contributes 0.75 percent to GDP*, www.thejakartapost.com/news/2018/02/14/e-commerce-contributes-0-75-percent-to-gdp.html.

Thomas, A. et al. (2017), "Taxation and investment in India", *OECD Economics Department Working Papers*, No. 1397, OECD Publishing, Paris, http://dx.doi.org/10.1787/4258e11a-en.

van Dender, K. (forthcoming), "Taxing vehicles, fuel and road use: What mix for road transport?", *OECD Taxation Working Papers*, OECD Publishing, Paris.

von Haldenwang, C. et al. (2015), "The Devolution of the Land and Building Tax in Indonesia", *Studies Deutsches Institut für Entwicklungspolitik*, No. 89, German Development Institute, Bonn.

WHO (2017), *WHO Report on the Global Tobacco Epidemic 2017*, World Health Organization, Geneva.

World Bank (2018), *March 2018 Indonesia Economic Quarterly: Towards Inclusive Growth*, World Bank, Jakarta.

World Bank (2017a), *December 2017 Indonesia Economic Quarterly: Decentralization that Delivers*, World Bank, Jakarta.

World Bank (2017b), *June 2017 Indonesia Economic Quarterly: Upgraded*, World Bank, Jakarta.

World Bank / PwC (2018), *Paying Taxes 2018*, www.pwc.com/payingtaxes.

World Economic Forum (2017), *The Global Competitiveness Report: 2017-2018*, World Economic Forum, Geneva.

Annex A.

As explained in Box 1.1, the potential tax revenue that an economy can generate depends on its structural features as well as its institutions. Following OECD (2015a) and earlier papers, the following equation is estimated using income per capita and structural variables (X_{it}) from the OECD SPIDER database (Égert, Gal and Wanner, 2017) and country fixed effects (c_i):

$$\frac{Tax}{GDP_{it}} = \alpha + \beta \ln(GDP\ per\ capita)_{it} + \gamma X_{it} + c_i + \varepsilon_{it}$$

The equation is estimated over 1997-2016 and 77 countries with annual income per capita ranging from USD 744 to USD 94 765 (PPP-adjusted). In general the results are in line with other studies (Table 1.8):

- GDP per capita is consistently related to higher tax capacity.
- A larger agricultural sector is associated with lower tax capacity.
- Greater trade openness (in log form) is associated with higher tax capacity. However, this is not statistically significant when using an alternative size-adjusted measure of openness (the residual from a regression of the absolute value of exports plus imports to GDP on population).
- Greater (perceived) control of corruption is associated with higher tax capacity but with diminishing effects as income rises.

Table 1.8. Estimating tax capacity

Dependent variable: tax-to-GDP ratio

	(1)	(2)	(3)	(4)	(5)	(6)	(7)
GDP per capita (log)	4.603***	2.466*	2.958**	2.527*	2.847**	5.461***	7.133***
	(1.181)	(1.397)	(1.397)	(1.390)	(1.309)	(0.820)	(1.462)
Agriculture share in GVA		-0.286***	-0.266***	-0.272***	-0.243***		0.157
		(0.0929)	(0.0978)	(0.0870)	(0.0802)		(0.172)
Openness (log)		2.082**		1.562*	1.927**		0.130
		(0.955)		(0.936)	(0.948)		(1.979)
Openness (size-adjusted)			0.00465				
			(0.00950)				
Control of corruption				-0.540	18.40***		
				(0.664)	(6.903)		
Control of corruption x GDP per capita					-1.993***		
					(0.706)		
Constant	-17.68	-4.057	0.0303	-2.187	-5.292	-25.92***	-43.96**
	(11.33)	(15.16)	(13.98)	(15.08)	(14.13)	(7.741)	(18.05)
Observations	1,462	1,374	1,374	1,234	1,234	1,462	1,374
R-squared	0.083	0.138	0.120	0.125	0.161	0.350	0.382
Number of countries	77	76	76	75	75		
Country fixed effects?	Yes	Yes	Yes	Yes	Yes	No	No

Note: Robust standard errors in parentheses. Errors are clustered at the country level in pooled regressions. *** p<0.01, ** p<0.05, * p<0.1
Source: OECD calculations

Chapter 2. Making the most of tourism to promote sustainable regional development

Tourism has boomed in Indonesia in recent years and is already one of the main sources of foreign-currency earnings. Indonesia has rich and diverse natural assets, whose tourism potential remains underutilised. The government has an ambitious target of attracting 20 million tourists by 2019, up from nearly 14 million in 2017. The main destination will continue to be Bali. Using Bali as the preferred development model, the government wants to develop other destinations, particularly through infrastructure programmes to improve connectivity, which is a longstanding challenge for tourism as well as for regional development more generally. Enhancing the tourism-related skills of local populations will provide them with expanded job opportunities. This calls for reforms to vocational education and training. Moreover, recent efforts by the authorities to improve the business environment need to continue, including through helping firms embrace digitalisation. Tourism may be growing too fast in some destinations without adequately taking into account sustainability issues, both for the environment and local communities. Better planning and co-ordination at all levels of government and across relevant policy areas can facilitate more sustainable tourism development.

Indonesia has diverse and rich landscapes and ecosystems that position the country as an attractive destination for tourists. However, the province of Bali, with less than half of 1% of Indonesia's landmass, has been the dominant destination, receiving half of all foreign visitors. Tourism also represents a smaller share of Indonesia's economy than comparator countries like Thailand or Malaysia. Traditionally, Indonesia has earned most of its foreign currency by exporting primary products. Government efforts to diversify the economy towards manufacturing have proved difficult. In 2014 the new President decided to use tourism as a new pillar of the economic strategy to achieve faster and more inclusive growth. Indonesia's competitiveness as a tourist destination improved from 70th in 2013 to 42nd in 2017, according to the World Economic Forum's Travel and tourism competitiveness index (WEF, 2017). Even so, the country still lags behind its regional competitors in a number of dimensions, particularly those related to infrastructure and environmental sustainability (Figure 2.1).

Tourism is special in that it touches many sectors of the economy including hotels, restaurants, agri-food and transport and also affects spatial development and the environment. It also involves multiple administrative levels (national, provincial, district and municipal). The horizontal and vertical nature of tourism complicates the role that governments can play in supporting the development of the industry. The Indonesian authorities expect a surge in the number of tourist arrivals in the near future, which will put pressure on infrastructure, local communities, cultural heritage and environmental assets like forests, coral reefs, beaches and wildlife. Digitalisation is also reshaping the tourism sector worldwide, which requires policy attention to ensure infrastructure and regulations are appropriate. Finally, the market is growing but is also increasingly competitive. In 2016 there were 1.2 billion international tourists, with an average annual growth rate of 4.4% since 2012 (UNWTO, 2018). Emerging economies, notably in Asia, have improved their competitiveness; for example, Thailand rose from 12th to 4th place in 15 years with regards to foreign visitor spending (WTTC, 2018).

Figure 2.1. Indonesia's competitiveness as a tourist destination

Score from 1 to 7 (best), 2017

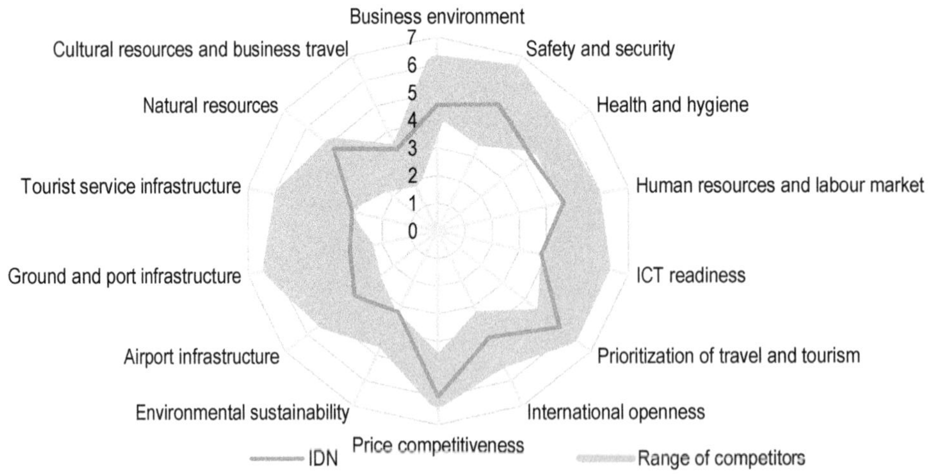

Note: Competitors are Malaysia, Philippines, Singapore and Thailand.
Source: WEF, *Travel and Tourism Competitiveness Report 2017*.

StatLink ⧉ https://doi.org/10.1787/888933833635

This chapter is organised into three sections. The first one summarises recent developments in Indonesia's tourism industry and examines the government's strategy. The second section considers how tourism can improve regional development in terms of employment, infrastructure and the business environment. The last part covers the sustainability of tourism development with particular attention to the environment and local communities.

Recent developments and tourism prospects in Indonesia

Recent developments and the size of the industry

At the national level the number of foreign tourist arrivals remained around 5 million per year over 1995-2007, despite a near doubling in worldwide tourism. Since 2007 the number of international arrivals has soared, reaching 14 million in 2017 and boosting Indonesia's market share to around 1% (Figure 2.2). The authorities aim to reach 20 million foreign visitors by 2019. Most of the recent increase has originated from Asian countries. Chinese tourists became the largest source market in 2017, surpassing Malaysia, Singapore and Australia. The tourism product portfolio is mostly culture and nature related, accounting for 95% (60% and 35%, respectively) of survey respondents' purpose of visit (Teguh, 2017). Only a small share of tourism is related to sport or business events (5%). Within culture, "culinary/gastronomy or shopping" represents the largest share (45%) of responses, followed by "city and village tourism" (35%). Nature-based tourism is focused on eco-tourism (45%) and marine tourism (35%).

Figure 2.2. Tourist arrivals in Indonesia

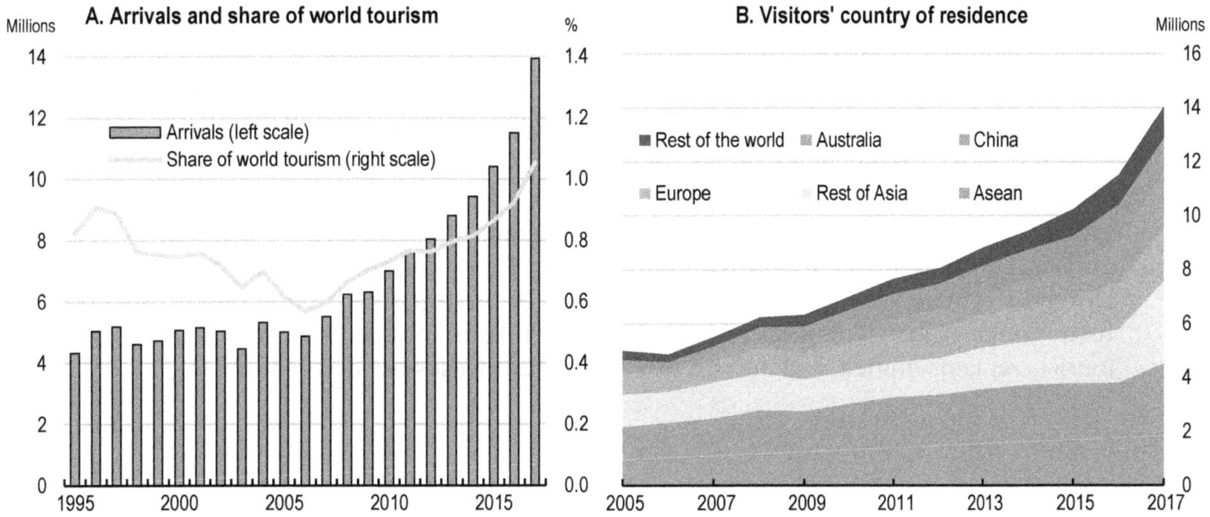

Source: CEIC.

StatLink ᵐˢᵖ https://doi.org/10.1787/888933833654

A more stable and welcoming environment likely contributed to the recent growth of foreign visitors. Terrorism damaged the country's reputation in the early 2000s; new attacks occurred in the recent past but did not specifically target tourists. In 2015 the government made visa policy changes to attract more foreign tourists. Now citizens of 169 countries do not require a visa to enter and stay in Indonesia (for a maximum period of 30 days). The free visa policy is expected to bring significant foreign exchange earnings per year, as the loss of the visa receipts (USD 35 per person) is more than compensated by the spending of additional tourists in the country (around USD 1000 per visit). In 2016 the government also legislated to allow international cruise liners to embark and disembark passengers at five seaports, which should facilitate arrivals by sea.

Bali remains the principal destination of foreign tourists, accounting for half of the rise in the number of arrivals over 2007-17 (Figure 2.3, Panel A). In 2018 tourists nominated it the preferred destination in Asia (TripAdvisor, 2018). Jakarta has also experienced strong growth over the same period (1.4 million additional tourists), partly driven by business tourism. Other areas (besides Batam island) also vastly increased their importance, with 2.5 million more tourists over 2007-17, and half of that growth in 2017 alone. Borobudur (Central Java) and Lake Toba (North Sumatra) are the two main new destinations. The growing importance of these new destinations can be linked to a recent government strategy to develop tourism outside Bali. As an expansive archipelago, air transport is the mode of transport used by the vast majority of inbound tourists, making effective air connectivity crucial (Panel B).

The direct contribution of tourism (domestic and foreign) to the economy, computed from the statistics office's Tourism Satellite Account, is in line with the average for OECD and G20 countries (at around 4.3% of GDP in 2015) but lower than countries that have a focus on tourism such as Spain, Croatia, Portugal, the Philippines or Mexico (Figure 2.4). The indirect measure also includes tourism's downstream effects. Assuming the direct and indirect effects to be of the same size (Box 2.1), the total contribution is estimated to be around 8.5% of GDP for 2015. Given that arrivals have increased by about one-third since then, the importance of tourism is likely to be higher now. Input-output tables also show that most of the value added is generated within the country.

According to UNWTO, there were nearly 120 million domestic guests in commercial accommodation in 2016, up from around 40 million in 2009. Domestic tourism is concentrated around the Muslim holiday Eid ul-Fitr (Lebaran); the authorities also increased the number of public holidays to facilitate and encourage travel. Internal movements both facilitated and were facilitated by the rapid growth of low-cost airlines (Schlumberger and Weisskopf, 2014). This will likely continue in the future with the growing middle class, the expansion of airports and the quality improvement of some airlines (no Indonesian airline was left on the European Union's ban list by 2018). However, a domestic tourist spends about USD 70 per trip compared to over USD 1 000 for a foreign visitor (Indonesia-Investments, 2016). Thus, the economic impact of domestic tourists remains limited, and the rest of this chapter focuses on foreign tourism.

Figure 2.3. Entry points and transport mode of foreign tourists

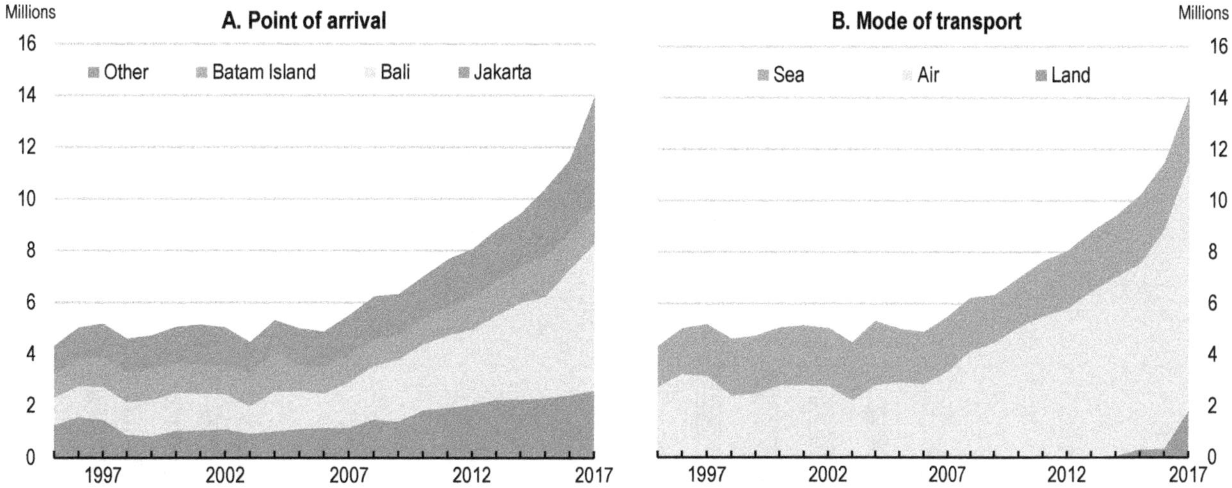

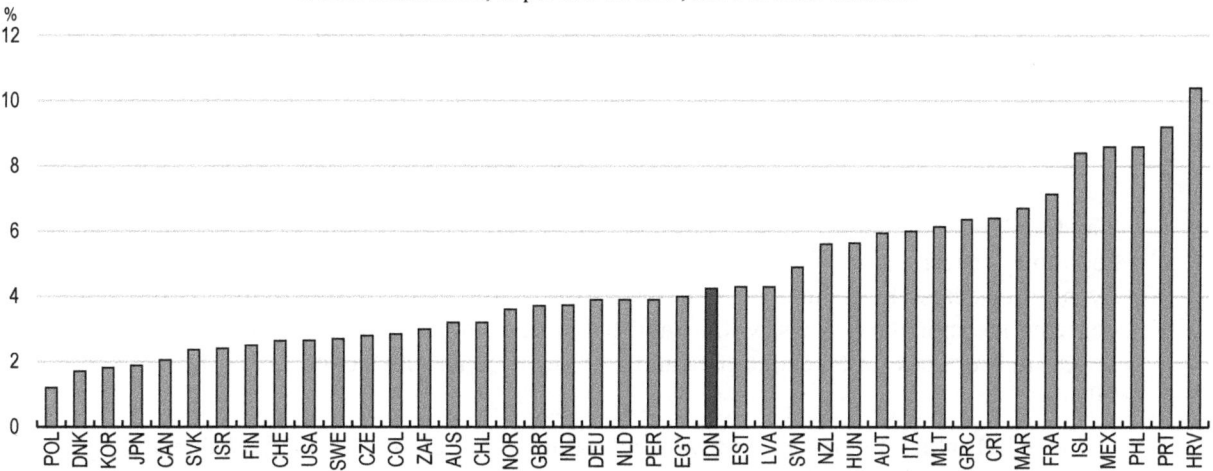

Source: CEIC.

StatLink ᵐᵍᴸ https://doi.org/10.1787/888933833673

Figure 2.4. Contribution of tourism to the economy

Direct contribution, in per cent of GDP, 2016 or latest available

Note: Direct contribution means that it only takes into account the output generated from a direct relationship between the visitor (foreign or domestic) and producer of a good or services. 2015 data for Indonesia. Data for France refers to internal tourism consumption. Data for Germany and Greece refer to gross value added.
Source: OECD, *Tourism Database*; Statistics Indonesia.

StatLink ᵐᵍᴸ https://doi.org/10.1787/888933833692

Tourism brings in substantial foreign-currency earnings, helping diversify Indonesia's exports away from natural resources (e.g. mining and crude palm oil). Foreign tourist spending has already gradually become one of the main sources of foreign currency for Indonesia (Figure 2.5, Panel A). However, the importance of tourism exports is still much lower than for other countries (Panel B). Input-output tables show that the biggest beneficiaries from foreign tourism are hotels and restaurants (8.5% of sector output), the transportation and storage sector (1.3%), and other community, social and personal services (1.3%). Using the same approach shows that these sectors benefit much more from foreign tourism in Thailand, with tourism representing 32%, 10% and 15% of sector output respectively. To some extent, this is related to the size of the domestic economy in Indonesia. There is considerable room to attract higher spending tourists: Indonesia ranks only 12th amongst 53 Asia-Pacific countries in terms of spending per arrival (UNWTO, 2017).

Figure 2.5. Foreign-currency earnings

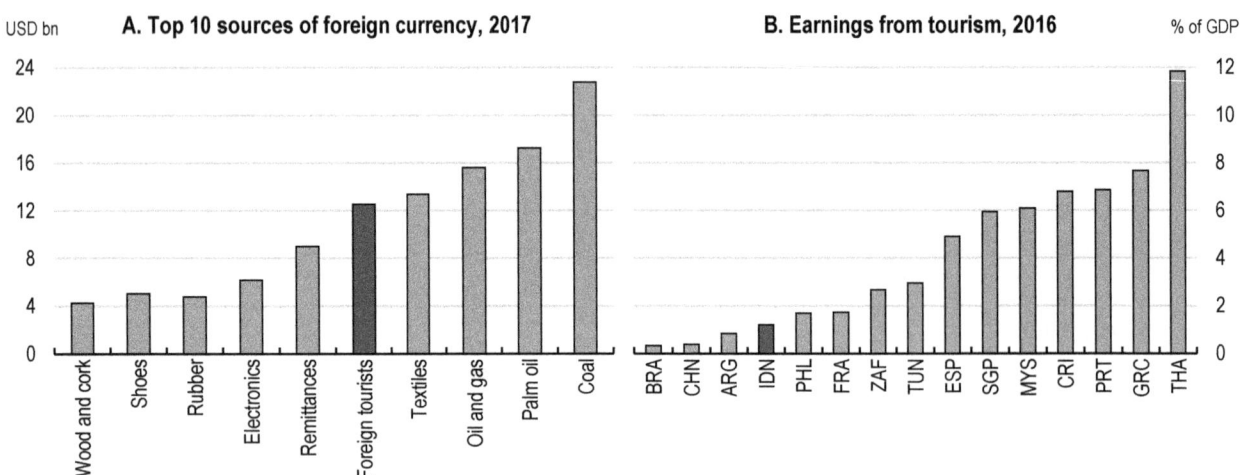

Note: Panel A refers to main sources of exports. Panel B uses tourism expenditure from UNWTO.
Source: CEIC; UNWTO; *OECD Economic Outlook Database*.

StatLink ᔕᓯᔚ https://doi.org/10.1787/888933833711

Box 2.1. Measuring the indirect economic impact of international tourism

The OECD Inter-Country Input-Output tables (ICIO) can provide new insights into the economic benefits of tourism activities by revealing the origin of value added generated by non-residents' household expenditures within a country. The current ICIO tables describe the monetary flows, within and between countries, of intermediate and final goods and services for 63 economies and 34 industrial activities over the period 1995 to 2011.

Using ICIO tables the *direct* and *indirect* value added embodied in final demand by tourists can be estimated. The direct value is computed from the sales of final goods and services to tourists (e.g. spending in a restaurant) while the indirect contribution comes from inputs, both domestic and imported, required for those sales (e.g. food purchased by restaurants).

On average for Indonesia, as well as for OECD countries, around half of the tourism value added comes directly from core industries that sell directly to tourists. Those sectors produce mostly services, while most industries indirectly related to tourism (such as agriculture and food manufacturing) provide goods. The importance of international tourism trade is estimated to be relatively low for Indonesia (Figure 2.6). However given the surge in tourism since 2011, the forthcoming update of the ICIO tables will likely show a larger contribution. Domestic value added in the purchases of non-residents was around 88% in 2011, down slightly from about 91% in 1995. In Thailand and Malaysia the domestic share has decreased more substantially since 1995 (by 11 percentage points), to 73% and 66%, respectively. This high share of domestic value-added means that future growth in tourism can benefit many parts of the economy.

Figure 2.6. Foreign tourists' expenditure

In % of GDP, 2011

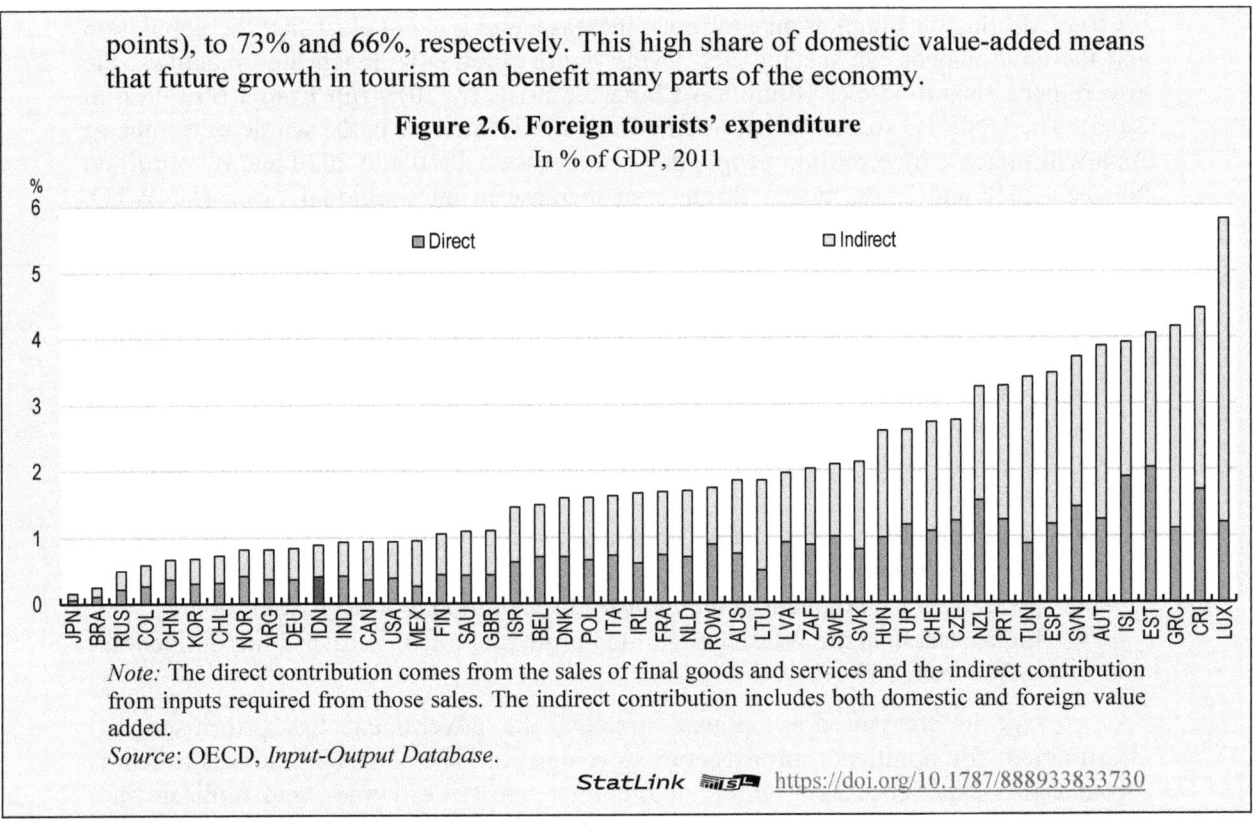

Note: The direct contribution comes from the sales of final goods and services and the indirect contribution from inputs required from those sales. The indirect contribution includes both domestic and foreign value added.

Source: OECD, *Input-Output Database*.

StatLink https://doi.org/10.1787/888933833730

The medium-term perspective

Since 2014 tourism has become one of the government's top priorities. The National Medium-Term Development Plan (RPJMN) for 2015-19 and the accompanying tourism strategy ("Pengembangan Destinasi dan Industri Pariwisata") set policy directions for the sector related to:

- Connectivity, basic services and tourist service infrastructure;
- Tourism workforce skills development and SME support;
- Tourism services, international marketing and investment promotion;
- Integrated destination master planning; and
- Institutions and mechanisms for programme implementation.

Different planning exercises at the central government level interact, including the medium-term plan, the Long-Term National Development Plan (RPJP) and the Long-Term National Tourism Development Plan (RIPPARNAS) for 2010-25. In the latter the government selected 50 tourism destinations nationwide to be developed by 2025. Bappenas (the national planning ministry) leads the planning stage, and the Ministry of Maritime Affairs co-ordinates the implementation of tourism-related plans across line ministries. Despite a high degree of decentralisation in government, planning is largely top-down; in addition to local stakeholder involvement, it also lacks *ex ante* and *ex post* evaluations.

The objectives set out in the medium-term plan are ambitious (Box 2.2) and will depend on massive infrastructure investment (more below). The initial focus on 10 "New Balis" has thus gradually switched to four priority destinations (Borobudur, Mandalika, Lake Toba and Labuan Bajo). So far, the increase in tourist arrivals has still been largely dependent on Bali, but from 2017, other destinations started to gain importance. The target for some destinations implies an enormous increase, and it is not clear that the population and the environment can sustain such levels (more below). To reach the objectives, the government aims to attract 10 million Chinese tourists by 2019 (up from 1.6 million in 2016). The UNWTO forecasts that international tourist arrivals in the whole of Southeast Asia will increase by 5 million people per year between 2010 and 2020 and by 6 million between 2020 and 2030, mostly through an increase in intra-regional flows (UNWTO, 2017). Competition in the region may delay the realisation of the government's target.

Box 2.2. The Government medium-term plan for tourism

The government's medium-term plan for 2015-19 set ambitious targets for 2019:

- 20 million international arrivals, up from 9 million in 2014.
- 275 million domestic visits, up from 250 million in 2014.
- 8% share in GDP, up from about 4% in 2013 (using the national tourism satellite account).
- Doubling of foreign exchange revenues from tourism to IDR 240 trillion (about USD 16 billion).
- Increase in employment in the industry by 2 million to nearly 12 million.
- Improvement in the World Economic Forum ranking of tourism competitiveness to 30th from 70th.

As part of its tourism development strategy, the government has prioritised 10 destinations for significant infrastructure development. The underlying aim is to learn from Bali's experience as a major international tourist destination and replicate the model in destinations across Indonesia with high potential. The selection of the destinations was in large part driven by the pre-existence of a tourism industry; however, it did not take into account locations' viability to develop as an international tourism destination including with respect to natural and cultural attractions. The need to promote geographical diversity also played a role. The 10 priority destinations are located in 10 of the 34 provinces with targets that represent sizeable increases (Table 2.1). Four destinations (Mandalika, Tanjung Lesung, Tanjung Kelayan and Morotai) have been designated as Special Economic Zones (SEZs).

Table 2.1. Tourist arrivals objectives for the 10 priority destinations

Number of people

	2013	2019 target
Borobudur (Central Java)	227 337	2 000 000
Mandalika (West Nusa Tenggara)	125 307	1 000 000
Lake Toba (North Sumatra)	10 680	1 000 000
Labuan Bajo (East Nusa Tenggara)	54 147	500 000
Morotai (Maluku Utara)	500	500 000
Mount Bromo (East Java)	33 387	1 000 000
Tanjung Kelayan (Belitung)	451	500 000
Tanjung Lesung (Banten)	1 739	1 000 000
Thousand Islands (DKI Jakarta)	16 384	500 000
Wakatobi National Park (Southeast Sulawesi)	3 315	500 000

Note: Respective provinces for each destination are in parentheses.
Source: Ministry of Tourism.

Figure 2.7. Locations of the 10 New Balis

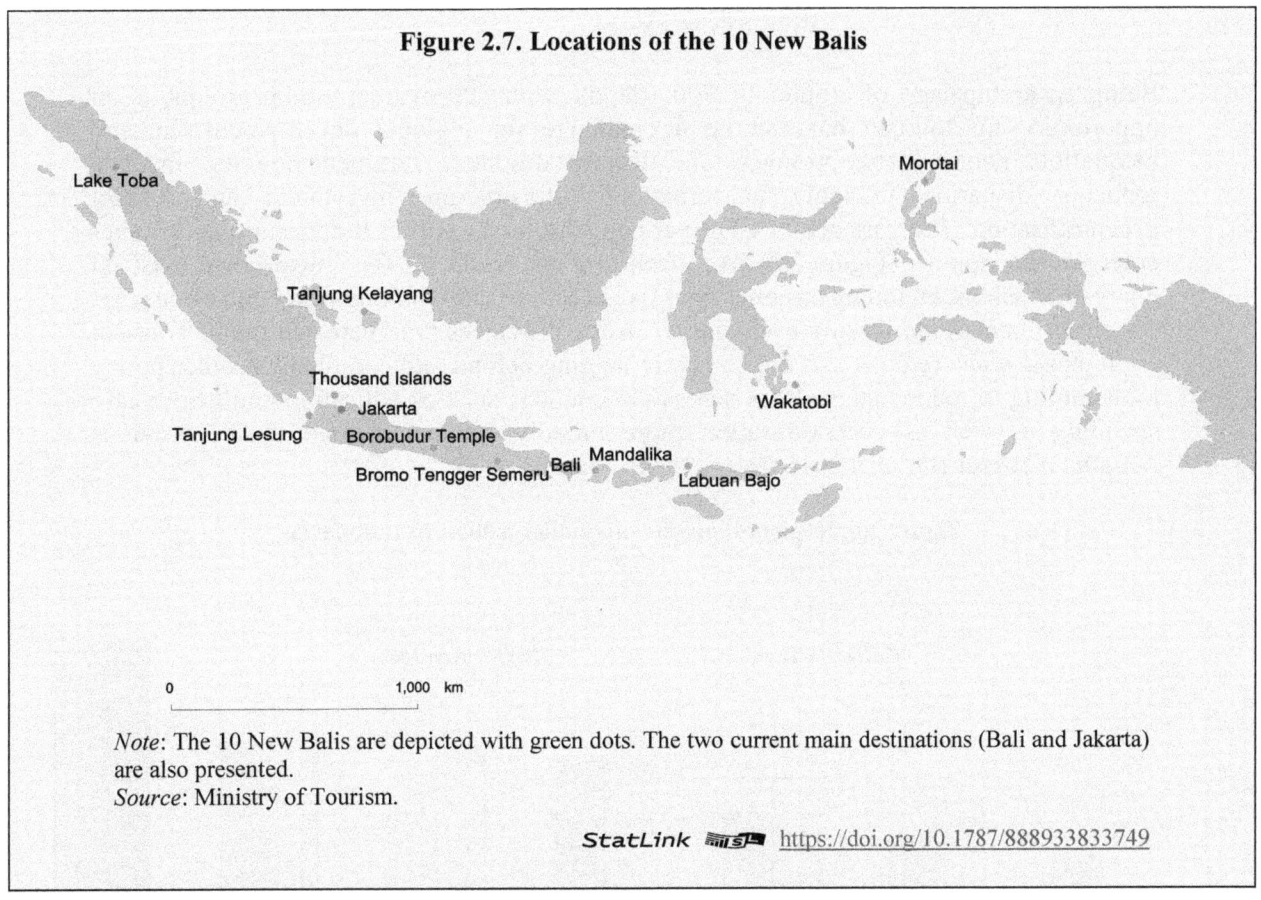

Note: The 10 New Balis are depicted with green dots. The two current main destinations (Bali and Jakarta) are also presented.
Source: Ministry of Tourism.

StatLink https://doi.org/10.1787/888933833749

The Ministry of Tourism is the lead institution for developing tourism in Indonesia. Its budget quadrupled in 2015 to IDR 1.2 trillion (about USD 80 million, less than 1% of public expenditure) mostly to improve tourism promotion (although it was cut by 30% in 2017). Marketing includes 100 *Pesona Indonesia* events for domestic visitors and 100 *Wonderful Indonesia* events for foreign tourists. WEF (2017) ranked the country's brand strategy 47th for its level of accuracy, ahead of Malaysia (85th) and Thailand (68th). However, the campaign's effectiveness in attracting tourists ranks only 51st, versus 7th for Malaysia and 20th for Thailand. The Ministry of Tourism bases its promotion efforts on market potential, using a weighted average of the number of tourists (40%), the previous rate of growth (30%) and total spending per visitor (30%); the latter favours Europeans because they tend to have a longer stay. At the end of 2017 this formula was prioritising spending on promotion in China, followed by Europe, Australia and Singapore. Digital tools help the Ministry to better focus its strategy (see below).

Another approach used by the authorities to grow the tourism industry is to promote events (Meetings, Incentives, Conferences and Exhibitions, MICE). Development of the MICE sector can bring benefits beyond short-term profits and jobs by adding competitive advantage to destinations and diversifying source markets. MICE can also hasten infrastructure development. In 2018 the biggest events are the summer Asian Games and the October IMF-World Bank annual meeting. For the latter Bank Indonesia estimates that the economic gain will be around IDR 5.7 trillion (nearly 0.1% of GDP), from around 15 000 delegates. The authorities have also promoted packages for attendees to visit other parts of the country. With MICE, it is crucial to ensure that the supporting infrastructure is in place and that relevant facilities are optimally utilised afterwards.

Boosting regional development through tourism

Being an archipelago of around 17 500 islands, with 300 distinct ethnic groups, is an opportunity for tourism but can be a challenge for regional development. Income inequalities persist across provinces and districts despite government policies aimed at reducing disparities, notably in terms of infrastructure investment and budget decentralisation. The variance in GDP per capita is larger within Indonesia than in other emerging economies (Figure 2.8). As discussed in OECD (2016a), disparities exist on many dimensions, including basic services like access to safe drinking water and electricity. Those differences are usually even starker inside provinces than between them. Tourism could boost some regions that are currently lagging behind and complement other policy tools aiming to reduce inequalities across the country, such as education and health care spending as well as decentralisation more broadly, as documented in the previous *Economic Survey* (OECD, 2016a).

Figure 2.8. Regional income inequality is high in Indonesia

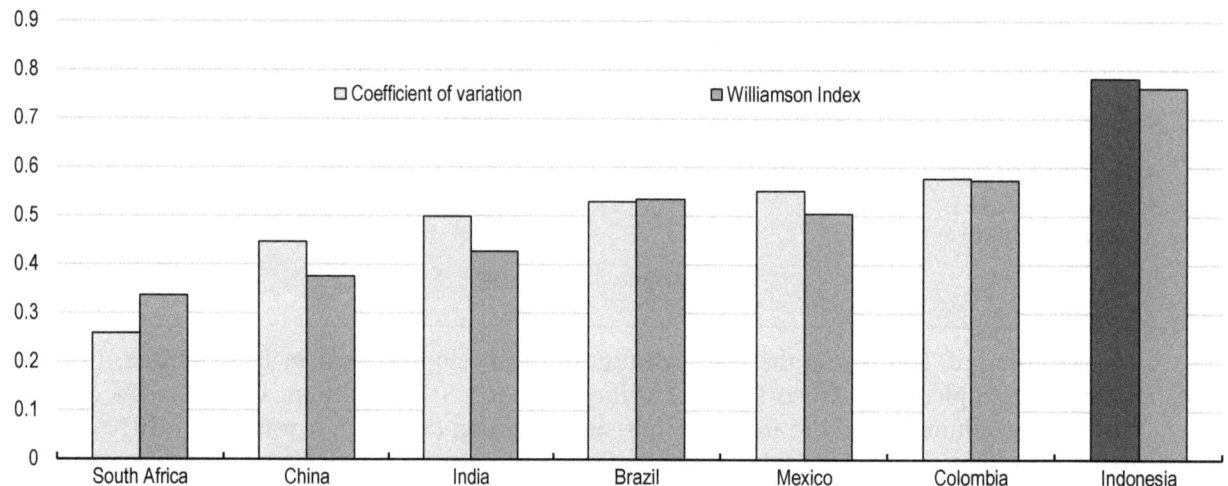

Note: The coefficient of variation is unweighted. The Williamson index is a similar measure of variance that weights regions by their share of the national population. Regional GDP per capita data are for 2016 for Indonesia and Mexico, 2015 for Colombia, 2014 for Brazil and 2013 for China and India.
Source: Statistics Indonesia; OECD, *OECD Regional Database*; OECD calculations.

StatLink ⟨⟩ https://doi.org/10.1787/888933833293

Building relevant infrastructure will be crucial for scaling up tourism

Achieving the planned growth of tourism requires substantial investment in infrastructure, notably in the area of transport connectivity. Transportation across Indonesia by road, sea and air has historically been difficult (OECD, 2016a). The government has pushed up public infrastructure investment, also supported by state-owned enterprises' active involvement. For example, 7 airports were recently built and 8 additional ones are planned by 2019 which should expand tourism to new regions; 27 airports have also been upgraded with runway extensions. However, the profitability of some projects is low in some remote regions. While infrastructure should also take into account the needs of local communities, tourism can be one way to improve returns on relevant infrastructure.

The close interdependence of transport and tourism activities requires coherence in policy formation, notably in terms of planning. Synergies between transport and tourism can improve visitor mobility and satisfaction, and help to secure the economic viability of local transport systems by servicing both residents and tourists. At a national level, rail, road, cruise and aviation policies are usually developed within separate Indonesian agencies in relatively segregated processes, even though there are consultative mechanisms that aim to facilitate communication and co-ordination. The effectiveness of information exchange and learning across policy sectors determines how transport interests are taken on board in tourism policies and how tourism interests are in transport policies (Haxton, 2015). For example, in Switzerland, various working groups, comprised of representatives of the tourism industry, cantons, municipalities and the federal administration identify challenges and develop potential solutions around the Tourism Forum Switzerland.

Infrastructure needs are enormous compared to government funding capacity. For example, it takes about 14 hours to drive the 810 kilometres from Jakarta to Surabaya, the second largest city. Needs are also important because the population is scattered across many islands (mostly Java, Sumatra, Kalimantan and Sulawesi). Adequate prioritisation is thus key. However, the selection of public investment projects in Indonesia suffers from a lack of transparency (World Bank, 2018a). Pre-feasibility studies and selection criteria are also not systematically applied. International best practice highlights the importance of socio-economic cost-benefit analysis to improve government decision-making, even though broader impacts should also be incorporated, such as the implications for relocation and reorganisation of households and businesses (ITF, 2017). Long-lived assets are especially risky and uncertain; thus, strategic planning by the central government with clear objectives is crucial to complement project-by-project assessment. Analytical tools such as scenario-based approaches – to include finance ability, public acceptance and sustainability – are also useful to assess project quality.

The emphasis on the initial investment should be complemented by attention to the future phases of the project lifecycle, including operation, maintenance and disposal (OECD, 2017a). Poor maintenance and operation weigh on quality and durability of infrastructure. For example, Jakarta's airport has a rating based on user reviews of only 65% compared with 80% for Bangkok and 94% for Singapore (Flightradar24, 2018). Skytrax (2018) ranks Jakarta's airport 44th out of 100 international airports, while Singapore's is 1st, Kuala Lumpur's 35th and Bangkok's 38th. Recent renovations at 12 airports should improve their quality. Road transport is also affected by a lack of proper maintenance. For example, in some provinces more than half of the roads are in disrepair due to co-ordination issues, ineffective planning and weak capacity in some institutions (OECD, 2016a).

New planned infrastructure should be built with ambitious targets of high-quality services, and existing facilities must be properly maintained to ensure their longevity and quality. Indonesia should conduct analysis of its infrastructure assets over their whole life cycle to monitor their state, as, for example, Turkey is doing (OECD, 2017a). Some government initiatives have already aimed to improve the management of roads with an asset-management system (James, 2016). In addition it is now possible to use private firms for maintenance. The government is also planning to contract out the operation of some airports, which could improve their efficiency.

Land acquisition difficulties have been the main reason for delays of many infrastructure projects. For instance, the 75km Batang-Semarang toll road was scheduled to open in 2018, but construction started in 2006, as various land acquisition issues slowed down the project; by end September the road was 88% complete (Jakarta Globe, 2018a; Kompas, 2018).

Several recent government economic policy packages have sought to ease land acquisition and the granting of permits (OECD, 2016a). The Land Acquisition Law (Presidential Regulation 71/2012), effective as of 2015, was an important improvement as it limits the procedure for land acquisition to 583 days and allows for revocation of private land rights in the public interest (PwC, 2016). In addition, the State Asset Management Agency (LMAN) has been capitalised with USD 2.5 billion to finance the acquisition of land for priority projects: the costs incurred for acquiring the land are reimbursed by LMAN when construction commences. Planning, capacity building, co-ordination between the central and sub-national governments together with law enforcement all need to improve. The lack of consolidated and accepted land-tenure information would be addressed by the rapid implementation of the One Map policy (a unique cadastre for Indonesia), which was launched in late 2015 and is to be completed by 2019.

Other infrastructure also matters. For example, waste and water treatment are important to ensure the sustainability of tourism (more below). In addition, internet access is increasingly a necessity. Indonesia's geography hampers easy deployment of optical fibre across the country, as it often implies crossing seas. The launch of Project Loom for Indonesia in 2015 may facilitate reaching remote and rural areas using balloons. However, the project appears to be making only slow progress. Some reports also point to the lack of ATMs in tourist areas; also, even when present, they often malfunction or do not accept foreign cards. In that regard, WEF (2017) reports that Thailand had twice as many ATMs per person, with 113 versus 55 per 100 000 adult population. In the end, the infrastructure needed to support significant and sustainable tourism growth is sizeable and will take years to be in place. Private investment has an important role to play. The focus of the government on four "new Balis" (Box 2.2) is a positive step, even though sustainability remains an issue (see below). Better planning will help reduce the major gaps (see below). The authorities should also continue removing hurdles for private investment, notably law and regulatory complexity, and improving the depth of local banking and capital markets.

Private infrastructure is also lacking in some areas. To accompany tourism targets, the medium-term government plan called for an additional 120 000 hotel rooms, 15 000 restaurants, 10 000 travel agencies, 300 international-class recreation parks, 2 000 diving operators and 100 marinas. To achieve these targets barriers to investment need to be removed and a more business-friendly environment supported (see below).

Tourism can generate employment opportunities in more areas

Statistics Indonesia produces tourism satellite accounts that indicate that tourism is labour intensive as it represented 10.4% of total employment and 4.3% of GDP in 2015 (compared to 6.8% and 4.3%, respectively, on average in the OECD). In 2016, employment in tourism-related activities increased further to reach 12.3% of total employment. Using that ratio for 2015 (employment over GDP) as a simple rule of thumb implies that additional activity in tourism will add at least twice as many jobs as an equal expansion in all sectors. The ILO (2011) also estimated that one extra job in Indonesia's core tourism industry (hotels and restaurants) indirectly generates roughly 1.5 additional jobs in the related economy. Overall, this implies that the tourism sector has huge job-creation potential. But this potential varies across regions. Using the share of workers in hotels, restaurants, wholesale and retail as a proxy – reveals huge differences (Figure 2.9). To some extent that can be partly explained by the level of income: a richer population spends more on services. A recent study highlighted that the employment multiplier, measuring the impact of one additional unit of final aggregate demand on regional employment, for the tourism-related sector is for instance over three times higher in East Nusa Tenggara than in Jakarta

(Faturay, Lenzen and Nugraha, 2017). There is an opportunity to develop tourism in areas with higher leverage on employment when such development is sustainable (see below).

The range of skills levels available in Indonesia corresponds well to the needs of the tourism sector, as tourism-related industries employ a relative high share of low-skilled workers (Figure 2.10). In Bali, the share of high-skilled workers in accommodation and food services is much higher: 17.5% compared to 5.5% at the national level; the share of low-skilled workers is also much lower in Bali at 37% compared to 60% for Indonesia. Bali's success in promoting higher-skilled jobs in tourism could be emulated, suggesting the potential for tourism development to not only provide job opportunities, but also to allow workers to climb the skills ladder. The sector is also well suited for women, young people and disadvantaged groups such as ethnic-minority populations (Ashley, Boyd and Goodwin, 2000). Some jobs can also be part-time and supplement income from other activities. The variety of jobs and the flexibility of the sector make it a natural and efficient tool for regional development.

Figure 2.9. Share of employment in the wholesale, retail, restaurant and hotel sectors

By province, 2017

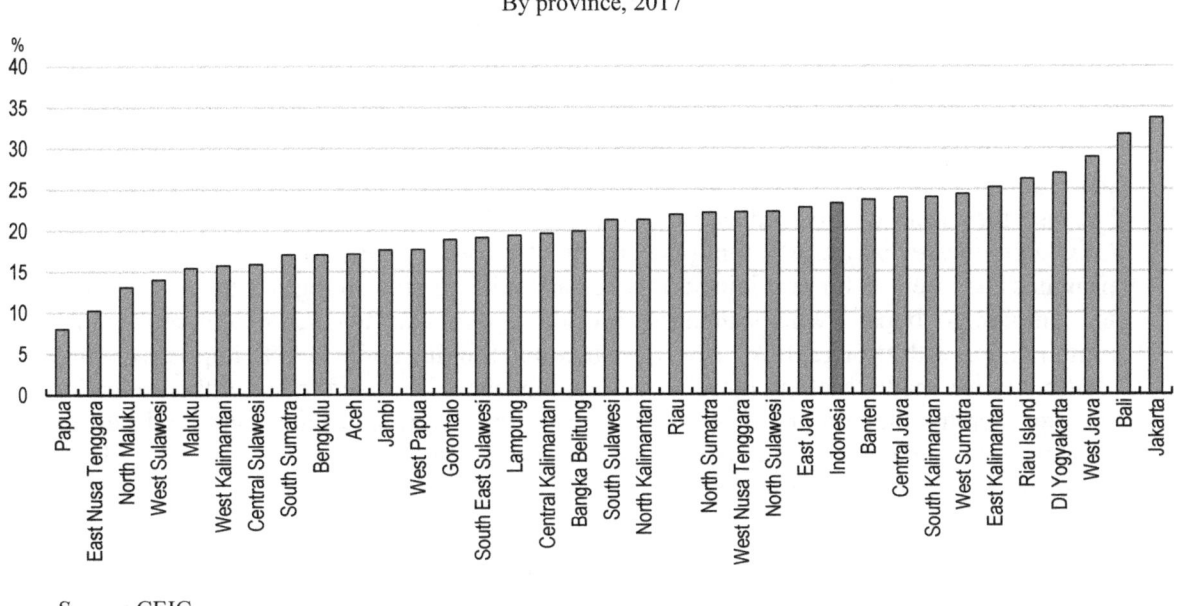

Source: CEIC.

StatLink https://doi.org/10.1787/888933833768

Figure 2.10. Educational attainment of employees across sectors
In percent, 2017

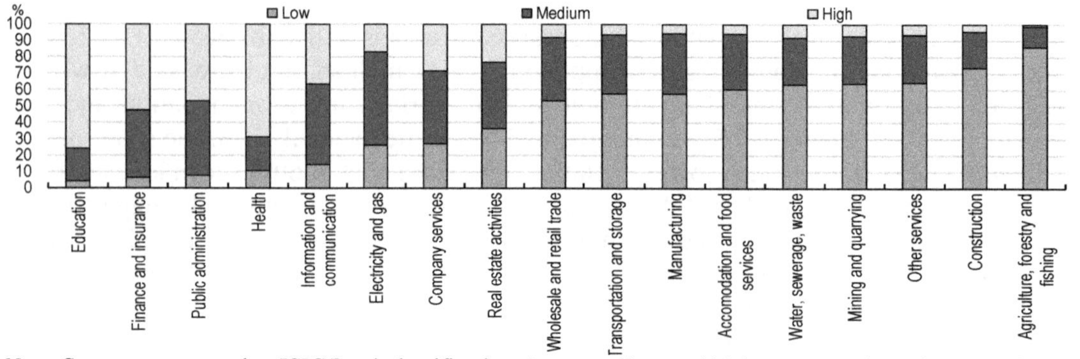

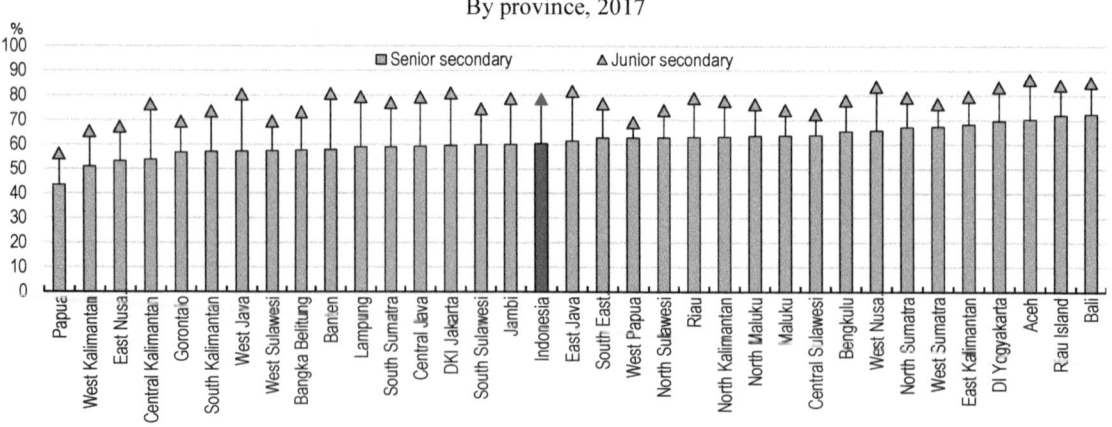

Note: Sectors correspond to ISIC Rev4 classification. Low, medium and high correspond to primary, to lower secondary and upper secondary and to tertiary educational attainment, respectively.
Source: Statistics Indonesia, *SAKERNAS Database*; and OECD calculations.

StatLink ⫘⫘ https://doi.org/10.1787/888933833787

The quality of human resources is weighing on Indonesia's ranking in tourism competitiveness compared to Singapore, Malaysia, Viet Nam, Thailand and the Philippines (WEF, 2017) (see Figure 2.1 above). This is partly related to lower educational attainment. Enrolment in primary education has improved nationwide and completion is close to universal, but stark differences remain across provinces in secondary education, likely hiding even larger disparities inside provinces (Figure 2.11). In 2016 a survey highlighted that tourism-related businesses in APEC economies have difficulties recruiting staff because they lack a proper education (APEC, 2017). As recommended in the previous OECD *Economic Survey*, improving the quality of secondary education, especially in some provinces, is essential for providing the necessary skills to give all regions the wherewithal to continue to boost living standards. Introducing regular teacher evaluations and a remuneration with stronger links to performance and training could help to improve quality. Better pay has made teaching more attractive; this should be used to strengthen selection into teacher training programmes so that over time retiring teachers are replaced by increasingly committed and competent teachers. Moreover, by improving basic competencies, more Indonesians will be able to upgrade their skills throughout their adult lives.

Figure 2.11. Net enrolment ratio in lower secondary schools

By province, 2017

Source: Statistics Indonesia.

StatLink ⫘⫘ https://doi.org/10.1787/888933833806

Going forward, there could be massive numbers of vacancies for various positions in tourism and intense global competition to recruit workers with necessary competencies; however, there are no official reports on the sector's current labour needs in Indonesia. The large tourism workforce in Bali is sometimes used to provide missing skilled workers, but training the local population would be preferable in the medium term. The authorities should promote the monitoring of shortages and give the education system enough flexibility to adapt curricula and class sizes quickly. This could be facilitated by setting up a national information service beyond the tourism sector that provides up-to-date labour market information for all involved parties including students and teachers (OECD/ADB, 2015). Such a system can take the form of a website providing trends in demand and supply by occupation, industry and district, complemented with skills shortages and surpluses. Information on occupation remuneration and requirements in terms of qualifications and experience could also contribute to increase the flexibility of the system. For example, ministries of education and labour in Peru provide data on the cost and employment outcomes at all higher-education institutions (McCarthy and Musset, 2016).

It is crucial to involve local communities more heavily in the development of tourism and eventually contribute to improving the matching between job opportunities and the skills of the local population. The government has launched several higher-education institutions specialised in tourism close to major tourist destinations. The government is now developing vocational higher-education institutions in Lombok, Medan and Palembang where there is evidence of skill shortages. There are plans to build similar institutions in Kalimantan, West Papua and Manado. There are also some specific projects like WISATA (with support from Switzerland) that aim to develop tourism education at vocational schools in some regions (Swisscontact, 2016). Nevertheless, co-ordination and capacity issues in Indonesia are slowing down progress in that direction. More consultation and collaboration with local authorities would help them to build their capacity to implement and monitor education reforms (OECD/ADB, 2015). One complementary solution could be to have a centralised pool of teachers and curricula to send directly to priority destinations. The Egyptian Tourism Workforce Development project, which aims at providing better levels of service and food safety in 12 tourism regions, addressed similar constraints by using mobile hospitality master trainers (Stacey, 2015).

Further investment in vocational education and training (VET) is important to meet the growing needs of the tourism sector. Indonesia has one of the highest rates of secondary school VET enrolment, with 45% of upper secondary students enrolled in VET in 2015, up from 20% in 2005 (ADB, 2018). However, the authorities should better monitor these schools, including private ones (as they are the major providers of education and training in tourism) since employers report that many graduates lack relevant skills (Kadir, Nirvansyah and Bachrul, 2016). Setting up regular retraining programmes for teachers would reduce the shortage of high-quality vocational teachers and lecturers. Training new and adequate teachers will become increasingly important to accompany the growth of the tourism sector. VET is also more expensive than academic education in Indonesia (at least twice as costly), which means that spending efficiency should be improved (OECD, 2016a). The government could introduce tools to measure activities to allow for benchmarking (OECD/ADB, 2015).

Tightening the relationship between firms and the education system could allow early detection of skills shortages and improve course content in VET. Brazil's experience with *Pronatec* – a publicly-funded programme that supports private and public vocational training courses – could provide useful insights. That system is more flexible because it is outside the main education system and tries to link training places in each region with skills needs using explicit requests from individual businesses (O'Connell et al., 2017). The Indonesian government is committed to promoting more vocational training and aims to train 1 million students in 2018 notably by having schools and firms signing agreements. This should benefit tourism too. The authorities should also promote work placements as a way to improve the school-to-work transition. Further developing on-the-job training is also crucial to allow for career progression and new technology adoption.

There are currently not enough incentives for employer involvement in tourism-related VET (Kadir, Nirvansyah and Bachrul, 2016), notably because the sector relies heavily on casual and temporary staff (Stacey, 2015). The focus is then more on initial skills provision rather than on up-skilling. One particular issue with the involvement of firms in VET is the fear that trained people leave the firm or the area after completing training. There could be more information to employers on the benefits of skills development for service quality and competitiveness. A tax incentive for providing training is also planned.

In the tourism sector mastering foreign languages is particularly important. For example, because of the language barrier Singaporeans tend to prefer Malaysia as holiday destination rather than Indonesia (Indonesia-Investments, 2016). English is important, but given that the country aims to attract more tourists from China, Mandarin training courses should also be further developed, especially in areas where China is a large and growing source market.

The use of foreign workers could be facilitated to help mitigate near-term skills shortages. The 2012 ASEAN mutual recognition agreements ease the procedure to recruit foreign tourism experts. More advertisements of that agreed procedure could encourage firms to use those opportunities more, for example to attract English-speaking Filipinos or Malaysians. The recent initiative, led by Indonesia, that facilitates mutual recognition of skilled workers amongst the members of the Organisation for Islamic Co-operation is also welcome (OIC, 2018). In addition, there are costs implied by migration, which are particularly high in APEC economies, notably due to fees charged by agents, intermediaries, travel agents and officials that are involved in the recruitment process. This represents a barrier to recruitment and reduces the demand for migrants (APEC, 2017). The government should promote and ease foreign migration as a tool to mitigate shortages of high-skilled workers in the tourism sector in the near term.

Improving the business environment to boost entrepreneurship

The tourism industry is characterised by the importance of micro and small firms: on average in OECD countries nearly half of all employees in accommodation and food services work in firms with 1-9 workers (nearly 60% for Turkey) (Stacey, 2015). A stable and conducive business environment can enable quick and robust growth in the number of firms in the tourism industry since not much capital is required. The environment in Indonesia has improved vastly: the 2015 World Bank Enterprise Survey shows that the average time to obtain an operating licence was reduced from 21 days in 2009 to just 6 in 2015 and is now much lower than the average for East Asia and Pacific (19 days) and lower-middle-income countries (22 days). Similarly, Indonesia's Ease of Doing Business ranking has improved considerably from 122nd in 2010 to 72nd in 2018. However, some issues remain and drag down its relative position; for example, even if getting an operating licence has become easier, starting a business and enforcing contracts are still complex (Table 2.2). Effective regulations are important to support tourism, especially regarding health and safety conditions in hotels, restaurants and transport.

Table 2.2. Ease of doing business

Ranking in 2018

	Malaysia	Thailand	Viet Nam	**Indonesia**	China	India	Philippines
Aggregate rank	24	26	68	**72**	78	100	113
Starting a business	111	36	123	**144**	93	156	173
Construction permits	11	43	20	**108**	172	181	101
Getting electricity	8	13	64	**38**	98	29	31
Registering property	42	68	63	**106**	41	154	114
Getting credit	20	42	29	**55**	68	29	142
Protecting minority investors	4	16	81	**43**	119	4	146
Paying taxes	73	67	86	**114**	130	119	105
Trading across borders	61	57	94	**112**	97	146	99
Enforcing contracts	44	34	66	**145**	5	164	149
Resolving insolvency	46	26	129	**38**	56	103	59

Note: Countries are ordered by the aggregate ranking. Indonesia's ranking is based on Jakarta and Surabaya.
Source: World Bank, *Ease of Doing Business Database*.

The authorities are developing some tourist destinations as Special Economic Zones (SEZs), which removes the local government's administrative burden. Amongst the 10 priority destinations, only some will be SEZs. In practice, SEZs can compete with another part of the same province for the same industry, potentially generating significant distortions. There is a risk that using SEZs bypasses the spirit of decentralisation and disconnects local governments from economic development in their areas. The previous *Economic Survey* argued that SEZs could serve to pilot new regulations, notably related to employment, but so far no such experimentation has taken place (OECD, 2016a). In parallel, to remove the need for SEZs, local governments should continue easing the administrative burden. To that end, the launch in June 2018 of the online single-submission system for all licensing and permits is most welcome even though its implementation is still in train. It is crucial that implementation be evaluated to ensure that it works well. More specifically related to tourism, the authorities could designate a central contact person in the government to assist proponents of significant tourism investments, as done in Australia (OECD, 2018a).

A more dynamic business environment would allow new linkages across different sectors to emerge more easily, for instance connecting farmers with restaurants, hotels with restaurants and transport (taxis, buses, boats) with accommodation. More information to tourists could also increase their satisfaction and create more opportunities for the sector. The integration of tourism activities in domestic value chains can foster activity and productivity. Bundling attractions and services together can increase visitors' spending by providing diverse tourism services and encouraging longer stays and facilitating access to local culture, which is the primary purpose for around 60% of visitors (see above). One way to achieve this is to improve tourist information and service centres, which rank poorly (96th) in the WEF (2017) tourism competitiveness indicators. Tourist information centres are a hub for reliable information and offer local knowledge to create packages. Financing for information centres could come from local government, visitors and local firms. Extra services could complement the trusted standard information for visitors, for instance ATMs, local artists' exhibitions and free Internet. In Australia tourist information centres have been shown to extend the time and money spent by visitors who appreciate local content (Ballantyne, Hughes and Ritchie, 2009). Districts could create such centres with provincial co-ordination and promotion on provincial websites.

Another approach is to encourage the expansion of the creative economy. In tourism, creative industries are knowledge-based activities "that link producers, consumers and locations by utilising technology, talent or skill to generate intangible cultural products, creative content and experiences" (OECD, 2014a). The creative economy can help offer new products and services for new target groups away from conventional models of environmental or heritage-based cultural tourism: that can be through unconventional media advertisements, arts creation in a specific building, and sound-and-light shows. Increasingly visitors are looking for experience-based, instead of destination-based, tourism. However, in Indonesia, the tourism-related creative economy mainly exists in the more service-based Javanese and Balinese economies, as they have access to a more highly educated workforce (Fahmi, Koster and van Dijk, 2016). Other places can leverage the diversity of their cultures and use a more traditional approach to attract visitors. Local governments can provide a platform – which can be a tourist service centre – to exhibit local arts and crafts, products and services.

Access to finance for small and medium-sized enterprises (SMEs) has improved across the board, notably driven by the KUR programme and the recent regulation requiring banks to dedicate at least 20% of their business loans to SMEs (OECD, 2018b). That can spur more start-ups and business dynamism in the tourism sector, of which the great majority are micro and small enterprises. However, banks holding more risk may increase lending interest rates in response. The lack of collateral and seasonal nature of tourism often drives difficulties for small enterprises seeking bank lending, all the more so given high rates of informality and extensive use of cash, which prevent many people from building a credit history. Indeed, in 2015 66% of SME business investment was financed by internal resources (*ibid*). In addition to the establishment of a collateral registry, a recent regulation by the banking regulator (OJK) requires banks to concentrate on business revenues in the loan decision-making process in the absence of collateral, while sub-national government entities offer guarantees to compensate for any such absence. However, further clarifying land property rights and developing credit bureaus would also be beneficial.

Foreign direct investment (FDI) could complement domestic capital to grow the tourism industry more quickly, given the sizeable investment gap. Foreign investors in the tourism sector can be more robust and stable than their domestic counterparts as they have more capital and experience (UNCTAD, 2007). FDI can also bring in new technologies and skills, including advanced management, environmental and financial systems. Foreign firms often generate proportionally more employment than local ones and tend to offer higher wages as on average they offer higher-quality services (*ibid*). However, restrictions to FDI in Indonesia remain relatively high compared to similar countries, as the negative investment list restricts foreign equity in certain sectors (OECD, 2016a).

Constraints on FDI are particularly significant in the transport sector and less so for hotels and restaurants (Figure 2.12). Foreign land ownership restrictions also put constraints on the development of hotels and restaurants although a right to build can be issued to foreign companies for 30 years (renewable for 20 years). Those in turn affect the development of tourism. For example, foreign ownership of airports is limited to 49%. In practice, none of the existing airports has any private capital, even though the President of Indonesia expressed interest in their privatisation. In the example of the recently constructed Kertajati airport, a regionally owned enterprise (PT BIJB) is participating in the project, illustrating a new approach with co-operation between the different levels of government and an enterprise (Jakarta Globe, 2018b). The development of airports could be faster if more foreign private investors were encouraged to participate, including by further revising the negative investment list. Removing limitations on foreign land ownership would also facilitate FDI.

Figure 2.12. Restrictions on foreign direct investment across emerging market economies

FDI Regulatory Restrictiveness Index from 0 (open) to 1 (closed), 2017

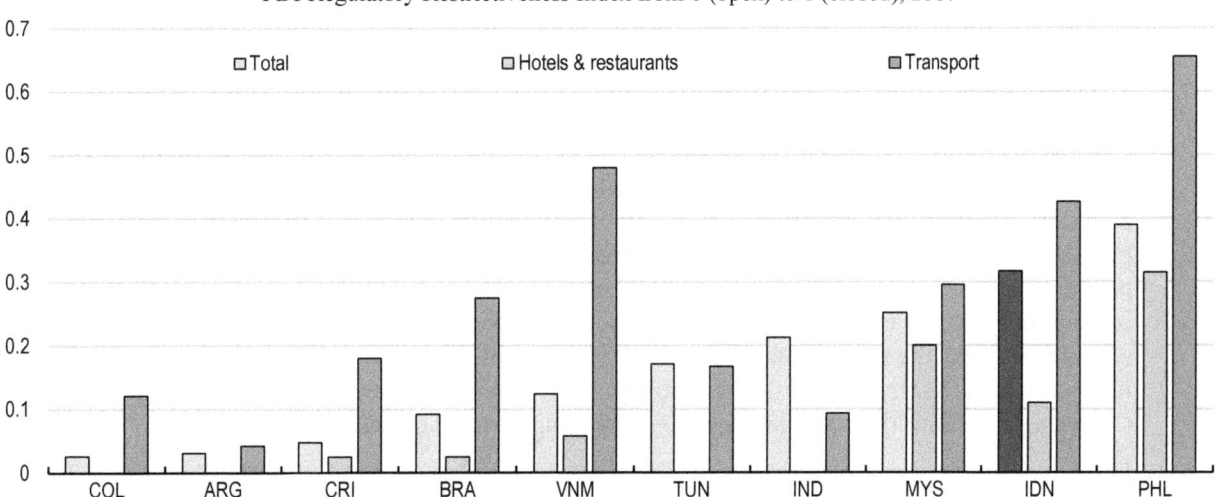

Note: The FDI Regulatory Restrictiveness Index measures statutory restrictions on foreign direct investment across 22 economic sectors. It gauges the restrictiveness of a country's FDI rules by looking at the four main types of restrictions on FDI: 1) foreign equity limitations; 2) discriminatory screening or approval mechanisms; 3) restrictions on the employment of foreigners as key personnel; and 4) other operational restrictions, e.g. on branching and on capital repatriation or on land ownership by foreign-owned enterprises.
Source: OECD, *FDI Regulatory Restrictiveness Index Database*.

StatLink https://doi.org/10.1787/888933833350

Firms in the tourism industry also face challenges with respect to taxation (Chapter 1). The administrative burden discourages firm registration. A turnover tax, introduced in 2013, aims to ease the burden for small firms, but the regime could focus more narrowly on very small firms, linked to additional non-financial support to encourage their participation. Many services are subject to a withholding tax on total revenue if the client elects to use this option. Tax from rental incomes, for instance through the sharing economy, is always fixed at 10%, whatever the person's income situation. Hotels and restaurants are exempted from the value-added tax (VAT), but pay a local sales tax usually at the same rate. That means that they pay more tax than with a VAT system as VAT is included in their inputs. In practice compliance rates are low. The tax regime would improve by shortening the list of exemptions. Merging the regimes into a fair and simple tax system would make compliance easier. Compensation through transfers for the sales tax would avoid a loss of revenues for local governments (Chapter 1).

Reaping the benefits of digitalisation

Digitalisation is a global phenomenon affecting all industries, including tourism. It changes the ways of doing business even for traditional players, including via the convergence of networks, the increasing connectivity of devices and changes in social interaction (OECD, 2018c). Some estimates evaluate the resulting gain for Indonesia at about 10% of GDP over 10 years (Das et al., 2016). The process of digitalisation as it applies to tourism is already well underway and provides tourism operators with direct access to international markets and customers. In Indonesia 80% of tourists use digital media to search destinations and share their experiences (ITX, 2018). One of the most visible changes is the development of online travel agents and digital platforms that intermediate between customers and providers like hotels, restaurants or taxis. Ongoing digitalisation of many other sectors – logistics, transport, culture, retail, finance – is also affecting the tourism sector, such as through cashless payments.

Digitalisation is an opportunity to attract more visitors, to increase competition, and to create jobs (OECD, 2017b). The growth of the digital economy challenges regulators to balance stimulating innovation and promoting tourism against the need to protect consumers and ensure a level regulatory playing field for traditional businesses (OECD, 2016b). Through digitalisation new products and services are created to expand supply. One case in point is the sharing economy; that is, the temporary sharing by individuals of what they own (for example, their car or their house) or do (for example, making meals or providing excursions). It establishes a direct connection between visitors and the local population, which can foster a feeling of ownership of tourism development. When such products or services meet demands that were not satisfied, the economic effect is undoubtedly positive. Some of them are developing only slowly, however, as Indonesia sometimes lacks the relevant facilities. For example, mobile payments are developing fast internationally, with 65% of Chinese tourists using them during overseas travel in 2017 (Nielsen, 2018) but their availability is still lagging in most of Indonesia.

Digital platforms are an example of one area developing particularly quickly: in 2017 Airbnb's 11 200 hosts received a median income of USD 2 100 (which is similar to the median income in Thailand and above that in the Philippines, Malaysia and Vietnam), adding up to a total of USD 85 million (Airbnb, 2017). The 900 000 guests represented a 69% increase over 2016. Airbnb is also estimated to have supported 48 100 jobs in 2016 across three Indonesian destinations – the highest for the firm amongst the 21 APEC countries excluding the United States (*ibid*). The government should work with digital platforms on how tax compliance can be best assured, looking at examples in other countries such as India.

Foreign and domestic tourists' use of the Internet is increasing rapidly, notably via mobile phones. It provides a strong argument for the expansion of infrastructure to offer similar service in tourist areas as in major cities – with benefits flowing to local residents as well as visitors. Notably, better reach and reliability of 4G technology would be beneficial as well as investing in 5G technology. In many destinations the uptake of digital technologies by tourism businesses and the provision of basic features, such as online booking and payment facilities, are limited by the available infrastructure and the necessary skills to fully reap the associated benefits. Their usage is unequal around the country. According to the Indonesia Internet Service Providers Association, nearly 55% of the population used the Internet in 2017, with a large gap between urban (72%) and rural areas (48%) (APJII, 2017). The gap is a sign of demand weakness but also supply constraints, which weigh on regional development. To alleviate inequality the government committed to offer fixed broadband with speeds of at least 2 Mb to all government offices, hotels, hospitals, schools and public spaces by 2019 (Andrews et al., 2018). That is welcome and can generate spillovers to surrounding areas. Wireless broadband internet can be easier to deploy in remote locations. As this expands it will reduce the gap between rural and urban areas.

More competition in the telecommunications market would encourage innovation, expand supply and hold down retail prices. According to the OECD's product market regulation indicators, competition in the telecommunications sector is limited; Indonesia has the most restrictive environment across all countries covered (Koske et al., 2015). The sector is highly concentrated with the largest company having more than half of the market share. The degree of public ownership is also relatively high. Regulatory restrictions, notably in the number of competitors, further limit competition. Lifting entry barriers and reducing government influence over PT Telkom Indonesia could encourage new entrants and greater innovation.

The Indonesian government was an early adopter of digital information systems to promote tourism. The Ministry of Tourism dedicated 30% of its 2016 budget to digital promotion with an objective of reaching 50% (Tempo, 2017). The Ministry has developed a digital dashboard to monitor Indonesia's tourism reputation on social media on a daily basis (at national and destination levels). The system compares the country with its nearby competitors to assess its relative performance. In addition, mobile positioning systems are utilised to monitor the number and distribution of tourists. This information allows decision makers to better understand visitor flows and perceptions, respond to issues as they arise and make better informed marketing decisions. In 2016 the Ministry launched Indonesia Travel X-Change (ITX), a business-to-business platform that helps connect sellers of tourism products and services with buyers (travel agents). The system provides a booking and online payment system plus analytical tools, and eases communication between sellers and buyers (Nurdin, 2018). However it is still being developed and manages only 2 270 rooms in 28 destinations. The platform should be finalised quickly and advertised more widely.

Digitalisation and the need to be visible to potential customers can also foster the formalisation of tourism-related businesses. Excessive bureaucracy tends to increase the share of the informal sector. The authorities could develop and promote online mobile applications for easing administrative tasks, for example to file income tax and VAT (Chapter 1). Initiatives such as the one by Bank Indonesia to create a mobile application (SI APIK) for small firms are welcome: standard and validated accounts and various financial reports, for example, are now much easier to produce for companies whose managers have low numeracy skills. Other applications could be developed, such as for paying local licence fees.

Ensuring growth in tourism is sustainable

Indonesia committed to achieving the United Nations Sustainable Development Goals (SDGs), which include eradicating poverty, improving health and education, achieving gender equality and protecting environmental assets. The development of tourism can directly contribute to all of the SDGs and especially in: "decent work and economic growth" (goal 8), "responsible consumption and production" (goal 12) and "life below water" (goal 14) (OECD, 2018a). Good policy planning is also important to preserve environmental assets.

Tourism and the environment are deeply interconnected

Indonesia's tourism competitiveness is boosted by its exceptional natural resources: it ranks 14th of 136 countries (WEF, 2017), not least thanks to its five Natural UNESCO World Heritage Sites and the sheer number of its known species (Figure 2.13, Panel A). However, Indonesia's overall competitiveness is dragged down by its dismal overall score on environmental sustainability, which leads to its ranking of 131st (see Figure 2.1 above). This poor performance is broad-based across measures of environmental sustainability but driven by the situation of threatened species, the change in forest cover and lack of wastewater treatment (Figure 2.13, Panel B). It is crucial that alterations to natural assets are valued against their potential use, including as a tourism asset. For example, forests and peatlands destroyed with man-made fires to clear land for plantations entail losing much more than only trees and grasses but also the economic returns from their sustainable use. The public value of those assets is higher than the private returns because of externalities and the fact that private actors are not bearing the cost. Given that those fires are prohibited, law enforcement should be stepped up, and campaigns should provide information about the economic loss from the associated environmental damage.

Figure 2.13. Components of tourism competitiveness related to the environment

Ranking out of 136 countries, 2017

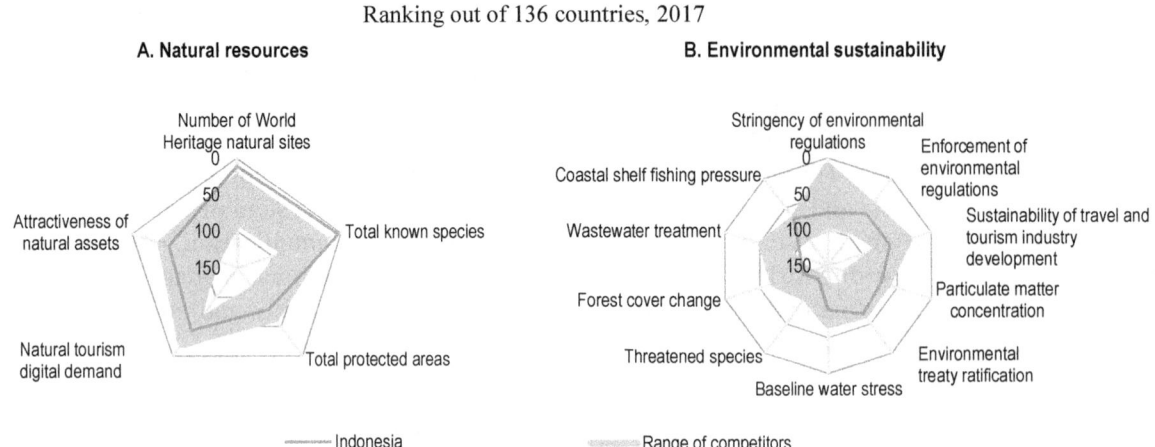

Note: Competitors are a simple average of Malaysia, Philippines, Singapore and Thailand.
Source: WEF, *Travel and Tourism Competitiveness Report 2017*.

StatLink ᵐˢᴾ https://doi.org/10.1787/888933833825

Sustainably developing tourism must take into account the impact of its growth on the environment. Uncontrolled tourism can have a range of negative impacts, including: depleting water resources (especially fresh water); changing land use and degradation; using local food, energy and other raw materials that may already be in short supply; generating air pollution and noise through increased transport; increasing solid waste, litter and sewage; creating aesthetic pollution; and other physical impacts such as construction activities, marina development, anchoring and other marine activities. That points to the need for assessment and monitoring of the environmental situation in each tourist destination, with for instance more involvement of the five Sustainable Tourism Observatories in Indonesia (a global network under UNWTO). In some cases, that would lead to mitigation plans to counteract the degradation. Conversely, tourism, if developed strategically, also has the potential to contribute to environmental protection and conservation. For instance, by raising awareness of environmental values it can serve as a tool to finance protection of natural areas and increase their economic importance.

Most of the expected increase in the volume of tourists will take place in few destinations. Thus, environmental pressures in these locations will be sizeable. For instance, sanitation services are already inadequate (Figure 2.14). In Bali, average daily water consumption per person is 60 litres in rural areas and 120 litres in cities, but tourists consume up to 200 litres, and capacity is already insufficient (Bali, 2015). Meeting the target for visitor numbers could degrade the natural environment, reducing future benefits from tourism. Growing pressures on the environment from mass tourism are already forcing some countries to shut some tourism destinations, at least temporarily. For example, the island of Boracay in the

Philippines (which received 2 million visitors in 2017) is being closed for six months in 2018, and direct boat access to Maya Bay in Thailand is forbidden from June to October 2018 (Jakarta Globe, 2018c). To raise the sustainability of the sector, medium-term planning should gradually refocus on increasing yield rather than numbers of tourists. That also means improving the availability and quality of data to allow accurately gauging such targets. As in New Zealand, the government could also have a fund to support some areas that face pressures from tourism growth and are financially constrained (OECD, 2018a).

Figure 2.14. The coverage of sanitation services is low in many areas

Basic and safely managed sanitation coverage by province, in per cent of the population, 2016

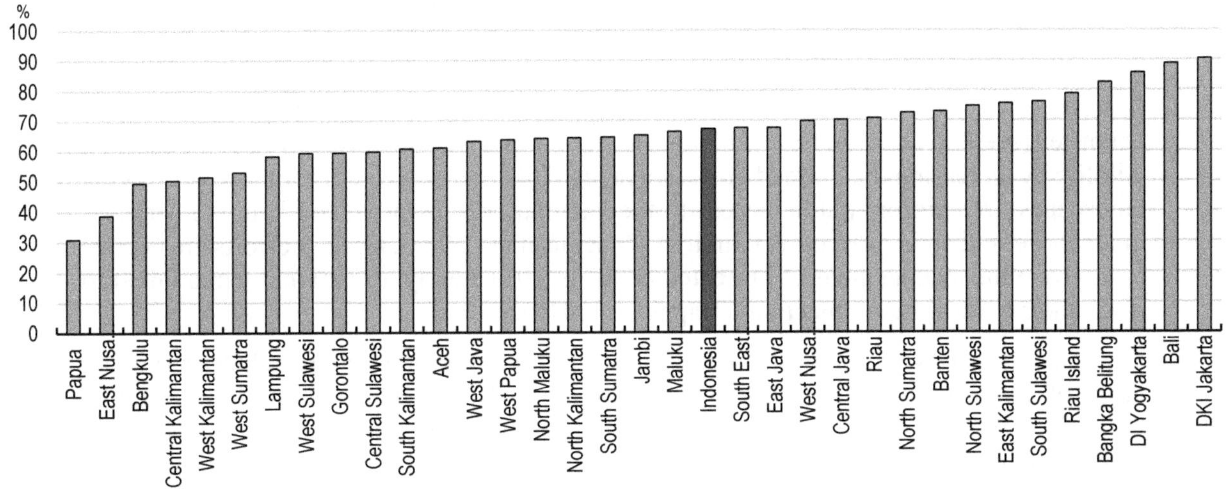

Source: Statistics Indonesia.

StatLink https://doi.org/10.1787/888933833844

Infrastructure projects that raise the number of visitors should be accompanied by other investment needed to support environmental sustainability. For example, when building a new airport that will bring hundreds of thousands of additional tourists, the capacity of waste and water treatment systems should also be raised, all the more so as foreign visitors are especially heavy users of water and producers of waste (Messenger, 2017). According to the Ministry of Environment and Forestry, 48% of the 61 million tonnes of waste produced in 2016 in Indonesia was sent to (mostly non-sanitary) landfills and 29% was unmanaged. Indonesia has become the second-largest contributor to plastic marine pollution with 80% of marine waste coming from improperly disposed waste from land. Coral reefs are consequently the most littered by plastic in the Asia-Pacific region (Lamb et al., 2018), potentially affecting the tourism experience. That suggests the need for appropriate integration of medium-term strategies and sustainability objectives into the plans for all infrastructure projects. An excise tax on plastic bags is planned and would indeed contribute to reduce waste and marine pollution. Introducing a deposit and collection scheme for water bottles would reduce plastic pollution.

Sustainable tourism development will require the integration of responsible consumption and production practices in the sector. Programmes already exist that aim to change tourists' behaviour in terms of water by encouraging guests in hotels to re-use towels rather than have them washed daily, for example. These should be intensified. Good examples of other private-sector initiatives include the lead taken by Chile's tourism association, Fedetur, to develop projects that aim to reduce energy consumption and CO_2 emissions from tourism, and the development of carbon calculators for tour operators and travel companies by the Tourism Institute of Bogota in Colombia. In the Yucatán Peninsula in Mexico, the government provides advice, training and financing to promote green energy (OECD, 2018a). Companies could benefit from such actions, which not only lower their energy costs but enhance their reputations as environmentally friendly operators and attract new customers. More important is to adopt the polluter-pays principle. For example, wastewater discharge monitoring should be stepped up with appropriate fees levied. Likewise, charges for water extraction and supply can help to control water demand and finance new treatment facilities.

There are many opportunities to make better use of environmental assets to attract more visitors while ensuring their preservation for the benefit of future generations. For example, Indonesia is home to 17% of the world's wildlife species but is not protecting them well enough, as evidenced by the megafauna conservation index, which ranks it only 89th (Lindsey et al., 2017). Less than 12% of land is protected, which is low relative to other countries (see Figure 2.13 above). Indonesia should intensify the protection of forests and wildlife by increasing the share of protected areas. This will be also contribute to preserving landscapes. In addition, public access to the vast majority of protected land is restricted, much more so than in most other countries (Mackie et al., 2017). Greater efforts are needed to improve the management of protected areas; in 2011 nearly all national parks failed to reach their conservation objectives (Bappenas, 2016).

The Ministry of Environment and Forestry's 2015-19 medium-term plan includes a specific target of 20 million visitors in conservation areas by 2019, of which 1.5 million would be foreigners. When the area can tolerate tourism activity, visitors should have access. User fees should be introduced and be set high enough to pay for the cost of basic infrastructure, maintenance and conservation, and the number of visitors to sensitive sites should be limited (Box 2.3). Some protected areas in Indonesia are already open with an entrance fee, such as Sungai Wain Protection Forest. The example of the Raja Ampat marine park in West Papua could be more widely replicated: since 2015 international visitors must pay an entry fee of IDR 1 million (USD 67) and Indonesians half as much; the funds are used to cover operational costs of the five marine protected areas, and for conservation and development programmes (Stay Raja Ampat, 2018).

When user fees cannot be set high enough to limit visitors to sustainable limits, infrastructure and regulations could also limit the number of potential visitors and restrict movement within opened protected areas. For example, in the Galapagos Islands, the number of ships allowed to cruise the archipelago is limited. In addition, concession fees could complement revenues and provide services to attract more tourists but with sensible restrictions under appropriate contracts. For some areas like cultural heritage sites, the authorities could encourage private investment to transform them into tourism facilities by granting concession rights free of charge, as practiced in Italy since 2014 (OECD, 2018a).

Ecotourism – visiting relatively undisturbed natural areas with low impact and often at small scale – is a way to promote some less developed regions. Costa Rica has successfully built a strong ecotourism sector by creating a well-recognised green trademark, which has also raised rural incomes through the resulting new job opportunities (OECD, 2016c). In Indonesia, the example of Kalibiru (special province of Yogyakarta) is encouraging: forestland was granted to the community and deforestation was stopped in the context of a small-scale tourism project, with particular attention to sustainability (Vitasurya, 2016). The authorities should encourage the development of small-scale ecotourism projects and provide capacity building and supporting infrastructure (including digital) to promote potential clusters.

Tourism development can have some direct positive environmental impacts. First, the increase in tourism will generate more revenue for all levels of government in terms of taxes, fees and other levies. While earmarking is not usually desirable, these additional revenues can help governments to preserve the environment. Second, tourism also has the potential to increase public appreciation of the environment and to spread awareness of environmental issues, including through greater domestic tourism as occurred in Brazil (OECD, 2015). Finally, the economic interests of the private sector for developing tourism can directly trigger some positive outcomes for the environment. For example, some tour operators are donating to the Sumatran Orangutan Conservation Programme, and Indonesian hotels regularly clean beaches in their vicinity. Efforts of the private sector to contribute to public goods and to co-ordinate with the public sector should be encouraged.

Box 2.3. Tourism in protected areas

Depending on the purpose, protected areas are generally classified under six categories ranging from a site reserved for scientific research and wilderness protection to a natural ecosystem used in a sustainable way (Dudley, Stolton and Shadie, 2013). Many sites are capable of supporting visitors, albeit in different forms, which can generate funds for environmental protection and awareness raising. Finding the right balance between short- to medium-term economic returns and long-term asset preservation will depend on the optimal number of visitors (Daubanes, 2017). Demand for visits increases with environmental quality and uniqueness, but more visitors mean more infrastructure is required, and risks to the quality of the protected area are higher. Eventually overuse leads to degradation, which lowers demand. Different tools can help regulate the volume of tourists and exploit their potential without blighting the future of the protected area:

- Visitor fees, such as for access and for additional activities (e.g. diving, trekking), can generate benefits that help cover the initial set-up costs (to organise facilities for tourists) and operating costs, and can fund environmental protection. The fees can be adapted to users' characteristics; for instance, they can be lower for locals than for foreigners. The price can be adjusted to the season to regulate flows. However, user fees are generally not sufficient to preserve an area, as they do not restrain bad behaviour and may not prevent excessive flows.
- Concession fees can complement revenues to protect the area. In some places private actors could run businesses related to food, lodging, transport, guiding, outdoor activities and retail services. Key challenges are to design adequate frameworks for contracts and then to monitor compliance.
- Specific regulations can be used to limit visitors to carrying capacity such as a maximum number of visitors at any given moment.
- A regulatory framework to control the use of the protected area can take different forms. First, rules are set to limit use and establish a minimum level of protection, but they need enforcement. Second, signs, pathways and similar measures can encourage visitors to follow the right principles. Third, information such as signs and flyers make visitors aware of the consequences of their actions but leaves them more freedom during their visit.

For successful management of protected areas, governments should establish national frameworks that take tourism into account as well as educate local populations and preserve the environment (Eagles, McCool and Haynes, 2002). Each protected area can then establish a management plan under the national policy. Local stakeholders'

---

involvement is important to ensure that they share in the economic benefits of opening up the protected area. Biosphere reserves (11 in Indonesia already) are part of the UNESCO's Man and the Biosphere Programme which aims to achieve the interconnected functions of conservation, development and logistic support, including through a multi-stakeholder approach, zoning schemes and education and training (UNESCO, 2017). Those reserves allow for the development of sustainable tourism and should be promoted.

Improving the planning process to better include local needs

There are three main development plans in Indonesia produced at the central level: long-term (20 years), medium-term (5 years) and short-term (1 year). The current long-term plan (*Rencana Pembangunan Jangka Panjang Nasional*, or RPJPN) covers 2005 to 2025 and is translated into the National Medium-Term Development Plan (*Rencana Pembangunan Jangka Menengah Nasional*, or RPJMN), currently in its third period (2015-19). Most of the SDG targets are aligned with national targets (under the President's agenda, known as "Nawacita", and the Medium-Term Development Plan), thereby securing resources for their achievement. Related tourism planning is also well established (see above). However, despite a highly decentralised system, the connection with sub-national governments is not working efficiently and local needs are then not sufficiently taken into account. The monitoring of sub-national government spending is weak and the inter-governmental fiscal transfer system lacks predictability (World Bank, 2018a). Co-ordination across multiple ministries and government units is also lacking (Ministry of Tourism and ILO, 2012).

Decentralisation can help align policies with local needs, but in practice its effectiveness is constrained by the limited capacity of officials at lower government levels and by insufficient co-ordination between actors (OECD, 2016a). For example, in 2014 the Ministry of Tourism, GIZ (the German Development Agency) and the province of West Nusa Tenggara established the first Tourism Masterplan for the island of Lombok. While a positive initiative, a lack of co-ordination with districts and villages prevented full implementation of the plan, justifying the need for a new masterplan that is being prepared in 2018 with the World Bank. For the development of Lake Toba, six district-level governments are involved in the development of the area's tourism, which again suggests the likelihood of co-ordination problems (Dong and Manning, 2017). That points to a role for provinces in improving co-ordination between lower-level governments in tourism matters. This could be through a provincial working group on tourism involving districts and villages, for example. Regional tourism satellite accounts would increase awareness of tourism at the sub-national level and also fully describe the local sectoral connections. Given the complexity of building such accounts, an initial step would be to enhance statistical collection at the provincial level.

The growth of tourism is expected to increase employment opportunities for the local population (see above). For this to happen, it is essential to have the acceptance and support of such development from the communities that will reap the benefits and costs associated with tourism development. As in many countries, destination management plans (DMP) can be used to support tourism development and take into account local needs and characteristics (OECD, 2018a). They can help to co-ordinate public and private actors. They can also help promote local ownership and encourage a more integrated and balanced approach to tourism development when undertaken in co-ordination with national strategic plans (see Box 2.4 for an example from Iceland). In France, "destination contracts" were signed in 2016 to develop specific local areas. The contracts were established gathering all tourism actors and aimed to attract more international visitors (French Ministry of Economic and Financial affairs, 2016). Masterplans, which are a form of DMP, will be delivered for the 10 priority tourist destinations in 2019 at the earliest, with the assistance of the World Bank and Switzerland. Strategic plans of this nature are necessary to put the appropriate framework in place to promote strategic and sustainable tourism growth and as such should involve key stakeholders from the outset. The authorities should therefore gradually produce masterplans for all strategic tourism areas, notably to incorporate needed infrastructure at the local level.

Box 2.4. Tourism management in Iceland: adapting to rapid growth

Tourism management issues are becoming more prominent in Iceland's tourism policy, as the rapid increase in tourist arrivals continues (OECD, 2017c). In addition to measures intended to maintain Iceland's competitiveness as a destination and improve the sector's productivity and profitability, the government has recognised that management measures are needed in order for tourism to continue to thrive in harmony with the community, the environment and other sectors of the economy. Measures need to be applied at many levels to moderate the growth in tourist arrivals, increase regional dispersion, reduce seasonality and better manage visitor flows at popular tourist sites. The following actions defined in Iceland's Road Map for Tourism 2015-20 have been implemented to improve the management and distribution of tourists around the country:

- A Route Development Fund has been established to relieve the pressure from Keflavik airport and encourage direct international flights to other airports in the country.
- Destination Management Plans are being prepared, taking into account the distribution and management of tourist flows in each of the seven regions.
- Reforms have been made to the Tourist Site Protection Fund together with the establishment of a new 12-year National Infrastructure Plan for the Protection of Nature and Sites of Cultural and Historical Value to improve infrastructure and encourage new developments in less visited areas.
- New legislation allows local authorities to apply parking fees in rural areas in order to better control tourist numbers at popular sites and for maintenance.
- Official tourist information was revised to improve service quality and visitor safety.

Destination Management Organisations (DMOs) are usually in charge of DMPs, and they can mitigate co-ordination issues amongst public institutions and effectively integrate the diverse views of all stakeholders. DMOs are formally constituted to deliver local tourism benefits with the involvement of the private sector. There is no unique and recommended DMO governance structure; they may be established at different levels of government, even outside of the government, and can mesh and network with one another. For example, Romania is implementing a three-tier structure for DMOs with representatives from central and regional governments and the private sector constituting at least 50% of membership (OECD, 2018a). In Thailand, there is one DMO doing promotion at the national level and local DMOs that are involved in marketing and management (McDowall, 2010). Langkawi island (Malaysia) is managed by an independent agency (LADA, 2018). The DMO in place in Bohol island (Philippines) is integrated in the provincial government (UNWTO and Griffith University, 2017).

In Indonesia DMOs have been created for some of the 10 tourism priority destinations, but they are constituted differently, depending on whether the destination is a SEZ or only a "tourism strategic area". For SEZs the role of the DMO is performed by the state-owned enterprise developing the site. This is the case for Mandalika, where the ITDC (Indonesia Tourism Development Corporation) is in charge of the site's development. For Lake Toba a decree (Presidential Regulation 49/2016) created the Lake Toba Authority – a DMO with representatives from line ministries and local governments. DMOs with shared responsibilities between public and private actors are preferable; local communities should also be involved. The previous example of Romania's approach can be inspiring. Another example is the Australia's Great Barrier Reef Marine Park Authority – an Australian government statutory agency – which manages to gather all involved stakeholders (including local communities) to both promote tourism (2 million visitors a year) and protect the site despite its geographical extent (344 400 km^2) and its vulnerability (Great Barrier Reef Marine Park Authority, 2017).

The size of the area covered by the DMO is also an important consideration. For example, on Lombok Island the development of Mandalika cannot be independent from nearby Senggigi and Gili Trawangan, which are already attracting many more tourists, even though they are not priority destinations and not in a SEZ. A new DMO could manage Lombok as a destination to build synergies and complementarities between different, but nearby, locations. More broadly, given that there is also a financial cost of running DMOs (which could be borne at least partly by the private sector), the authorities should assess and integrate all direct tourism linkages before designing the geographical coverage of a DMO.

Indonesia's gain from tourism will depend on local governments' capacity to provide a good framework and services. To make decentralisation work better local governments should raise a larger share of revenues themselves rather than through transfers, as recommended in the previous *Survey* (OECD, 2016a). A small tourist tax on accommodation, as levied in many other countries, could complement local revenues. Tourists have typically a greater willingness to pay than residents (because of preferences and higher income), and taxation can price in any negative externalities (OECD, 2014b). Given that Indonesia's tourism price competitiveness is already very high – ranked 5th by WEF (2017) – the impact will be negligible on foreigners. But to limit the burden on domestic tourists the tax rate should not be set too high. The tax should be part of a reform package discussed above and in Chapter 1. Associated revenues could potentially fund tourism-related projects (like tourist information centres) and marketing and promotion activities and improve services more generally. With more revenues, there can also be more local public initiatives, which can serve as examples for other regions and stimulate healthy competition amongst them. Districts are likely to be the right level of government to collect such a tax, as they have experience in collecting the hotel and restaurant sales tax; OECD countries tend to use municipal governments for such taxation.

Local initiatives increase chances of success. The experience of Banyuwangi regency (East Java) is enlightening: the number of tourists is about 10 times higher than in 2010 and reached nearly 5 million in 2016 (mostly domestic) through festivals and a strong participation of the population. And in 2016 Banyuwangi won the UNWTO Award for Excellence and Innovation in Tourism for the category "Public Policy Innovation and Governance". Local small-scale initiatives are facilitated with a special allocation fund (or DAK, part of central government transfer to subnational entities) targeted for tourism development. In 2018, IDR 632 billion (USD 42.5 million) was allocated for 319 local government tourism-related projects, up from 58 projects and IDR 92 billion in 2016. Such projects can be co-financed and have potentially large returns for local communities: for example, to finance an additional bus line, a taxi hub or information panels in a tourist site. However, as recommended in the previous *Survey,* monitoring of those transfers should be stepped up. With more promotion especially to local policy makers and with DAK transfers, there could be opportunities to develop more destinations. Technical support to assist local governments to let them prepare tourism-related projects could also be expanded. Provinces should gradually become the main provider of such support.

Tourism as an opportunity to promote female labour participation

Gender equality is one of the SDGs. Indonesia is committed to using female labour force participation as an enabling factor in achieving all of its SDGs (Republic of Indonesia, 2017). Globally, according to UNWTO, women make up most of the tourism workforce and the same is true in Indonesia (Figure 2.15). Therefore women could be expected to fill many of the new jobs generated by the development of tourism in Indonesia. However, there is a gap in literacy and educational attainment in favour of men, as their school enrolment was higher in the past (Figure 2.16). This is particularly the case in rural areas and for those with lower educational attainment. Nevertheless, enrolment gaps have been shrinking over time. For younger cohorts only a small difference exists: in 2015 the enrolment rate for the 15-19–year-old age group was 69% and 71% for women and men, respectively. Indeed, equality in education seems to be achievable in the near future, thanks to active government policies (OECD/ADB, 2015).

Figure 2.15. Share of women in total employment

In per cent, 2017

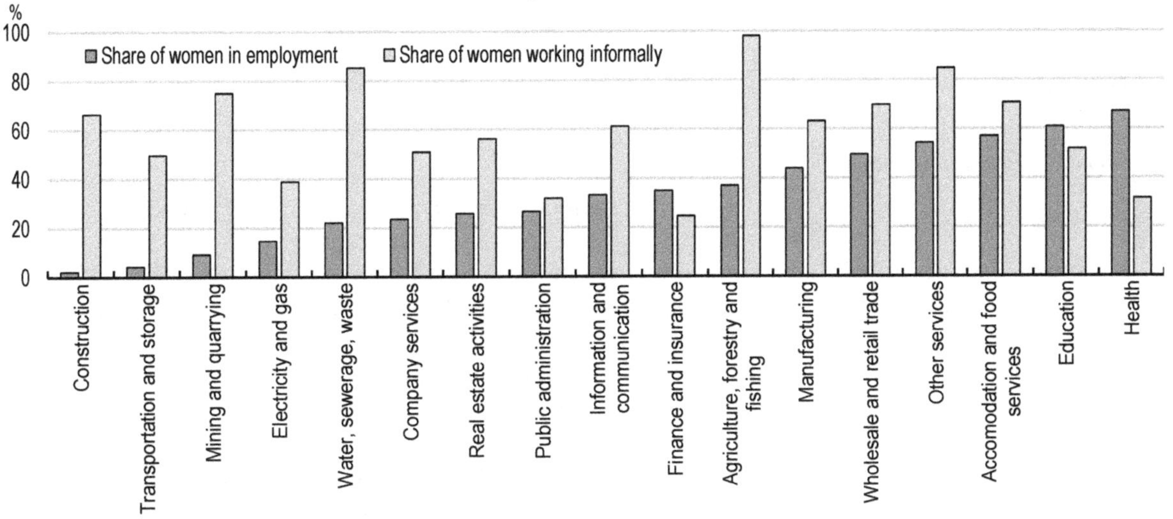

Source: Statistics Indonesia, *SAKERNAS Database*; OECD calculations.

StatLink ⬛ https://doi.org/10.1787/888933833863

Figure 2.16. Illiteracy rates and educational attainment by gender

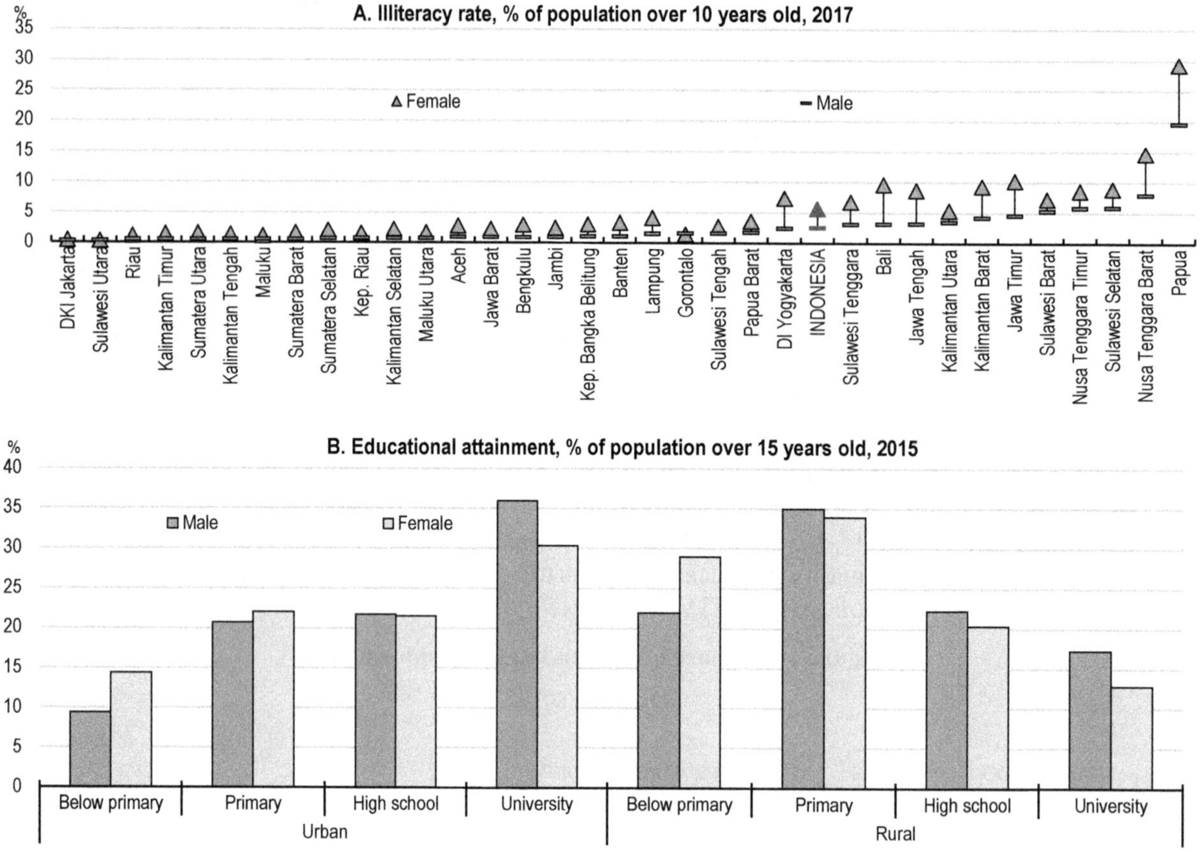

A. Illiteracy rate, % of population over 10 years old, 2017

B. Educational attainment, % of population over 15 years old, 2015

Source: Statistics Indonesia.

StatLink ⫘ https://doi.org/10.1787/888933833882

Women also tend to participate less than men in the labour force, but with large differences across provinces (Figure 2.17). As expected, where the female participation rate is higher, the difference with men is also lower. The smallest differences between men and women in labour participation are in provinces with relatively large tourism sectors, like Bali. In 2014 women represented about 40% of employment across all industries; but using the current structure, women would fill 6 out of 10 new jobs in the accommodation and food services sector (see Figure 2.15 above). The development of tourism can therefore increase their role in the workforce. Some of the inter-provincial differences could also decline with the development of tourism. For example, Banten, which has one of the lowest female participation rates and also has one of the 10 priority destinations, could have more women working in the future if the sector grows. An exception in that regard is Jakarta where employment in hotels and restaurants is mostly male.

Raising the skills of the female workforce will contribute to addressing the sector's employment needs. The lack of female skills is evidenced by the higher share of women in the informal sector: about 27% of them work in the formal sector compared to 31% for men. Being in the formal sector usually translates into higher wages and better social protection. The increasing digitalisation of the tourism sector can ease formalisation (see above), which will benefit women only if the official minimum wage does not exceed what their skills can command in the labour market. Expanding access to adult training can help address the gender skills gap: the literacy rate of women over 40 is only around half of that of similar-aged men (OECD/ADB, 2015).

A second earner will raise household revenues, which will be especially beneficial for welfare in regions where poverty is high. In many countries women tend to work in tourism in non-regular and part-time jobs (Stacey, 2015). This can enable them to maintain caring duties, but it also contributes to the earnings gap with men. Rural areas are poorer and have lower female participation rates. Thus, the development of tourism in such areas could be particularly beneficial for women and their households.

Figure 2.17. Labour force participation rates by gender across provinces

In per cent of total population, 2017

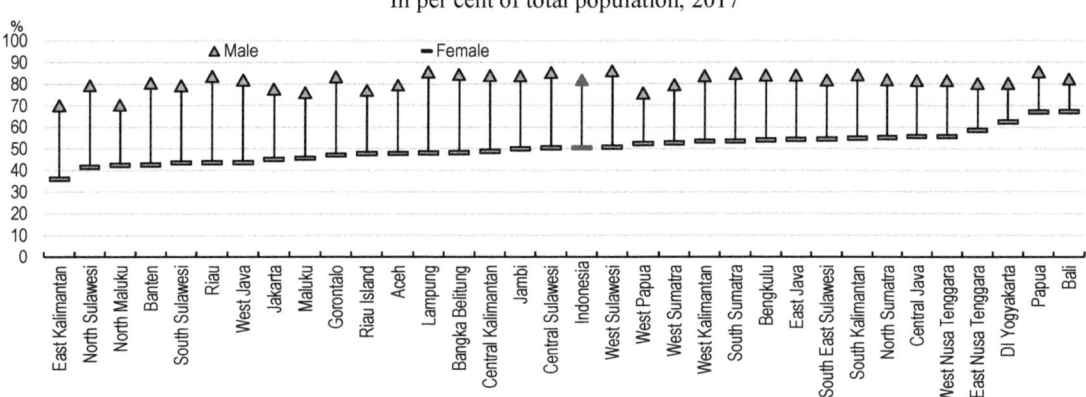

Source: CEIC; OECD calculations.

StatLink ▆▇▊ https://doi.org/10.1787/888933833901

Facilitating female entrepreneurship will boost tourism activity and gender equality. Small and medium-sized enterprises employ about 97% of the Indonesian working population, and half of them are owned by women (FT, 2018; OECD, 2018b). Access to finance is more difficult for women, despite better credit performance than for men (IFC, 2016). Part of the problem lies in a lack of demand for loans, discrimination by banks against women and their requirement of collateral (like land or buildings) when wives and daughters do not have equal inheritance rights (World Bank, 2018b). The authorities should use training and awareness campaigns to mitigate these problems. Financial literacy and education could enhance the financial inclusion of micro-enterprise owners in particular. The government is implementing a national strategy targeting in particular women (OECD, 2018b). Clearer property rights, anti-discrimination laws and facilitating inheritance would help women to access finance.

Recommendations for using tourism for sustainable regional development

(Key recommendations are shown in bold)

Government planning

- **Give more prominence to revenue-based targets for tourism in future plans.**
- Better interconnect government plans across sectors, in particular ensuring coherence between tourism, transport and environment policy.
- Incorporate expected tourism growth in all government planning, notably in the expansion of waste and water infrastructure and of broadband Internet.
- Develop destination management plans, and establish destination management organisations in all strategic tourist areas. Adjust the size of destination areas covered by management plans to better balance management costs and local tourism linkages.

Local areas

- **Incorporate needed infrastructure in forthcoming destination management plans to ensure sustainable development of tourism.**
- Create a small tourist tax on accommodation nights to fund local governments.
- Build tourist service centres to promote local businesses, provide trusted information for tourists and offer specific services like free internet and ATMs.
- Expand technical support to local governments on how to prepare tourism projects.
- Finalise the tourism satellite account update, and collect more detailed information at the regional level.

Labour and entrepreneurship

- **Expand vocational and on-the-job training to build tourism-related skills in the workforce, especially in areas with skills shortages.**
- Increase interaction between high-level institutions and employers to better monitor missing skills and design appropriate curricula.
- Further ease access to finance for female entrepreneurs.
- Increase capacity building for firms by developing online applications and training, to facilitate start-ups and help them tap into foreign markets.

Environment

- **Increase the coverage of protected areas, and consider opening more for tourism use, but with visitor controls including regulations, and appropriate user and concession fees.**

- Take social and environmental impacts into account when selecting tourism-related infrastructure projects.

Bibliography

ADB (2018), *Indonesia: Enhancing Productivity through Quality Jobs*, Asian Development Bank, http://dx.doi.org/10.22617/TCS189213-2.

Airbnb (2017), *Airbnb & APEC - closing tourism gaps with healthy travel*.

Andrews, D., G. Nicoletti and C. Timiliotis (2018), "Digital technology diffusion: a matter of capabilities, incentives or both", *OECD Economics Department Working Papers*, No. 1476, OECD Publishing, Paris, https://doi.org/10.1787/7c542c16-en.

APEC (2017), *Developing the Tourism Workforce of the Future in the APEC region*, Asia-Pacific Economic Cooperation.

APJII (2017), *Penetration and Behavior of Indonesian Internet User 2017, Indonesia Internet Service Provider Association*, https://blog.apjii.or.id/index.php/2018/02/19/survei-apjii-penetrasi-internet-indonesia-jangkau-547-persen-populasi-di-2017/.

Ashley, C., C. Boyd and H. Goodwin (2000), "Pro-poor tourism: Putting poverty at the heart of the tourism agenda", *Natural Resource Perspective*, Vol. 51.

Bali (2015), *Sustainable Tourism on Bali?*, www.bali.com/news_Sustainable-Tourism-on-Bali-_161.html.

Ballantyne, R., K. Hughes and B. Ritchie (2009), "Meeting the needs of tourists: The role and function of Australian visitor information centers", *Journal of Travel & Tourism Marketing*, Vol. 26/8, pp. 778-794, http://dx.doi.org/10.1080/10548400903356178.

Bappenas (2016), *Indonesian Biodiversity Strategy and Action Plan (IBSAP) 2015-2020*.

Das, K., M. Gryseels, P. Sudhir and K. Tee Tan (2016), *Unlocking Indonesia's Digital Opportunity*, McKinsey&Company.

Daubanes, J. (2017), "The sustainable management of a productive natural capital", *IFRO Working Paper*, 2017/08.

Dong, S. and C. Manning (2017), "Labour-market developments at a time of heightened uncertainty", *Bulletin of Indonesian Economic Studies*, Vol. 53/1, pp. 1-25, http://dx.doi.org/10.1080/00074918.2017.1326201.

Dudley, N., S. Stolton and P. Shadie (2013), *IUCN WCPA Best Practice Guidance on Recognising Protected Areas and Assigning Management Categories and Governance Types*, International Union for Conservation of Nature.

Eagles, P., S. McCool and C. Haynes (2002), *Sustainable Tourism in Protected Areas – Guidelines for Planning and Management*, World Commission on Protected Areas, United Nations Environment Programme, World Tourism Organisation and IUCN.

Fahmi, F., S. Koster and J. van Dijk (2016), "The location of creative industries in a developing country: The case of Indonesia", *Cities*, http://dx.doi.org/10.1016/j.cities.2016.06.005.

Faturay, F., M. Lenzen and K. Nugraha (2017), "A new sub-national multi-region input–output database for Indonesia", *Economic Systems Research*, http://dx.doi.org/10.1080/09535314.2017.1304361.

Flightradar24 (2018), www.flightradar24.com/data/ (accessed on 9 March 2018).

French Ministry of Economic and Financial Affairs (2016), "Les 20 contrats de destination – présentation des contrats" [The 20 destination contracts – presentation], Directorate of Enterprises, www.entreprises.gouv.fr/files/files/directions_services/tourisme/territoires/Contrats_de_destination/Fiches_de_Presentation_des_contrats_de_destination.pdf.

FT (2018), *How the Gender Pay Gap Varies Across South-East Asia*, Financial Times, www.ft.com/content/1f62b27a-2ddf-11e8-9b4b-bc4b9f08f381.

Great Barrier Reef Marine Park Authority (2017), *2016-17 Annual Report*, www.gbrmpa.gov.au/about-us/about-us/annual-report.

Haxton, P. (2015), "A review of effective policies for tourism growth", *OECD Tourism Papers*, No. 2015/1, OECD Publishing, Paris, http://dx.doi.org/10.1787/5js4vmp5n5r8-en.

IFC (2016), *Access to Credit for Businesswomen in Indonesia*, International Finance Corporation.

ILO (2011), *Measuring Employment: A Case Study of Indonesia*, International Labour Organisation.

Indonesia-Investments (2016), *Tourism Industry Indonesia*, www.indonesia-investments.com/business/industries-sectors/tourism/item6051 (accessed on 9 March 2018).

ITF (2017), *Quantifying the Socio-economic Benefits of Transport*, OECD Publishing, Paris, http://dx.doi.org/10.1787/9789282108093-en.

ITX (2018), *About ITX*, http://itx.co.id/ (accessed on 15 April 2018).

Jakarta Globe (2018a), *Batang-Semarang Toll Road to Be Ready for Idul Fitri Exodus*, http://jakartaglobe.id/business/batang-semarang-toll-road-ready-idul-fitri-exodus/.

Jakarta Globe (2018b), *Indonesia Improves in Getting Private Money for Infrastructure*, http://jakartaglobe.id/business/indonesia-among-top-5-countries-utilizing-the-most-private-money-for-infrastructure-last-year/.

Jakarta Globe (2018c), *Southeast Asia's Idyllic Islands Buckle Under Tourism Strain*, http://jakartaglobe.id/business/southeast-asias-idyllic-islands-buckle-tourism-strain-2/.

James, E. (2016), "Improving Indonesia's national road assets maintenance outcomes", *Prakarsa*, 24.

Kadir, S., Nirvansyah and B. Bachrul (2016), *Vocational Education and Technical Training in Indonesia: Challenges and Opportunities for the Future*, Lee Kuan Yew School of Public Policy.

Kompas (2018), *Tol Batang-Semarang Diresmikan Akhir 2018* [Batang-Semarang toll inaugurated end of 2018], https://regional.kompas.com/read/2018/09/29/09490231/tol-batang-semarang-diresmikan-akhir-2018.

Koske, I., I. Wanner, R. Bitetti and O. Barbiero (2015), "The 2013 update of the OECD's database on product market regulation: Policy insights for OECD and non-OECD countries", *OECD Economics Department Working Papers*, No. 1200, OECD Publishing, Paris, http://dx.doi.org/10.1787/5js3f5d3n2vl-en.

LADA (2018), *Langkawi Development Authority*, www.lada.gov.my/en/.

Lamb, J. et al. (2018), "Plastic waste associated with disease on coral reefs", *Science*, Vol. 359/6374, pp. 460-462, http://dx.doi.org/10.1126/science.aar3320.

Lindsey, P. et al. (2017), "Relative efforts of countries to conserve world's megafauna", *Global Ecology and Conservation*, Vol. 10, pp. 243-252, http://dx.doi.org/10.1016/J.GECCO.2017.03.003.

Mackie, A., S. Sentier, I. Haščič and M. Linster (2017), "Indicators on terrestrial and marine protected areas: Methodology and results for OECD and G20 countries", *OECD Environment Working Papers*, No. 126, OECD Publishing, Paris, http://dx.doi.org/10.1787/e0796071-en.

McCarthy, M. and P. Musset (2016), *A Skills beyond School Review of Peru*, OECD Reviews of Vocational Education and Training, OECD Publishing, Paris, http://dx.doi.org/10.1787/9789264265400-en.

McDowall, S. (2010), "International tourist satisfaction and destination loyalty: Bangkok, Thailand", *Asia Pacific Journal of Tourism Research*, Vol. 15/1, pp. 21-42, http://dx.doi.org/10.1080/10941660903510040.

Messenger, B. (2017), *Waste-to-Energy Asia Summit: Indonesia Ready for Solution to Growing Waste Problem*, https://waste-management-world.com/a/waste-to-energy-asia-summit-indonesia-ready-for-solution-to-growing-waste-problem.

Ministry of Tourism and ILO (2012), *Sustainable Tourism and Green Jobs for Indonesia*, International Labour Organisation.

Nielsen (2018), *Outbound Chinese Tourism and Consumption Trends: 2017 Survey*, Nielsen.

Nurdin, H. (2018), *Indonesia Tourism Exchange*, http://pemasaranpariwisata.com/2018/02/26/indonesia-tourism-exchange/.

O'Connell, S., L. Mation, J. Basto and M. Dutz (2017), "Can business input improve the effectiveness of worker training? Evidence from Brazil's Pronatec-MDIC", *Policy Research working paper*, World Bank, No. 8155.

OECD (2018a), *OECD Tourism Trends and Policies 2018*, OECD Publishing, Paris, http://dx.doi.org/10.1787/tour-2018-en.

OECD (2018b), *Country Review of SME and Entrepreneurship Policy: Indonesia*, OECD Publishing, Paris.

OECD (2018c), *Economic Outlook for Southeast Asia, China and India 2018: Fostering Growth through Digitalisation*, OECD Publishing, Paris, http://dx.doi.org/10.1787/9789264286184-en.

OECD (2017a), *Gaps and Governance Standards of Public Infrastructure in Chile: Infrastructure Governance Review*, OECD Publishing, Paris, http://dx.doi.org/10.1787/9789264278875-en.

OECD (2017b), *Key Issues for Digital Transformation in the G20*, Report prepared for a joint G20 German Presidency/OECD conference, OECD Publishing, Paris.

OECD (2017c), *OECD Economic Surveys: Iceland 2017*, OECD Publishing, Paris, http://dx.doi.org/10.1787/eco_surveys-isl-2017-en.

OECD (2016a), *OECD Economic Surveys: Indonesia 2016*, OECD Publishing, Paris, http://dx.doi.org/10.1787/eco_surveys-idn-2016-en.

OECD (2016b), *OECD Tourism Trends and Policies 2016*, OECD Publishing, Paris, http://dx.doi.org/10.1787/tour-2016-en.

OECD (2016c), *OECD Economic Surveys: Costa Rica 2016: Economic Assessment*, OECD Publishing, Paris, http://dx.doi.org/10.1787/eco_surveys-cri-2016-en.

OECD (2015), *OECD Environmental Performance Reviews: Brazil 2015*, OECD Environmental Performance Reviews, OECD Publishing, Paris, http://dx.doi.org/10.1787/9789264240094-en.

OECD (2014a), *Tourism and the Creative Economy*, OECD Studies on Tourism, OECD Publishing, Paris, http://dx.doi.org/10.1787/9789264207875-en.

OECD (2014b), *OECD Tourism Trends and Policies 2014*, OECD Publishing, Paris, http://dx.doi.org/10.1787/tour-2014-en.

OECD/ADB (2015), *Education in Indonesia: Rising to the Challenge*, Reviews of National Policies for Education, OECD Publishing, Paris, http://dx.doi.org/10.1787/9789264230750-en.

OIC (2018), *Resolution of the 4th Islamic Conference of Labour Ministers*, 21-22 February.

Pro Natura Foundation (2018), "Priority Projects: 2017-2019 Sungai Wain Balikpapan", http://support.pronaturafoundation.org/projects-sungai-wain/.

PwC (2016), *Indonesian Infrastructure: Stable Foundations for Growth*, PwC Indonesia.

Republic of Indonesia (2017), *Voluntary National Review: Eradicating Poverty and Promoting Prosperity in a Changing World*, United Nations.

Schlumberger, C. and N. Weisskopf (2014), *Ready for Takeoff?: The Potential for Low-Cost Carriers in Developing Countries*, The World Bank, http://dx.doi.org/10.1596/978-1-4648-0282-9.

Skytrax (2018), *World's Top 100 Airports 2018*, www.worldairportawards.com/Awards/world_airport_rating.html.

Stacey, J. (2015), "Supporting quality jobs in tourism", *OECD Tourism Papers*, No. 2015/2, OECD Publishing, Paris, http://dx.doi.org/10.1787/5js4rv0g7szr-en.

Stay Raja Ampat (2018), *Raja Ampat Marine Park entry permit*, www.stayrajaampat.com/ultimate-raja-ampat-guide/information/raja-ampat-marine-park-entry-permit/.

Swisscontact (2016), *The Swisscontact WISATA II program*, www.swisscontact.org/fileadmin/user_upload/COUNTRIES/Indonesia/Documents/Publications/Progress_Report_2016.pdf.

Teguh, F. (2017), *Resources Efficiency, Safeguarding Natural and Cultural Resources: Sustainable Tourism Policy and Practices*, Presentation, Papua New Guinea, 21 March.

Tempo (2017), *Indonesia Boosts Promotion of Digital Tourism*, https://en.tempo.co/read/news/2017/09/05/199906020/Indonesia-Boosts-Promotion-of-Digital-Tourism.

TripAdvisor (2018), *Top 25 Destinations - Asia – Travelers' choice*, www.tripadvisor.com/TravelersChoice-Destinations-cTop-g2.

UNCTAD (2007), *FDI in Tourism: The Development Dimension*, United Nations.

UNESCO (2017), *A New Roadmap for the Man and the Biosphere (MAB) Programme and its World Network of Biosphere Reserves*, United Nations Conference on Trade and Development.

UNWTO (2018), *UNWTO World Tourism Barometer*, World Tourism Organisation.

UNWTO (2017), *UNWTO/GTERC Annual Report on Asia Tourism Trends*, 2017 Edition, World Tourism Organisation, http://dx.doi.org/10.18111/9789284419111.

UNWTO and Griffith University (2017), *Managing Growth and Sustainable Tourism Governance in Asia and the Pacific*, World Tourism Organisation.

Vitasurya, V. (2016), "Local wisdom for sustainable development of rural tourism, case on Kalibiru and Lopati village, province of Daerah Istimewa Yogyakarta", *Procedia - Social and Behavioral Sciences*, Vol. 216, pp. 97-108, http://dx.doi.org/10.1016/J.SBSPRO.2015.12.014.

WEF (2017), *The Travel and Tourism Competitiveness Report 2017: Paving the Way for a More Sustainable and Inclusive Future*, World Economic Forum, Geneva.

World Bank (2018), *Women, Business and the Law*, http://wbl.worldbank.org/en/data/exploreeconomies/indonesia/2017.

World Bank (2018), *Indonesia - Public Expenditure and Financial Accountability: Assessment Report 2017*, World Bank.

WTTC (2018), *Country League Table Summary*, World Travel and Tourism Council.

ORGANISATION FOR ECONOMIC CO-OPERATION AND DEVELOPMENT

The OECD is a unique forum where governments work together to address the economic, social and environmental challenges of globalisation. The OECD is also at the forefront of efforts to understand and to help governments respond to new developments and concerns, such as corporate governance, the information economy and the challenges of an ageing population. The Organisation provides a setting where governments can compare policy experiences, seek answers to common problems, identify good practice and work to co-ordinate domestic and international policies.

The OECD member countries are: Australia, Austria, Belgium, Canada, Chile, the Czech Republic, Denmark, Estonia, Finland, France, Germany, Greece, Hungary, Iceland, Ireland, Israel, Italy, Japan, Korea, Latvia, Lithuania, Luxembourg, Mexico, the Netherlands, New Zealand, Norway, Poland, Portugal, the Slovak Republic, Slovenia, Spain, Sweden, Switzerland, Turkey, the United Kingdom and the United States. The European Union takes part in the work of the OECD.

OECD Publishing disseminates widely the results of the Organisation's statistics gathering and research on economic, social and environmental issues, as well as the conventions, guidelines and standards agreed by its members.

OECD PUBLISHING, 2, rue André-Pascal, 75775 PARIS CEDEX 16
(10 2018 22 1 P) ISBN 978-92-64-30492-5 – 2018

9 789264 304925